WRITER: **JONATHAN HICKMAN**

ARTISTS: **GREG TOCCHINI** [#6-7], **STEVE EPTING** [#8-9] & **BARRY KITSON** [#10-11]

INKER, ISSUE #9: **RICK MAGYAR**

FINISHERS, ISSUE #11: **BARRY KITSON, SCOTT HANNA, SCOTT KOBLISH, JAY LEISTEN & MARK PENNINGTON**

COLOR ARTIST: **PAUL MOUNTS**

LETTERER: **VIRTUAL CALLIGRAPHY'S CLAYTON COWLES**

COVER ARTISTS: **MARK BAGLEY, ANDY LANNING & PAUL MOUNTS** [#6-7]; **DANIEL ACUÑA** [#8-9]; **AND STEVE EPTING** [#10-11]

ASSOCIATE EDITOR: **LAUREN SANKOVITCH**

EDITOR: **TOM BREVOORT**

COLLECTION EDITOR: **JENNIFER GRÜNWALD**
ASSISTANT EDITORS: **ALEX STARBUCK & NELSON RIBEIRO**
EDITOR, SPECIAL PROJECTS: **MARK D. BEAZLEY**
SENIOR EDITOR, SPECIAL PROJECTS: **JEFF YOUNGQUIST**
SENIOR VICE PRESIDENT OF SALES: **DAVID GABRIEL**
SVP OF BRAND PLANNING & COMMUNICATIONS: **MICHAEL PASCIULLO**

EDITOR IN CHIEF: **AXEL ALONSO**
CHIEF CREATIVE OFFICER: **JOE QUESADA**
PUBLISHER: **DAN BUCKLEY**
EXECUTIVE PRODUCER: **ALAN FINE**

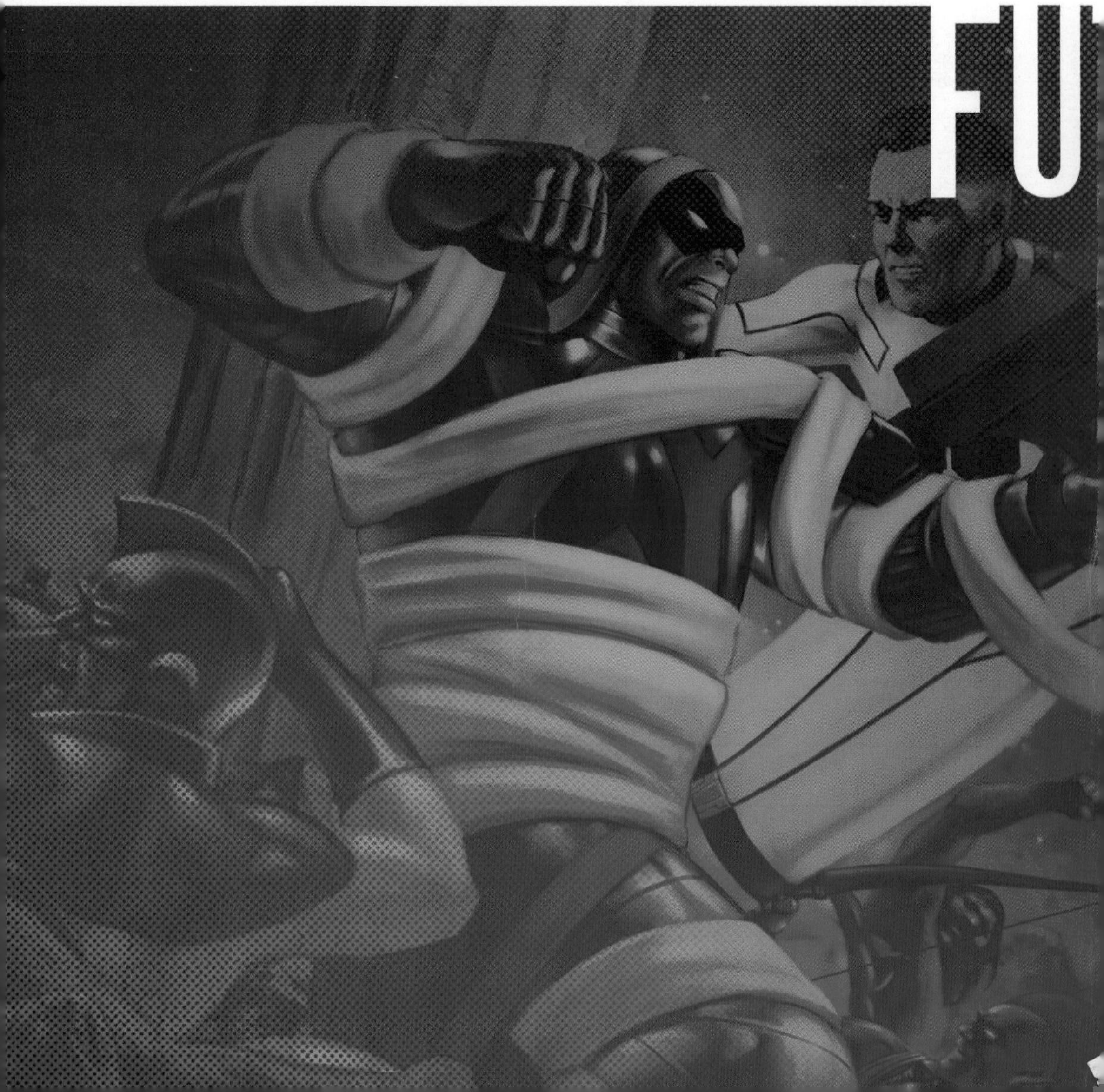

TURE FOUNDATION

UNIFIED FIELD THEORY: STAN LEE & JACK KIRBY

FF BY JONATHAN HICKMAN VOL. 2. Contains material originally published in magazine form as FF #6-11. First printing 2012. ISBN# 978-0-7851-5769-4. Published by MARVEL WORLDWIDE, INC., a subsidiary of MARVEL ENTERTAINMENT, LLC. OFFICE OF PUBLICATION: 135 West 50th Street, New York, NY 10020. Copyright © 2011 and 2012 Marvel Characters, Inc. All rights reserved. Hardcover: $24.99 per copy in the U.S. and $27.99 in Canada (GST #R127032852). Canadian Agreement #40668537. All characters featured in this issue and the distinctive names and likenesses thereof, and all related indicia are trademarks of Marvel Characters, Inc. No similarity between any of the names, characters, persons, and/or institutions in this magazine with those of any living or dead person or institution is intended, and any such similarity which may exist is purely coincidental. **Printed in the U.S.A.** ALAN FINE, EVP - Office of the President, Marvel Worldwide, Inc. and EVP & CMO Marvel Characters B.V.; DAN BUCKLEY, Publisher & President - Print, Animation & Digital Divisions; JOE QUESADA, Chief Creative Officer; DAVID BOGART, SVP of Business Affairs & Talent Management; TOM BREVOORT, SVP of Publishing; C.B. CEBULSKI, SVP of Creator & Content Development; DAVID GABRIEL, SVP of Publishing Sales & Circulation; MICHAEL PASCIULLO, SVP of Brand Planning & Communications; JIM O'KEEFE, VP of Operations & Logistics; DAN CARR, Executive Director of Publishing Technology; SUSAN CRESPI, Editorial Operations Manager; ALEX MORALES, Publishing Operations Manager; STAN LEE, Chairman Emeritus. For information regarding advertising in Marvel Comics or on Marvel.com, please contact John Dokes, SVP Integrated Sales and Marketing, at jdokes@marvel.com. For Marvel subscription inquiries, please call 800-217-9158. **Manufactured between 12/12/2011 and 1/9/2012 by R.R. DONNELLEY, INC., SALEM, VA, USA.**

10 9 8 7 6 5 4 3 2 1

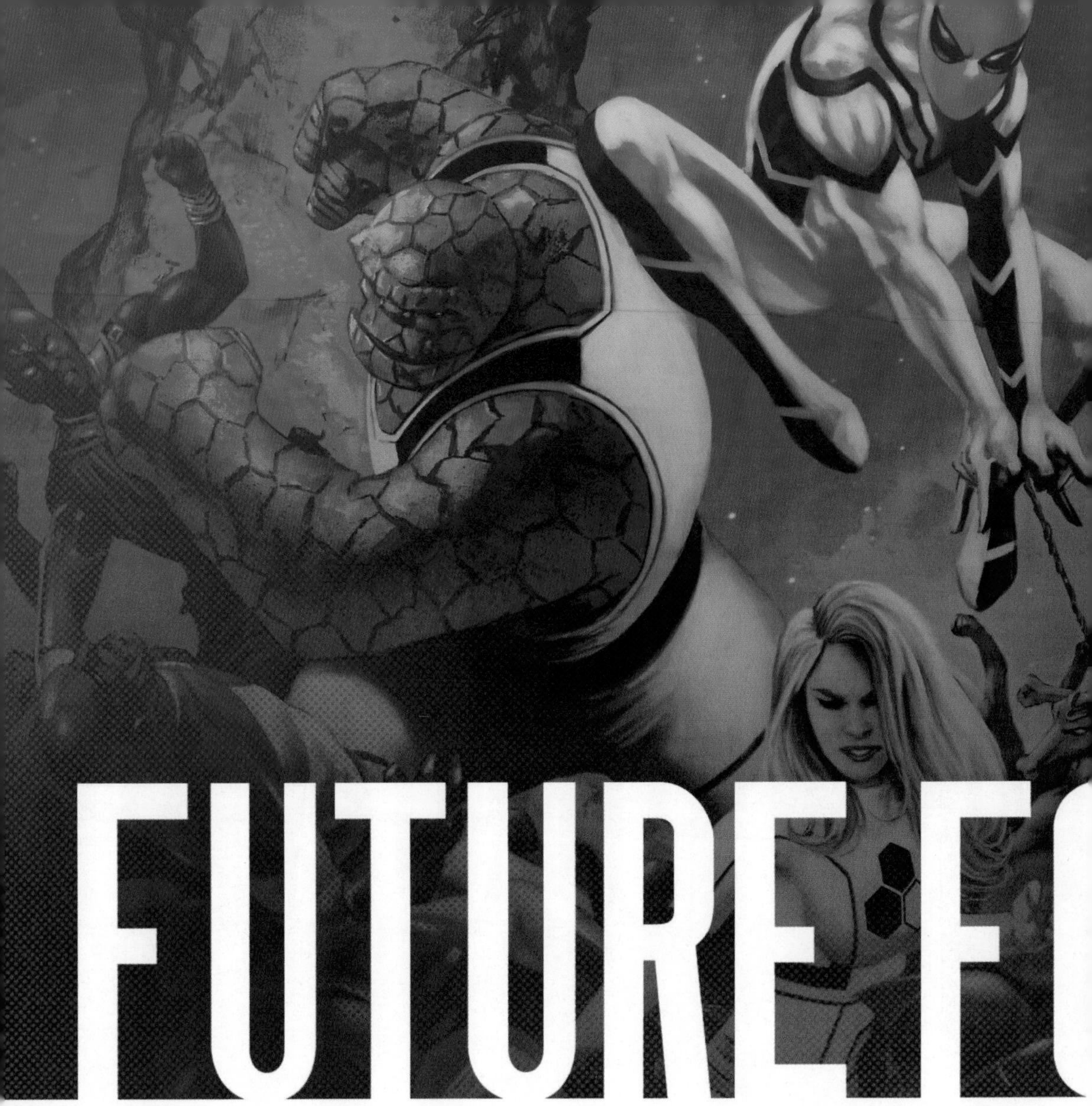
FUTURE

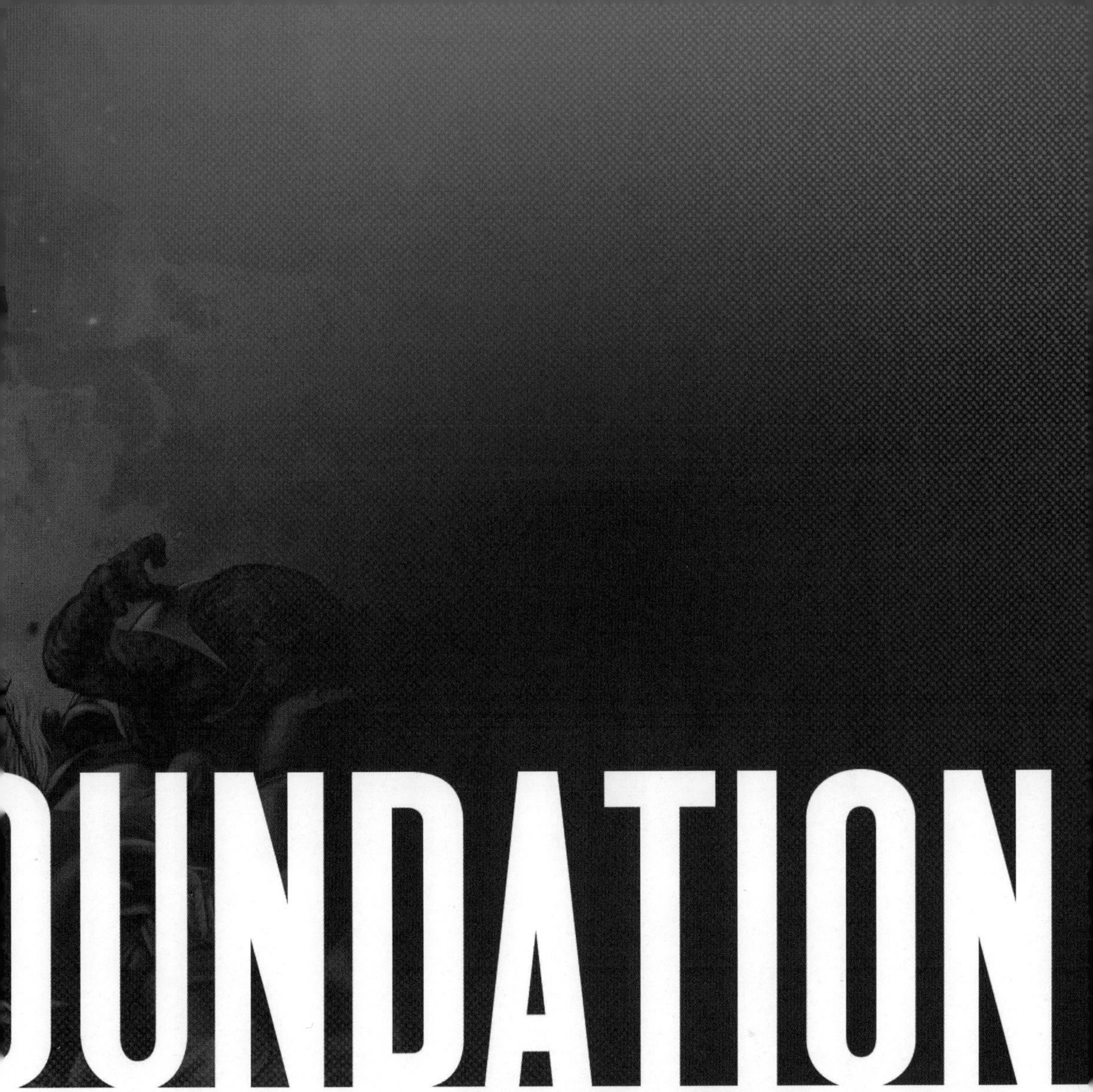

OUNDATION

VOL TWO THE SUPREMOR SEED

THIS WILL REQUIRE A WITNESS

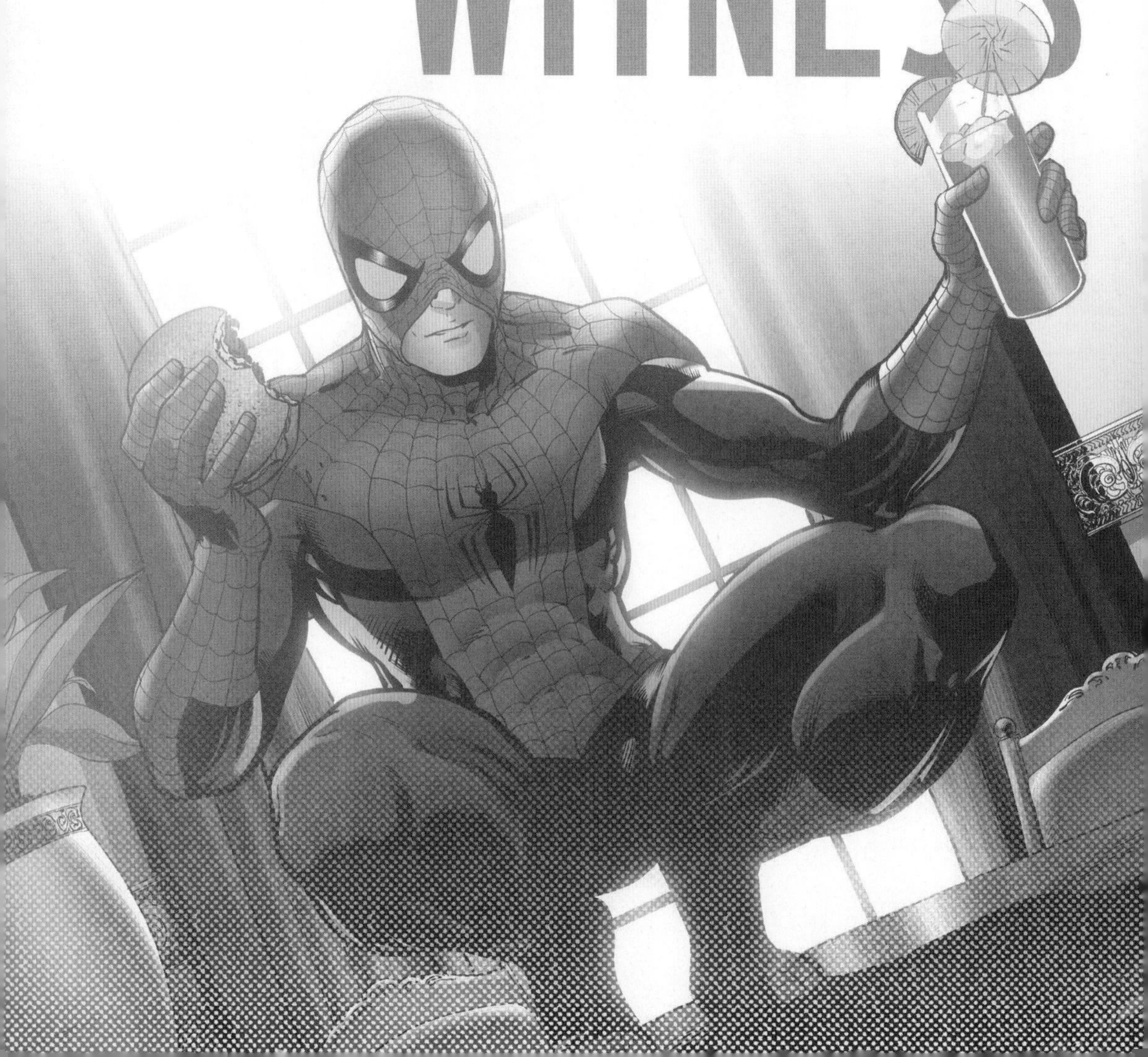

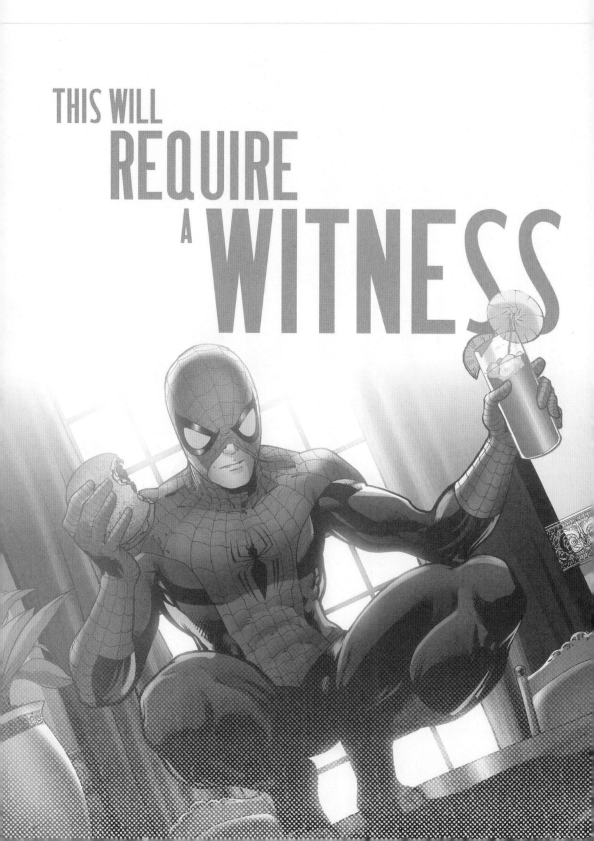

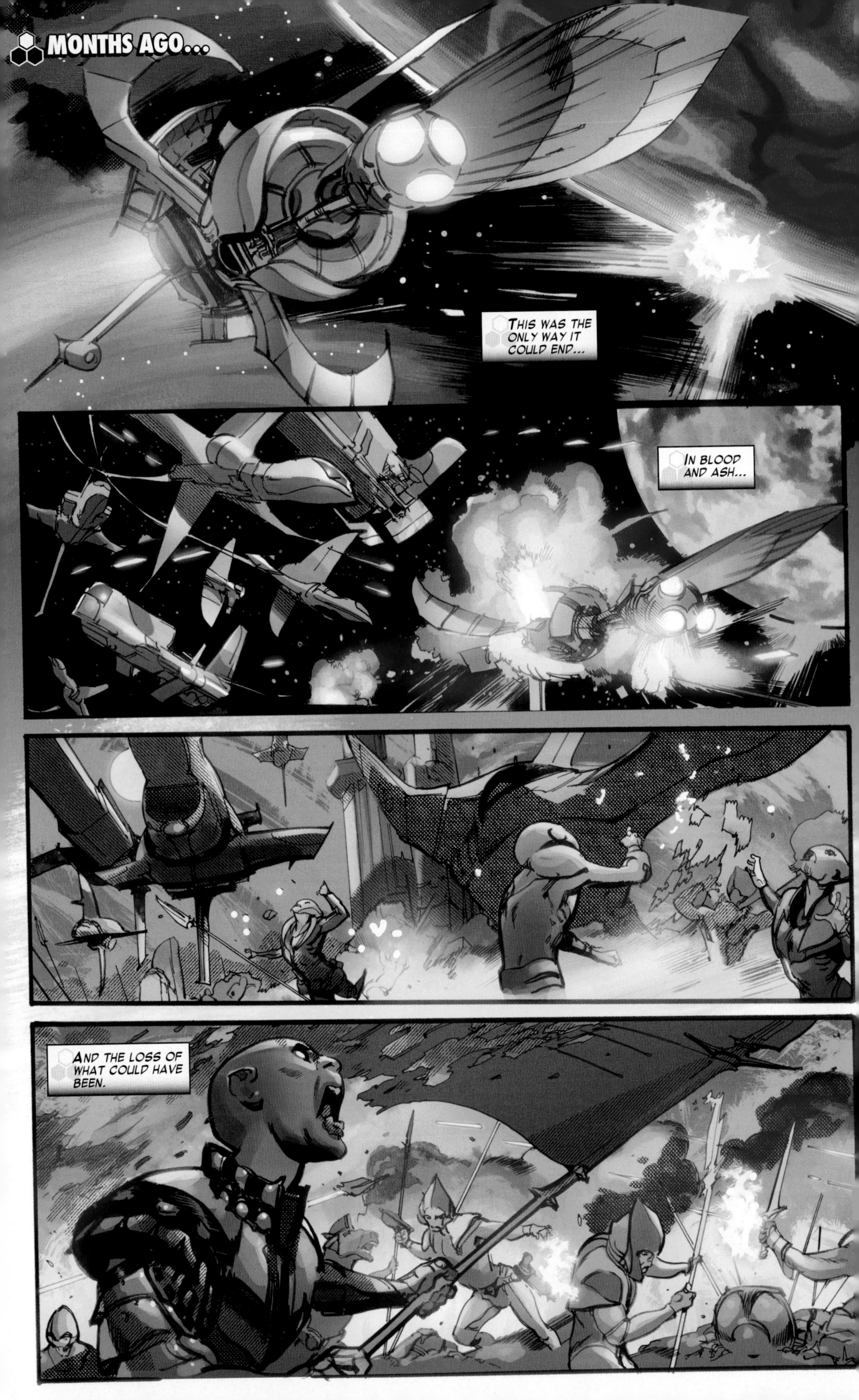
MONTHS AGO...
THIS WAS THE ONLY WAY IT COULD END...
IN BLOOD AND ASH...
AND THE LOSS OF WHAT COULD HAVE BEEN.

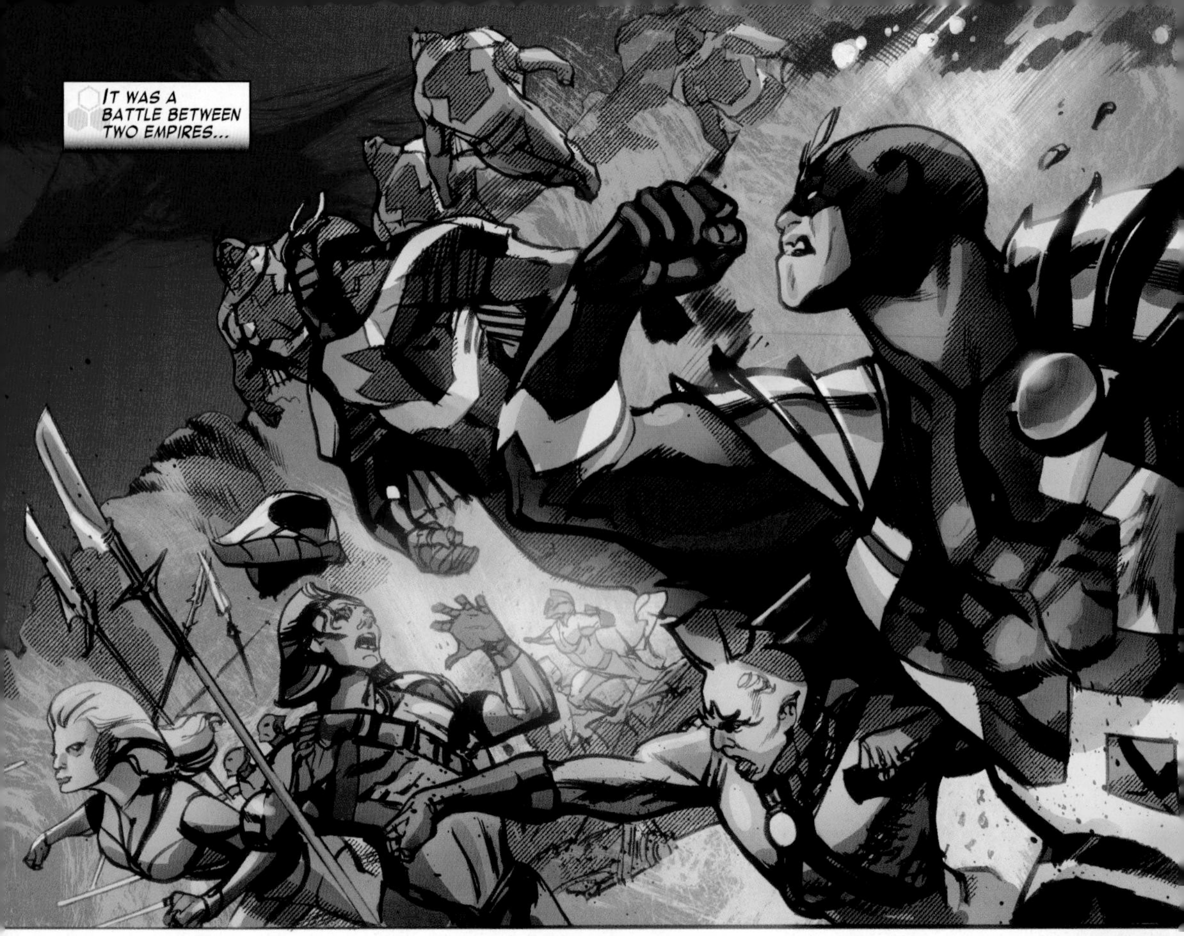
IT WAS A BATTLE BETWEEN TWO EMPIRES...

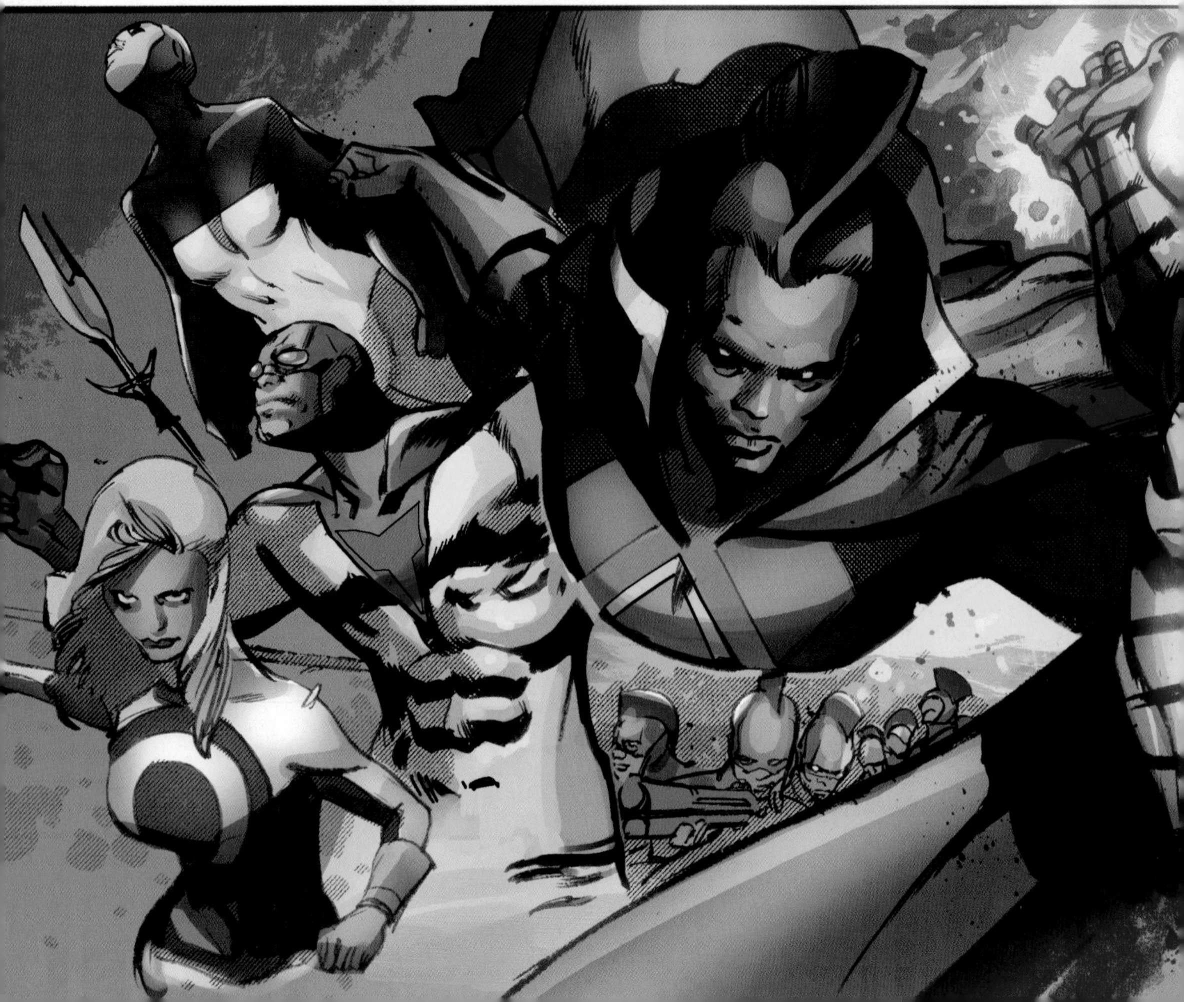

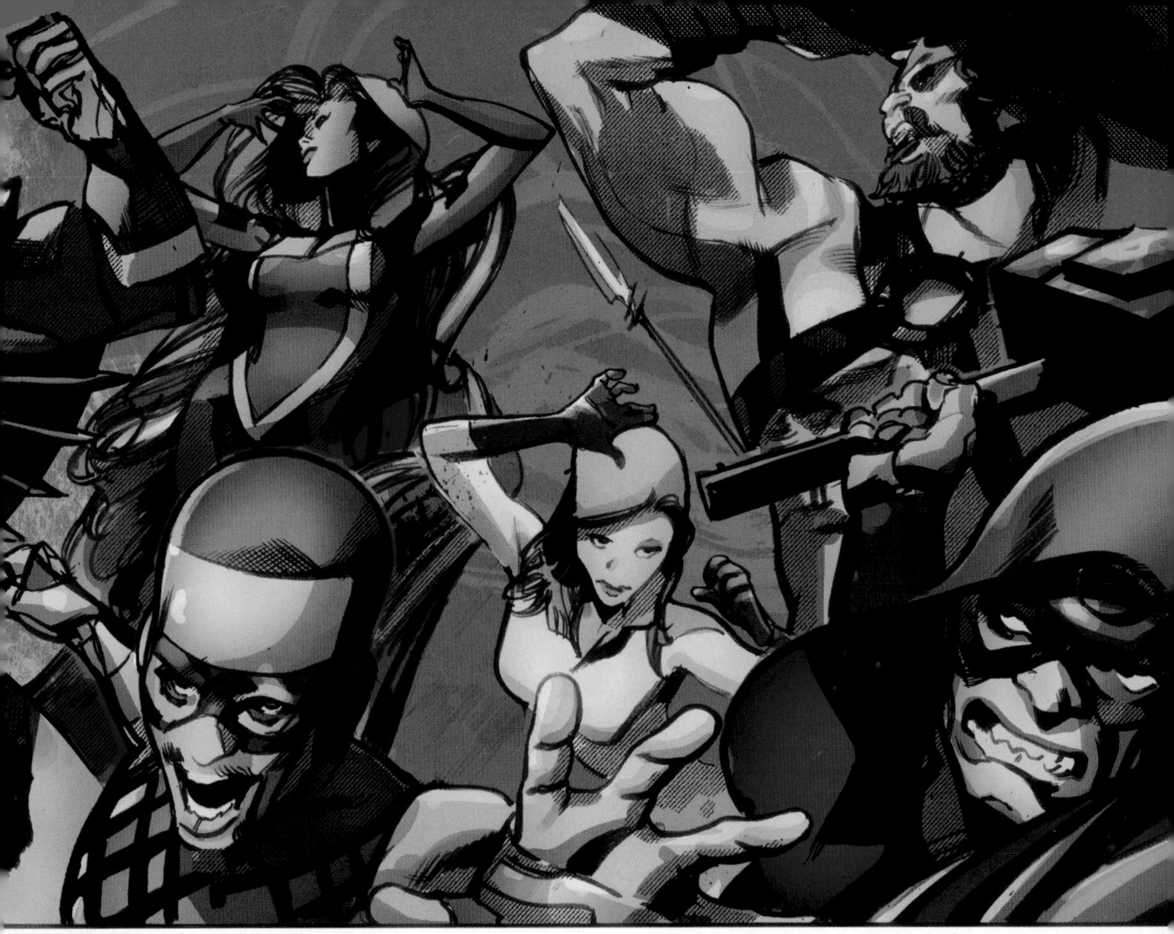

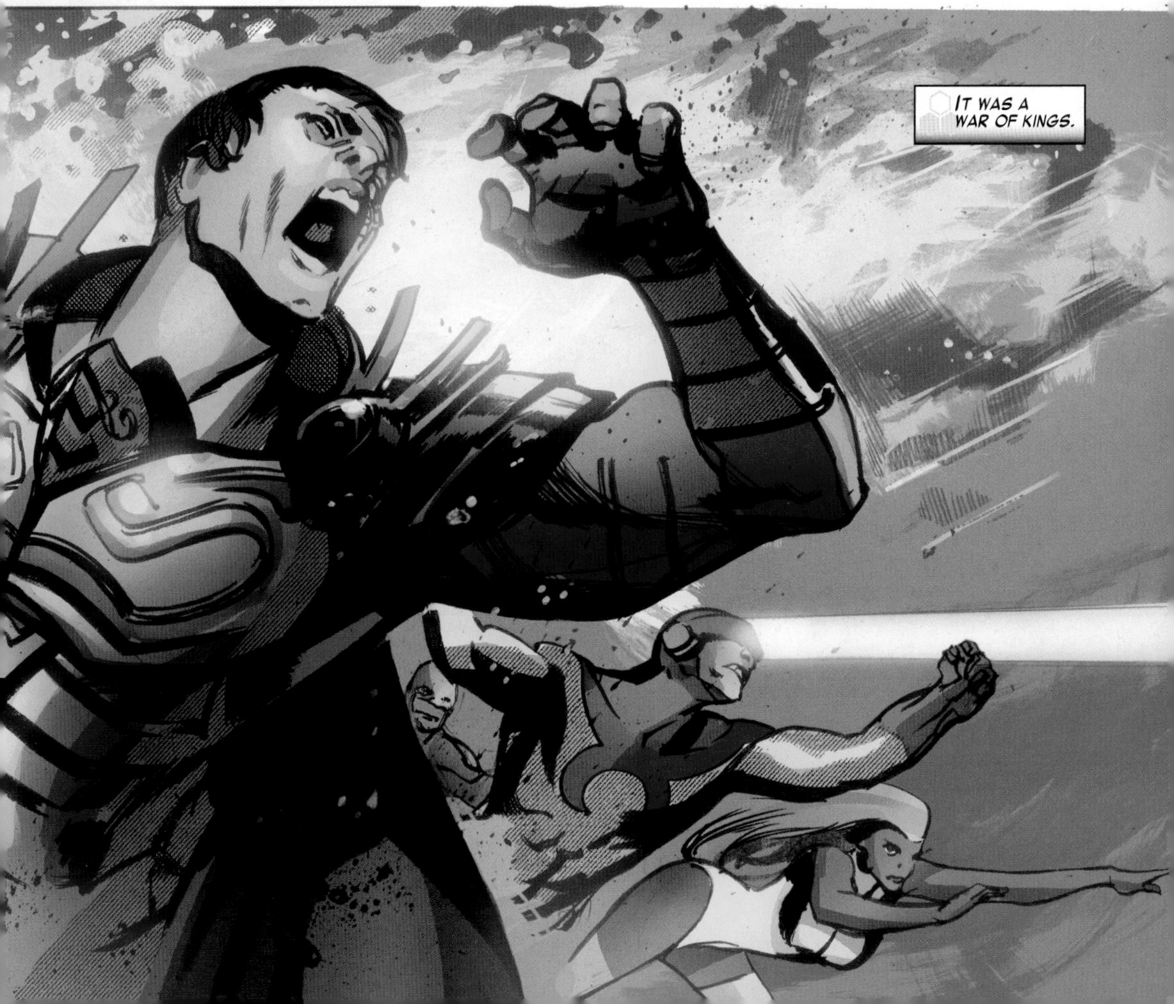
IT WAS A
WAR OF KINGS.

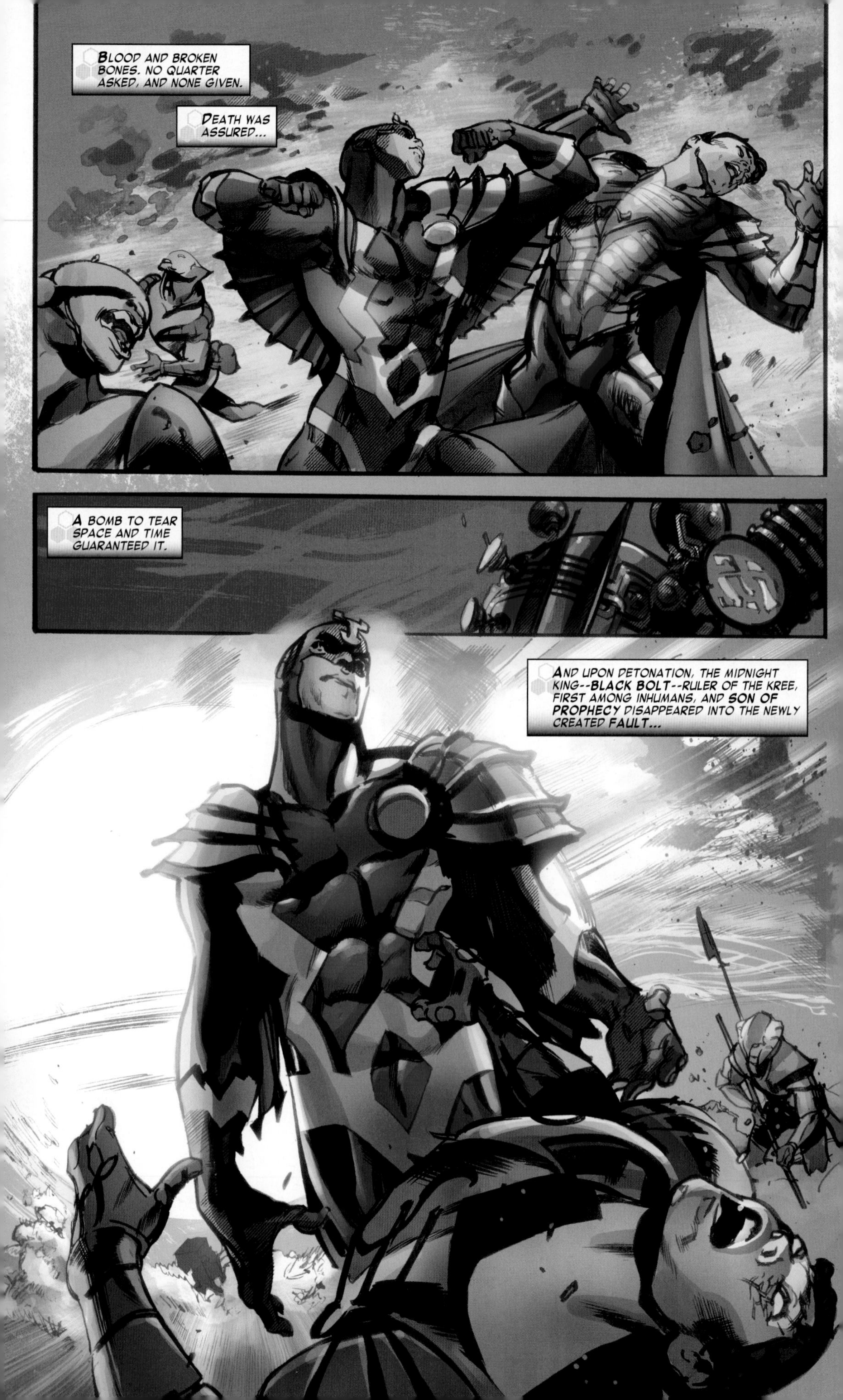
BLOOD AND BROKEN BONES. NO QUARTER ASKED, AND NONE GIVEN.
DEATH WAS ASSURED...
A BOMB TO TEAR SPACE AND TIME GUARANTEED IT.
AND UPON DETONATION, THE MIDNIGHT KING--BLACK BOLT--RULER OF THE KREE, FIRST AMONG INHUMANS, AND SON OF PROPHECY DISAPPEARED INTO THE NEWLY CREATED FAULT...

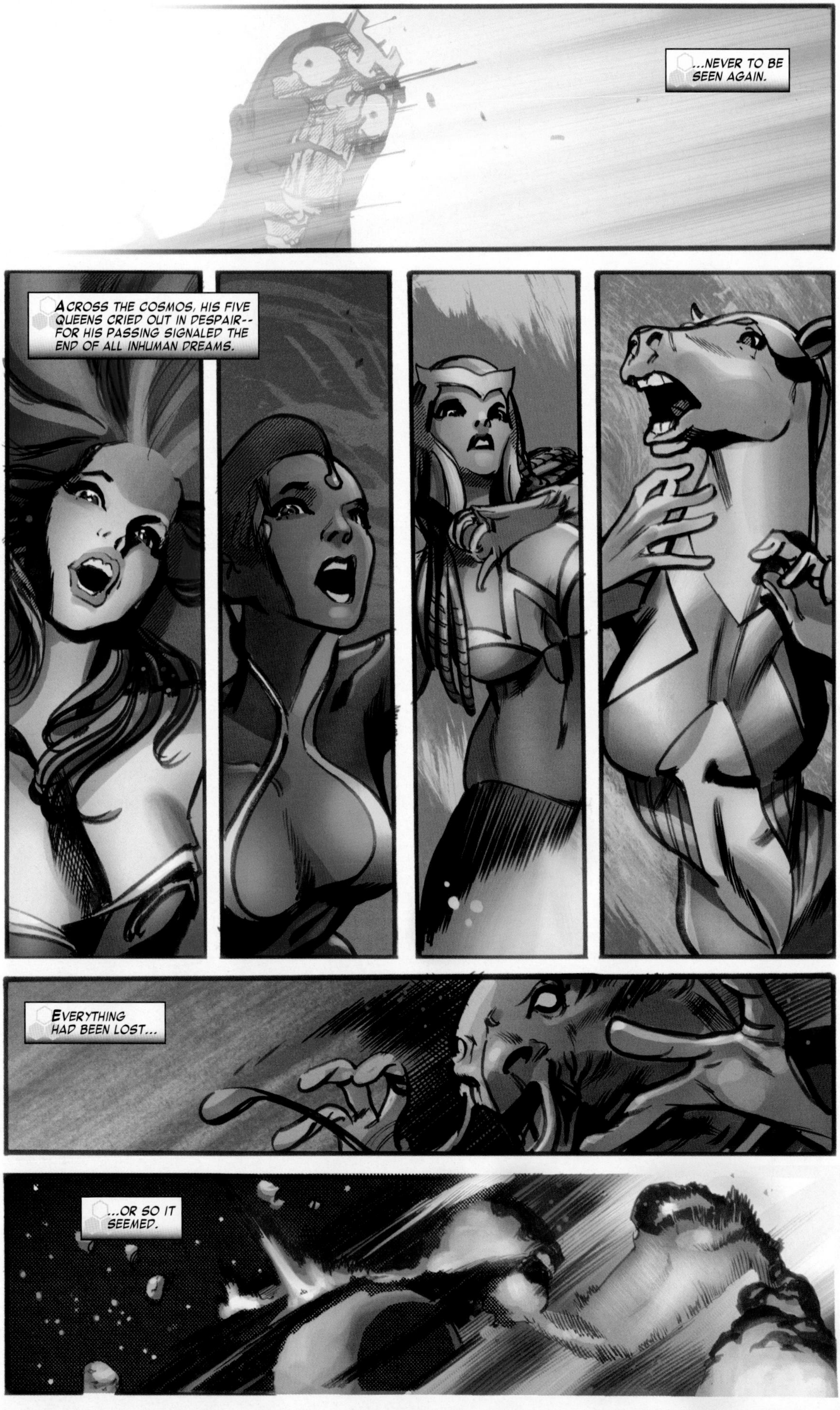
...NEVER TO BE SEEN AGAIN.
ACROSS THE COSMOS, HIS FIVE QUEENS CRIED OUT IN DESPAIR--FOR HIS PASSING SIGNALED THE END OF ALL INHUMAN DREAMS.
EVERYTHING HAD BEEN LOST...
...OR SO IT SEEMED.

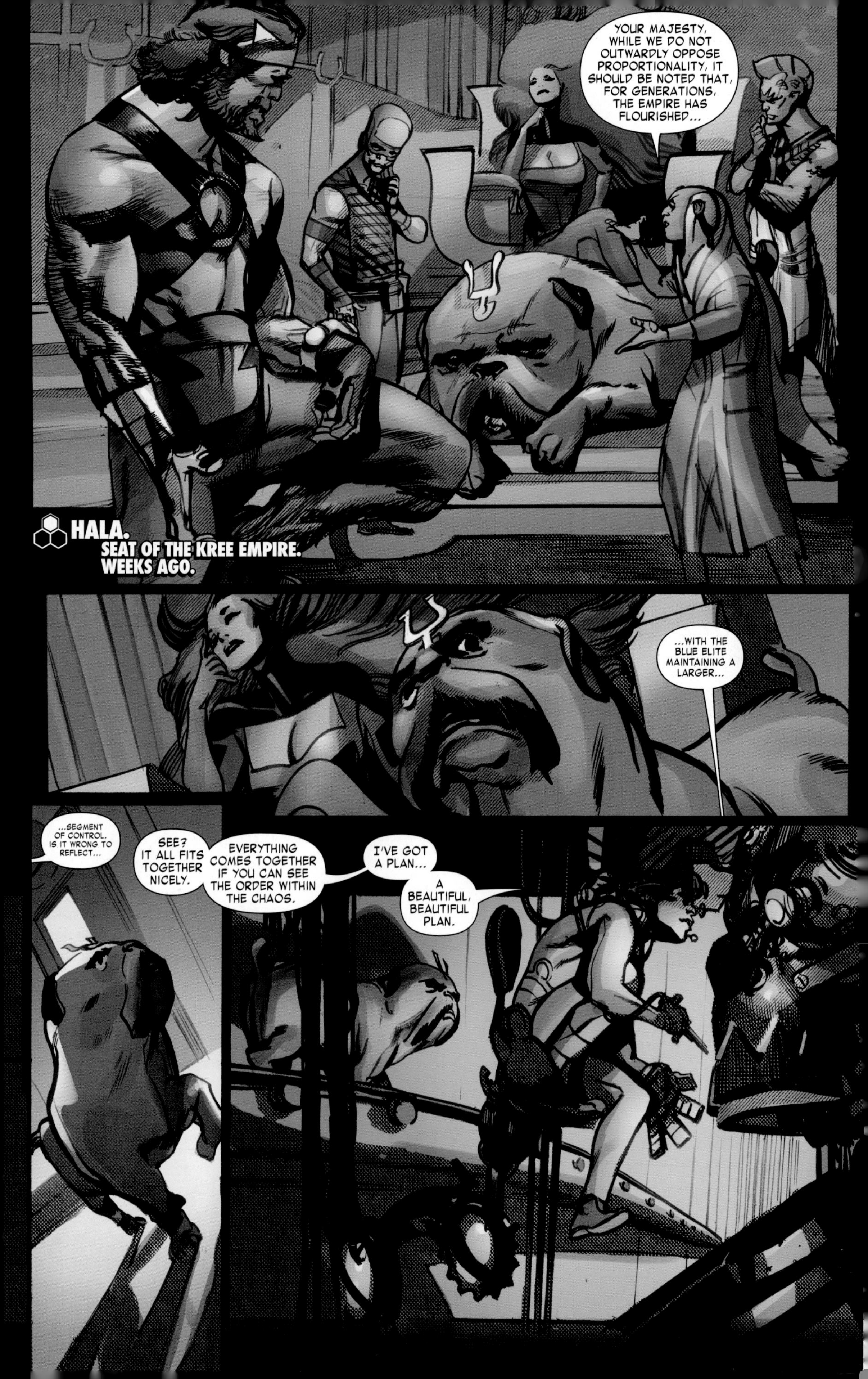
YOUR MAJESTY, WHILE WE DO NOT OUTWARDLY OPPOSE PROPORTIONALITY, IT SHOULD BE NOTED THAT, FOR GENERATIONS, THE EMPIRE HAS FLOURISHED...
HALA.
SEAT OF THE KREE EMPIRE.
WEEKS AGO.
...WITH THE BLUE ELITE MAINTAINING A LARGER...
...SEGMENT OF CONTROL. IS IT WRONG TO REFLECT...
SEE? IT ALL FITS TOGETHER NICELY.
EVERYTHING COMES TOGETHER IF YOU CAN SEE THE ORDER WITHIN THE CHAOS.
I'VE GOT A PLAN...
A BEAUTIFUL, BEAUTIFUL PLAN.

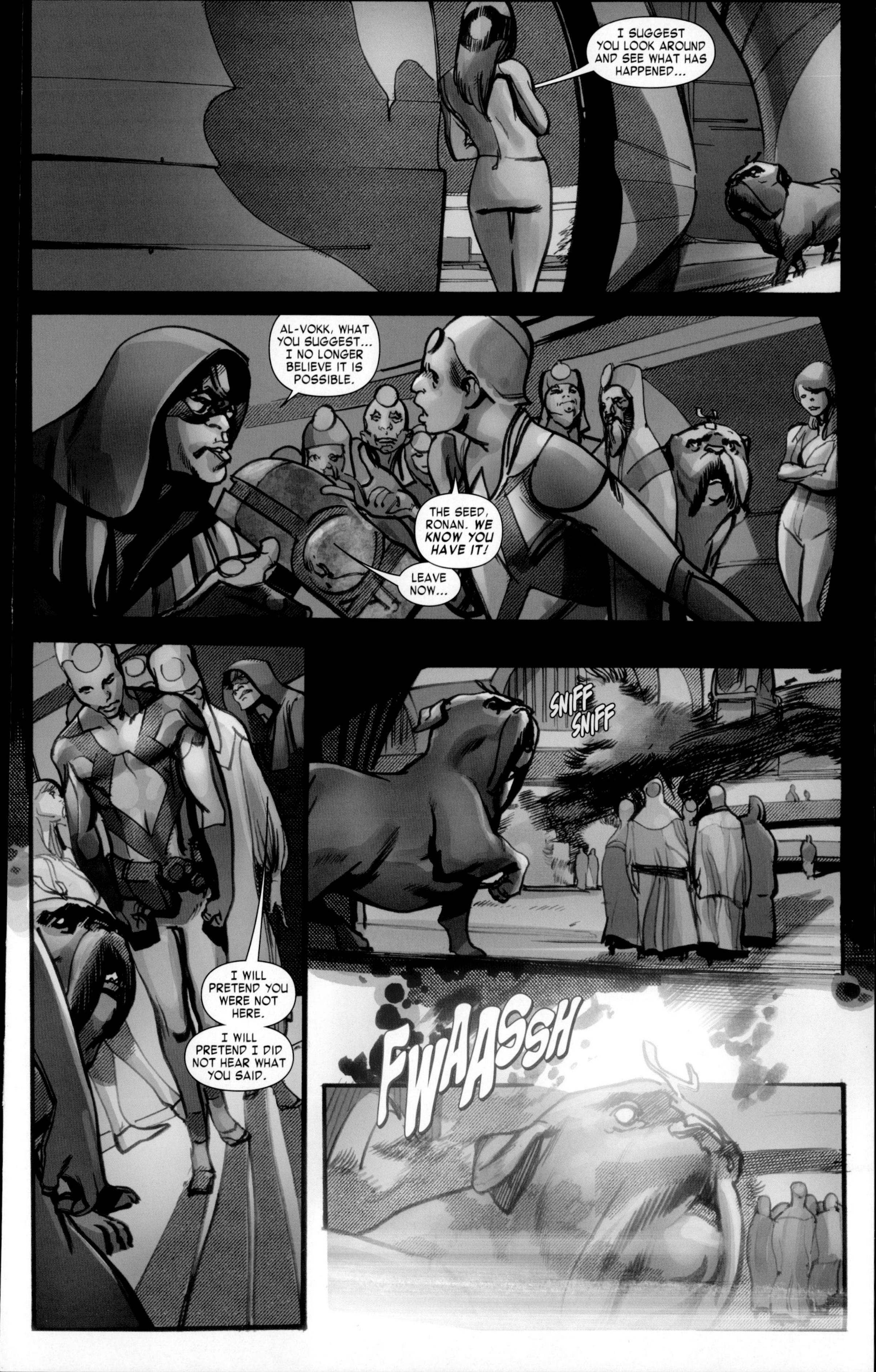
I SUGGEST YOU LOOK AROUND AND SEE WHAT HAS HAPPENED...
AL-VOKK, WHAT YOU SUGGEST... I NO LONGER BELIEVE IT IS POSSIBLE.
THE SEED, RONAN. WE KNOW YOU HAVE IT!
LEAVE NOW...
I WILL PRETEND YOU WERE NOT HERE.
I WILL PRETEND I DID NOT HEAR WHAT YOU SAID.
SNIFF SNIFF
FWAASSH

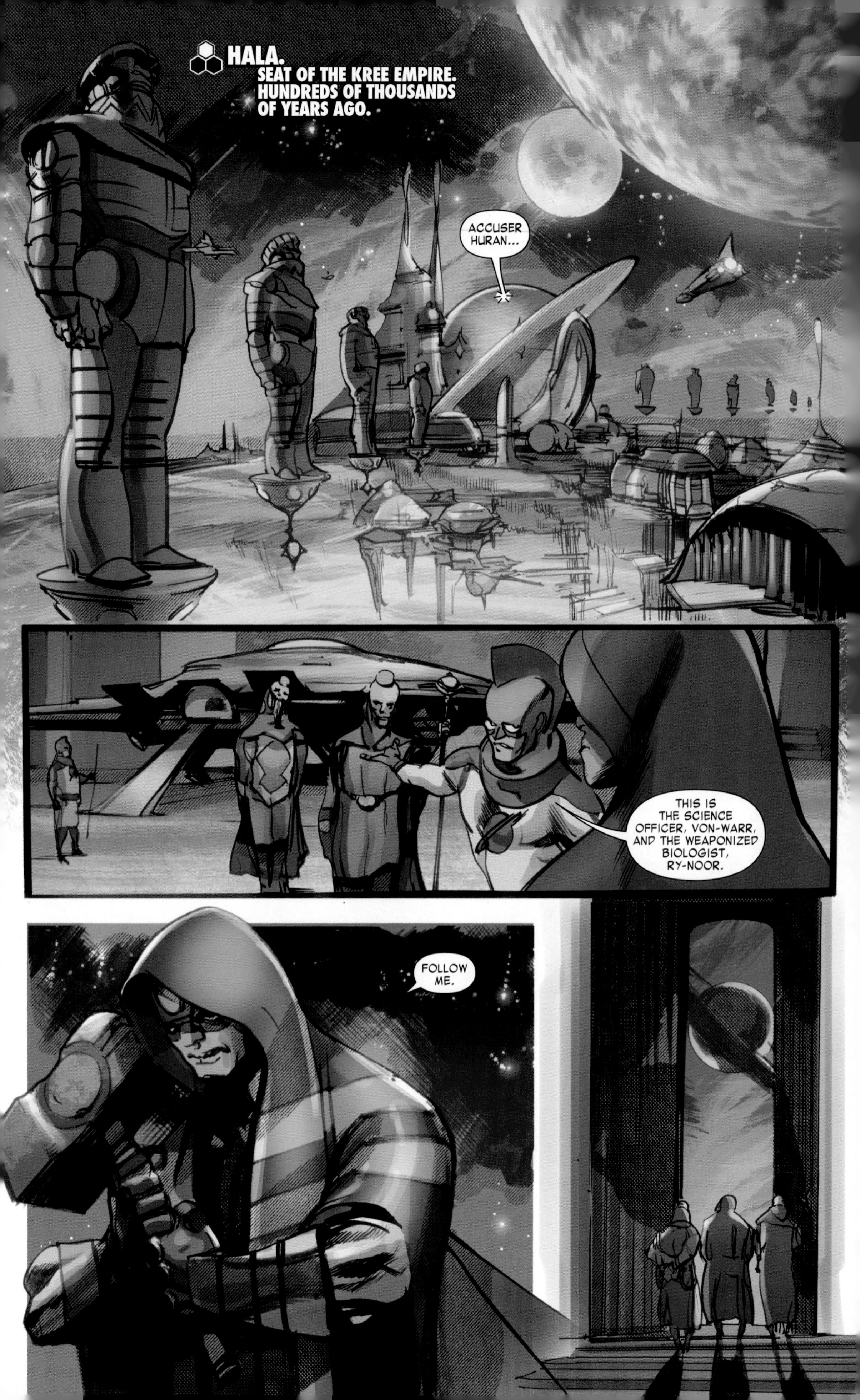
HALA.
SEAT OF THE KREE EMPIRE.
HUNDREDS OF THOUSANDS
OF YEARS AGO.
ACCUSER HURAN...
THIS IS THE SCIENCE OFFICER, VON-WARR, AND THE WEAPONIZED BIOLOGIST, RY-NOOR.
FOLLOW ME.

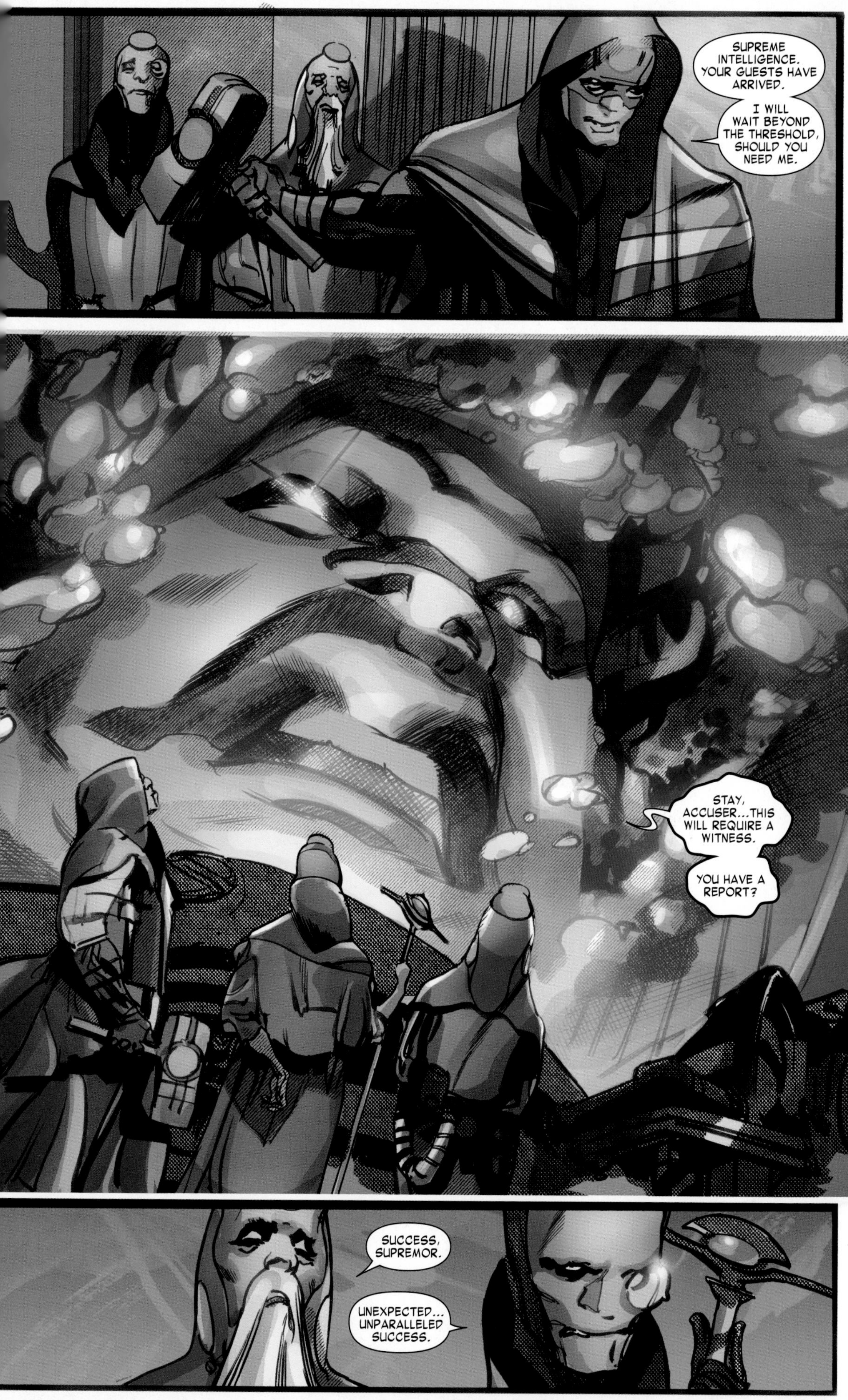
SUPREME INTELLIGENCE. YOUR GUESTS HAVE ARRIVED.
I WILL WAIT BEYOND THE THRESHOLD, SHOULD YOU NEED ME.
STAY, ACCUSER...THIS WILL REQUIRE A WITNESS.
YOU HAVE A REPORT?
SUCCESS, SUPREMOR.
UNEXPECTED... UNPARALLELED SUCCESS.

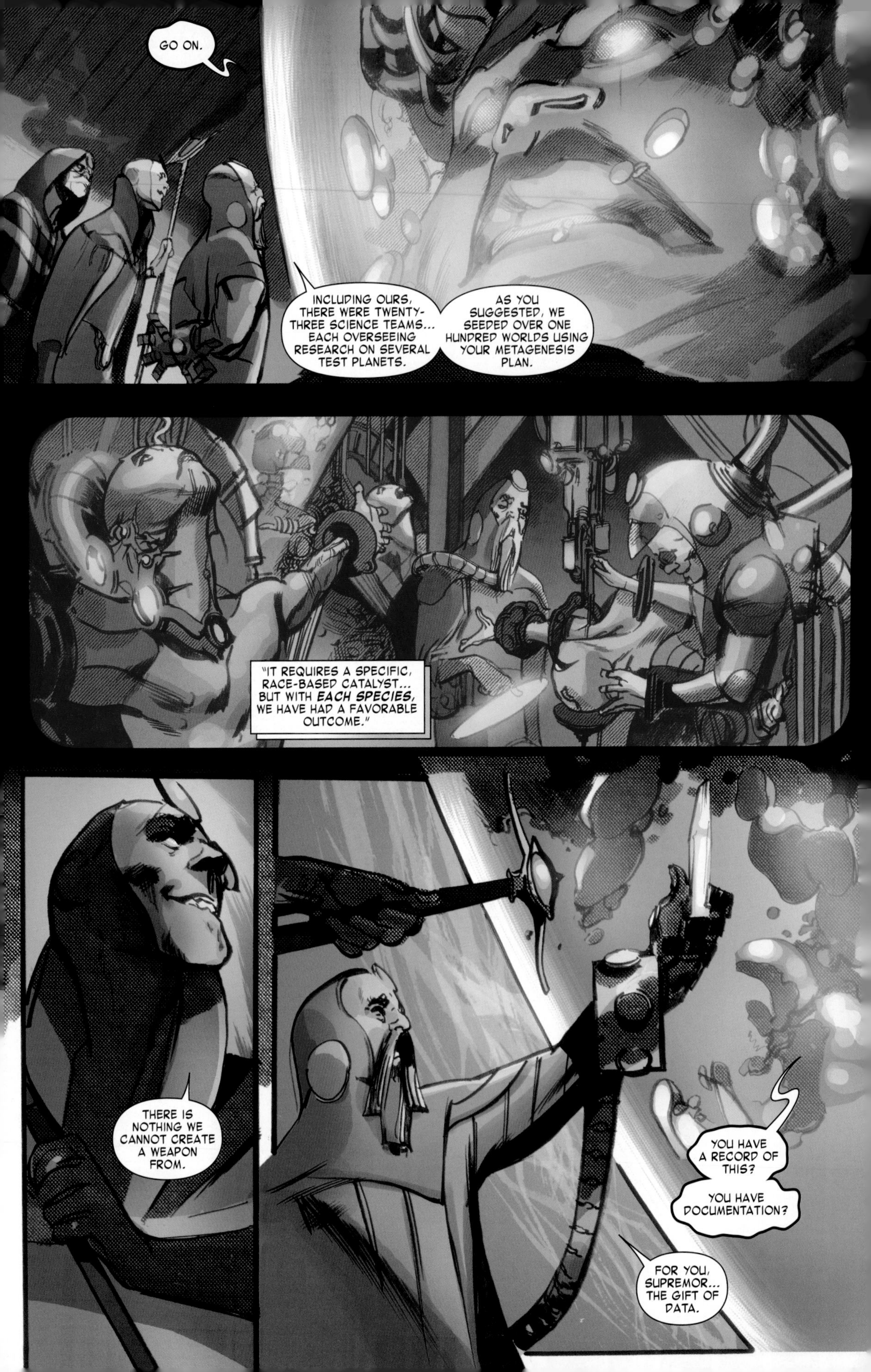
GO ON.
INCLUDING OURS, THERE WERE TWENTY-THREE SCIENCE TEAMS... EACH OVERSEEING RESEARCH ON SEVERAL TEST PLANETS.
AS YOU SUGGESTED, WE SEEDED OVER ONE HUNDRED WORLDS USING YOUR METAGENESIS PLAN.
"IT REQUIRES A SPECIFIC, RACE-BASED CATALYST... BUT WITH EACH SPECIES, WE HAVE HAD A FAVORABLE OUTCOME."
THERE IS NOTHING WE CANNOT CREATE A WEAPON FROM.
YOU HAVE A RECORD OF THIS?
YOU HAVE DOCUMENTATION?
FOR YOU, SUPREMOR... THE GIFT OF DATA.

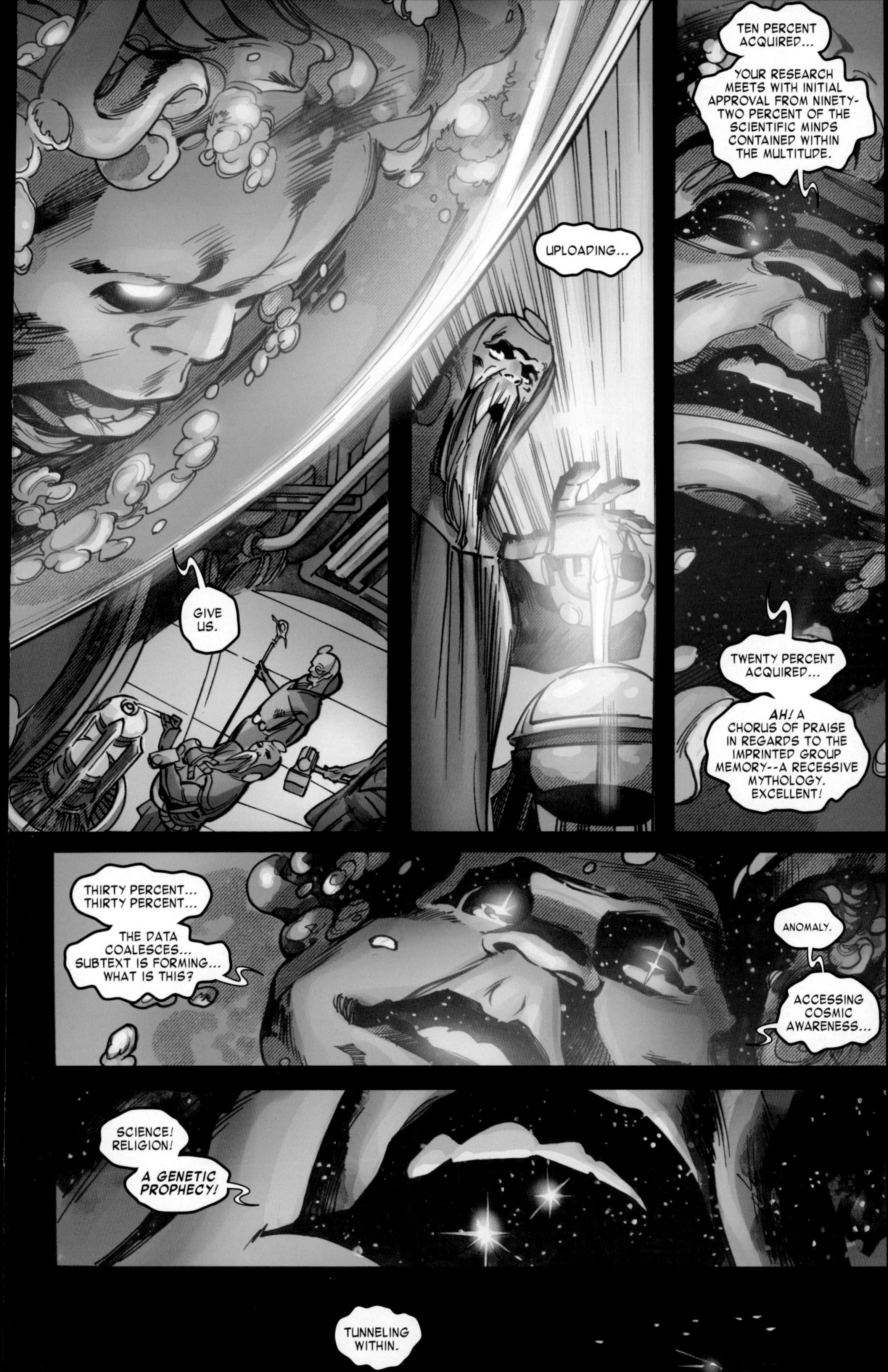
TEN PERCENT ACQUIRED...
YOUR RESEARCH MEETS WITH INITIAL APPROVAL FROM NINETY-TWO PERCENT OF THE SCIENTIFIC MINDS CONTAINED WITHIN THE MULTITUDE.
UPLOADING...
GIVE US.
TWENTY PERCENT ACQUIRED...
AH! A CHORUS OF PRAISE IN REGARDS TO THE IMPRINTED GROUP MEMORY--A RECESSIVE MYTHOLOGY. EXCELLENT!
THIRTY PERCENT... THIRTY PERCENT...
THE DATA COALESCES... SUBTEXT IS FORMING... WHAT IS THIS?
ANOMALY.
ACCESSING COSMIC AWARENESS...
SCIENCE! RELIGION!
A GENETIC PROPHECY!
TUNNELING WITHIN.

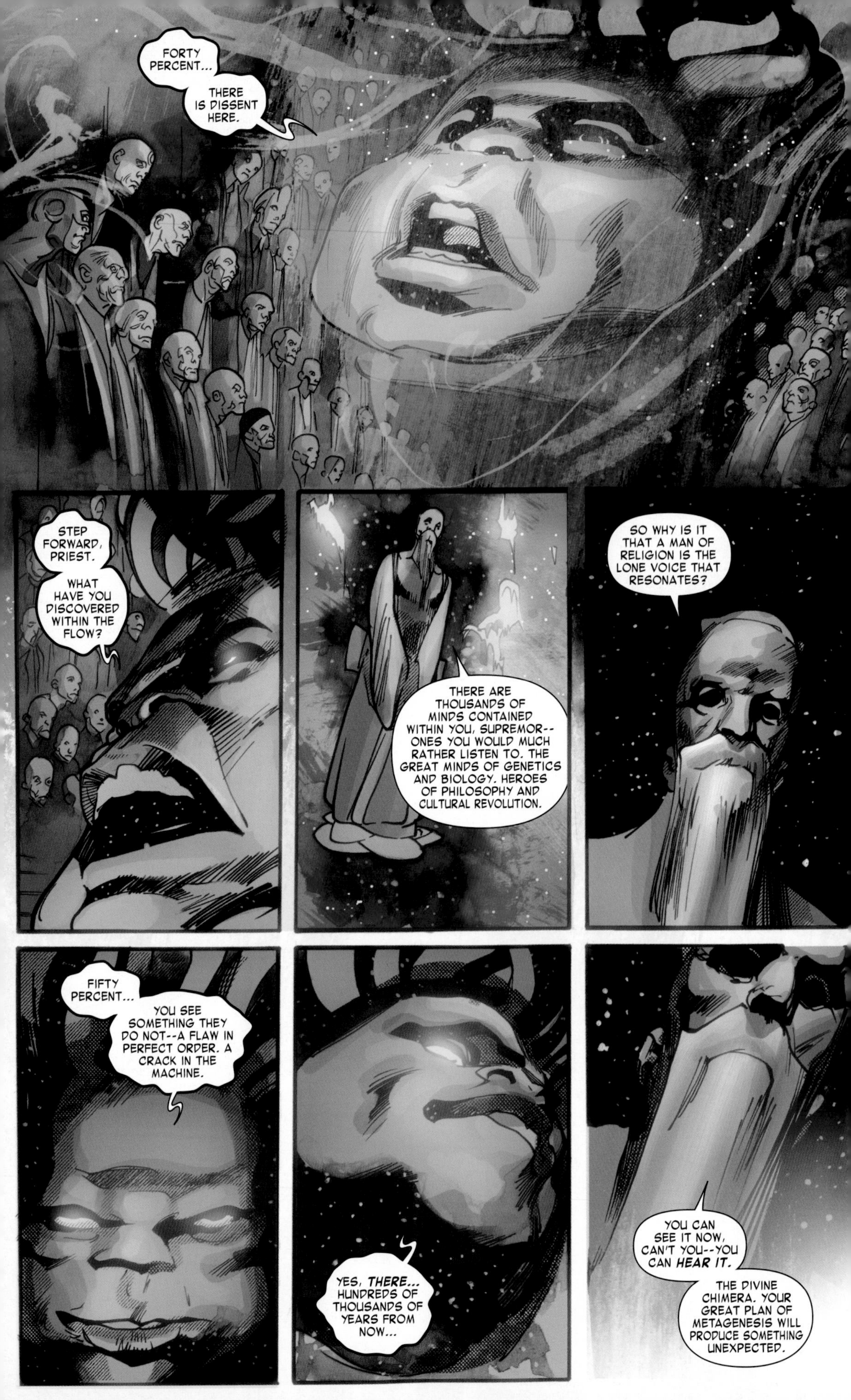
FORTY PERCENT...
THERE IS DISSENT HERE.
STEP FORWARD, PRIEST.
WHAT HAVE YOU DISCOVERED WITHIN THE FLOW?
THERE ARE THOUSANDS OF MINDS CONTAINED WITHIN YOU, SUPREMOR-- ONES YOU WOULD MUCH RATHER LISTEN TO. THE GREAT MINDS OF GENETICS AND BIOLOGY. HEROES OF PHILOSOPHY AND CULTURAL REVOLUTION.
SO WHY IS IT THAT A MAN OF RELIGION IS THE LONE VOICE THAT RESONATES?
FIFTY PERCENT...
YOU SEE SOMETHING THEY DO NOT--A FLAW IN PERFECT ORDER. A CRACK IN THE MACHINE.
YES, *THERE...* HUNDREDS OF THOUSANDS OF YEARS FROM NOW...
YOU CAN SEE IT NOW, CAN'T YOU--YOU CAN *HEAR IT.*
THE DIVINE CHIMERA. YOUR GREAT PLAN OF METAGENESIS WILL PRODUCE SOMETHING UNEXPECTED.

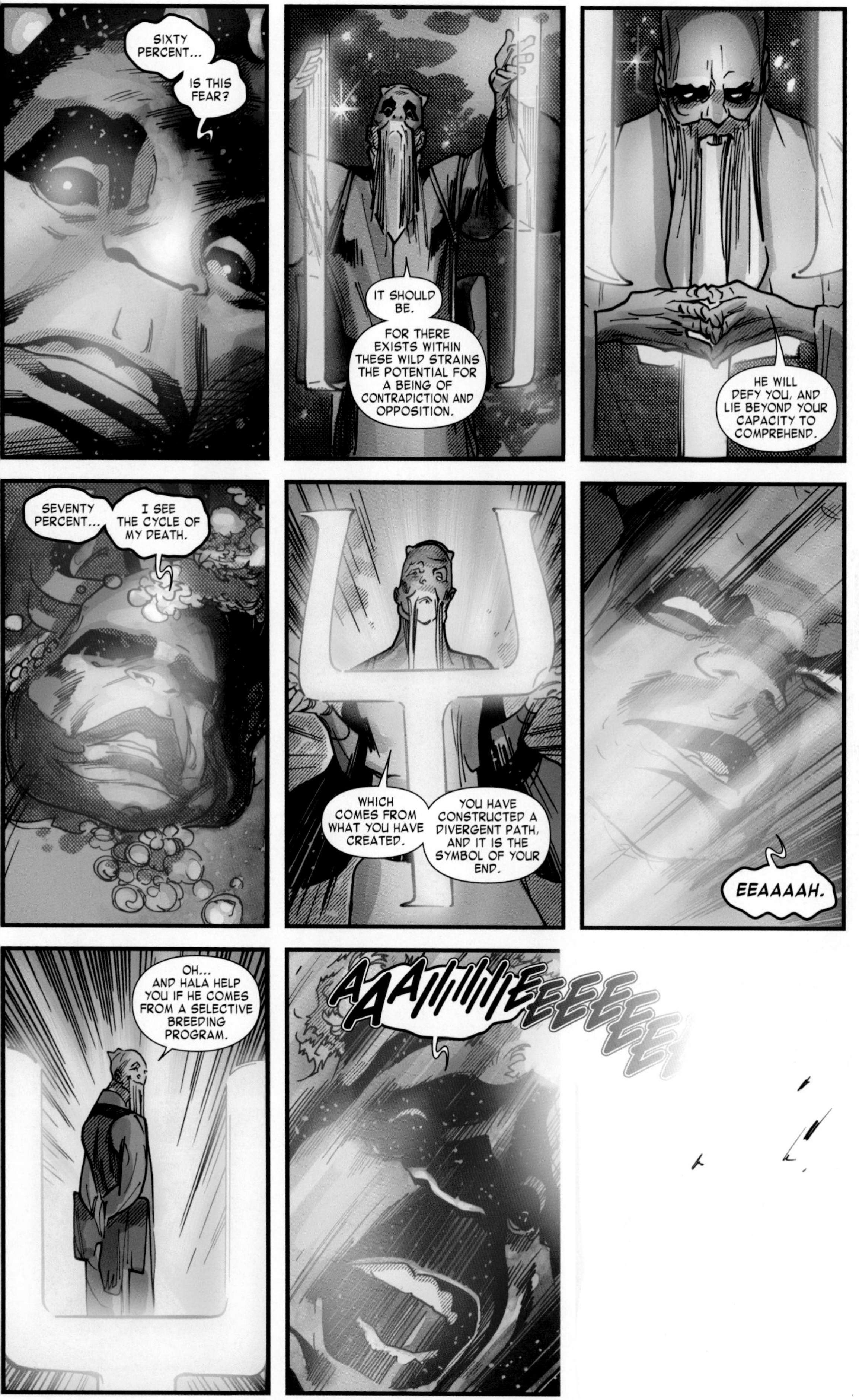
SIXTY PERCENT...
IS THIS FEAR?
IT SHOULD BE.
FOR THERE EXISTS WITHIN THESE WILD STRAINS THE POTENTIAL FOR A BEING OF CONTRADICTION AND OPPOSITION.
HE WILL DEFY YOU, AND LIE BEYOND YOUR CAPACITY TO COMPREHEND.
SEVENTY PERCENT...
I SEE THE CYCLE OF MY DEATH.
WHICH COMES FROM WHAT YOU HAVE CREATED.
YOU HAVE CONSTRUCTED A DIVERGENT PATH, AND IT IS THE SYMBOL OF YOUR END.
EEAAAAH.
OH... AND HALA HELP YOU IF HE COMES FROM A SELECTIVE BREEDING PROGRAM.
AAAIIIIIIIEEEEEE

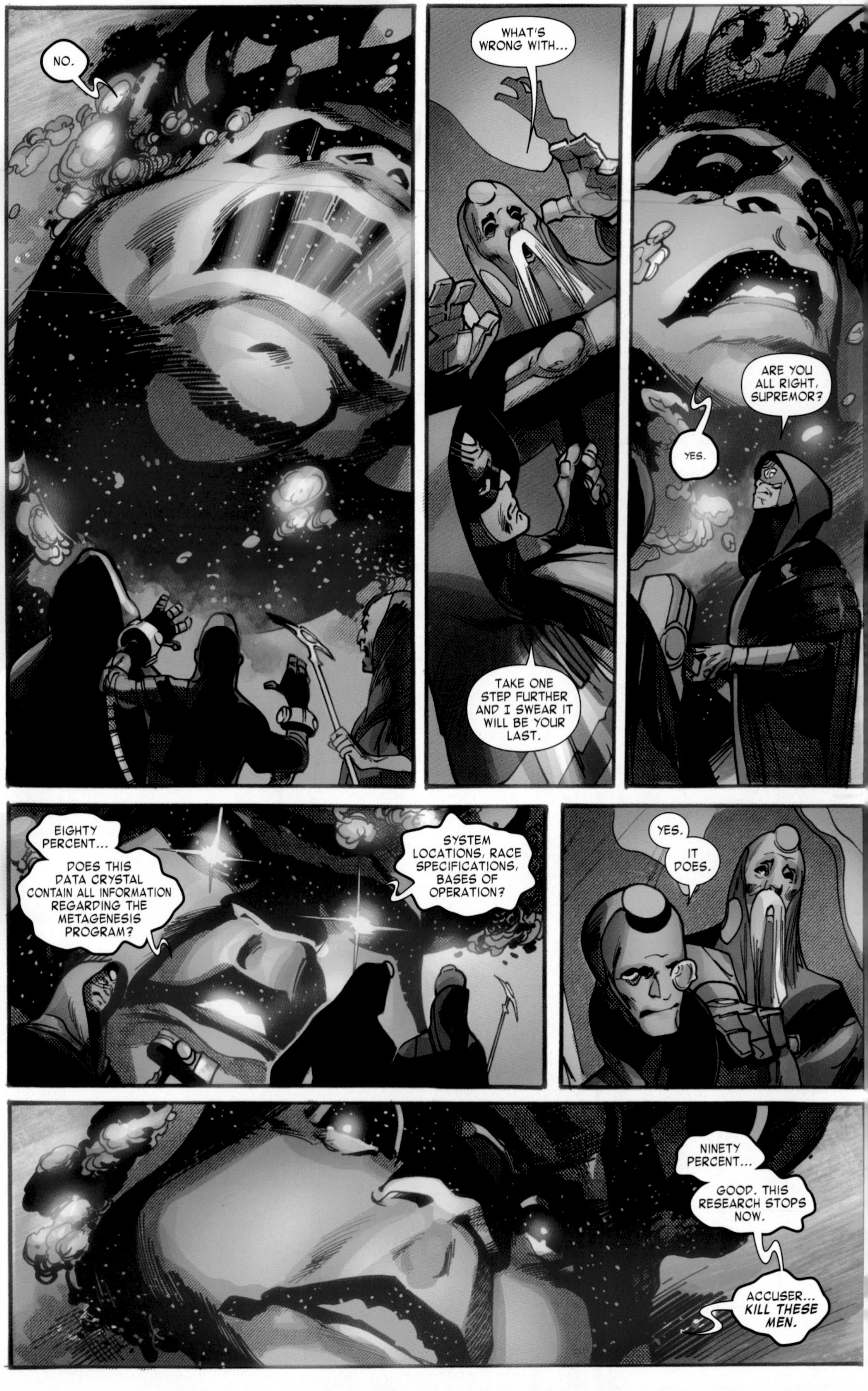
NO.
WHAT'S WRONG WITH...
TAKE ONE STEP FURTHER AND I SWEAR IT WILL BE YOUR LAST.
ARE YOU ALL RIGHT, SUPREMOR?
YES.
EIGHTY PERCENT...
DOES THIS DATA CRYSTAL CONTAIN ALL INFORMATION REGARDING THE METAGENESIS PROGRAM?
SYSTEM LOCATIONS, RACE SPECIFICATIONS, BASES OF OPERATION?
YES.
IT DOES.
NINETY PERCENT...
GOOD. THIS RESEARCH STOPS NOW.
ACCUSER... KILL THESE MEN.

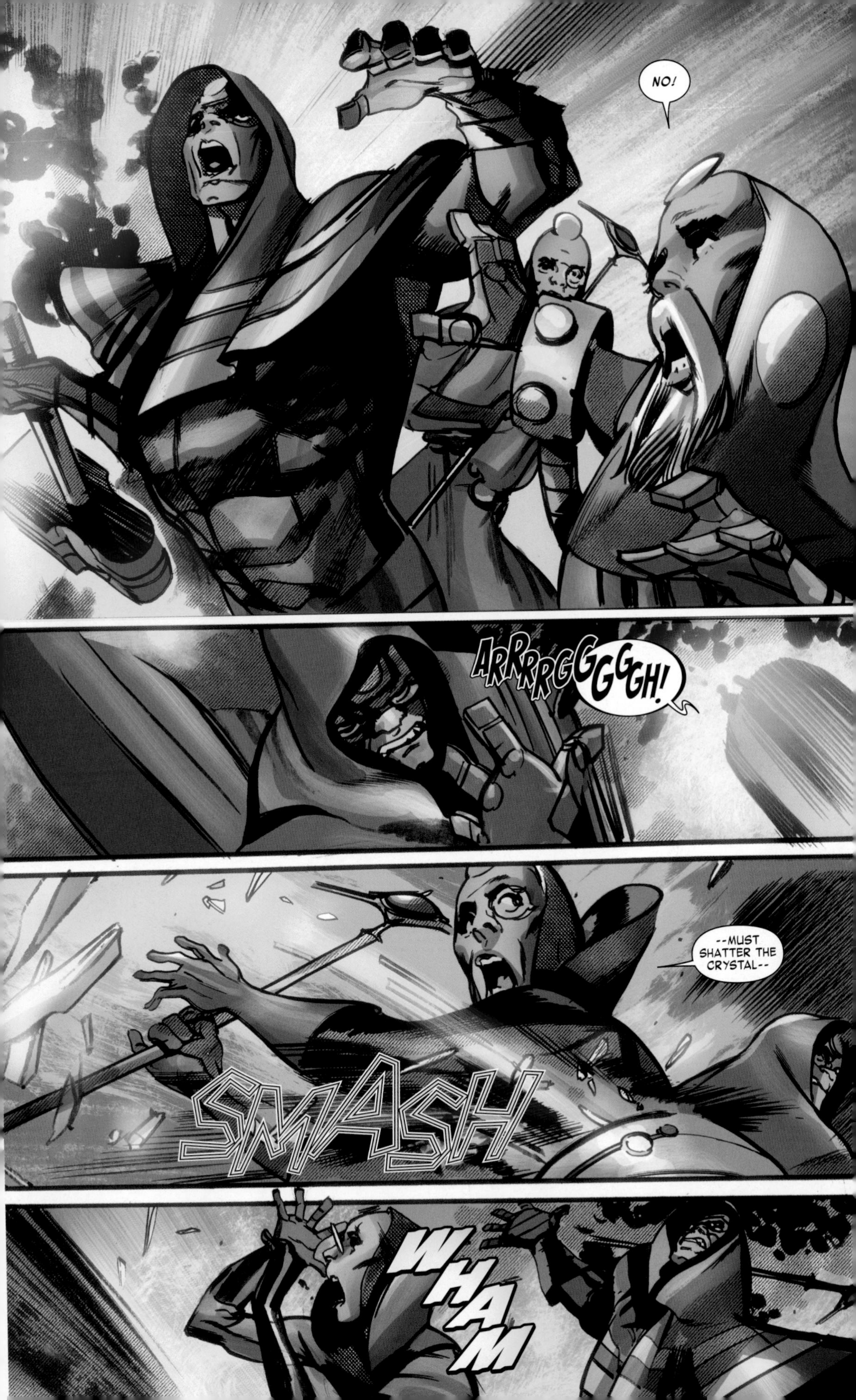
NO!
ARRRRGGGGGH!
--MUST SHATTER THE CRYSTAL--
SMASH
WHAM

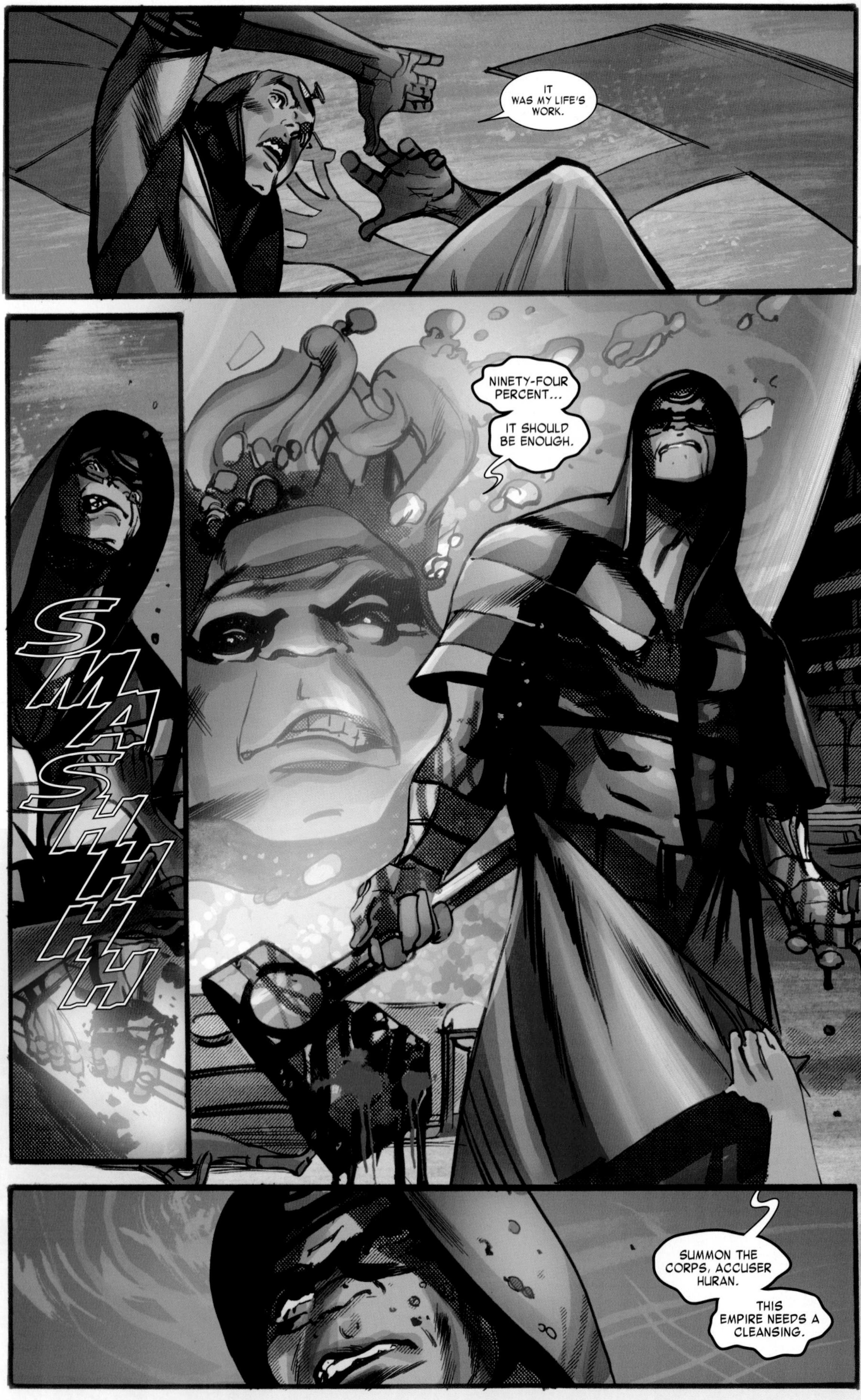
IT WAS MY LIFE'S WORK.
NINETY-FOUR PERCENT...
IT SHOULD BE ENOUGH.
SMASHHHH
SUMMON THE CORPS, ACCUSER HURAN.
THIS EMPIRE NEEDS A CLEANSING.

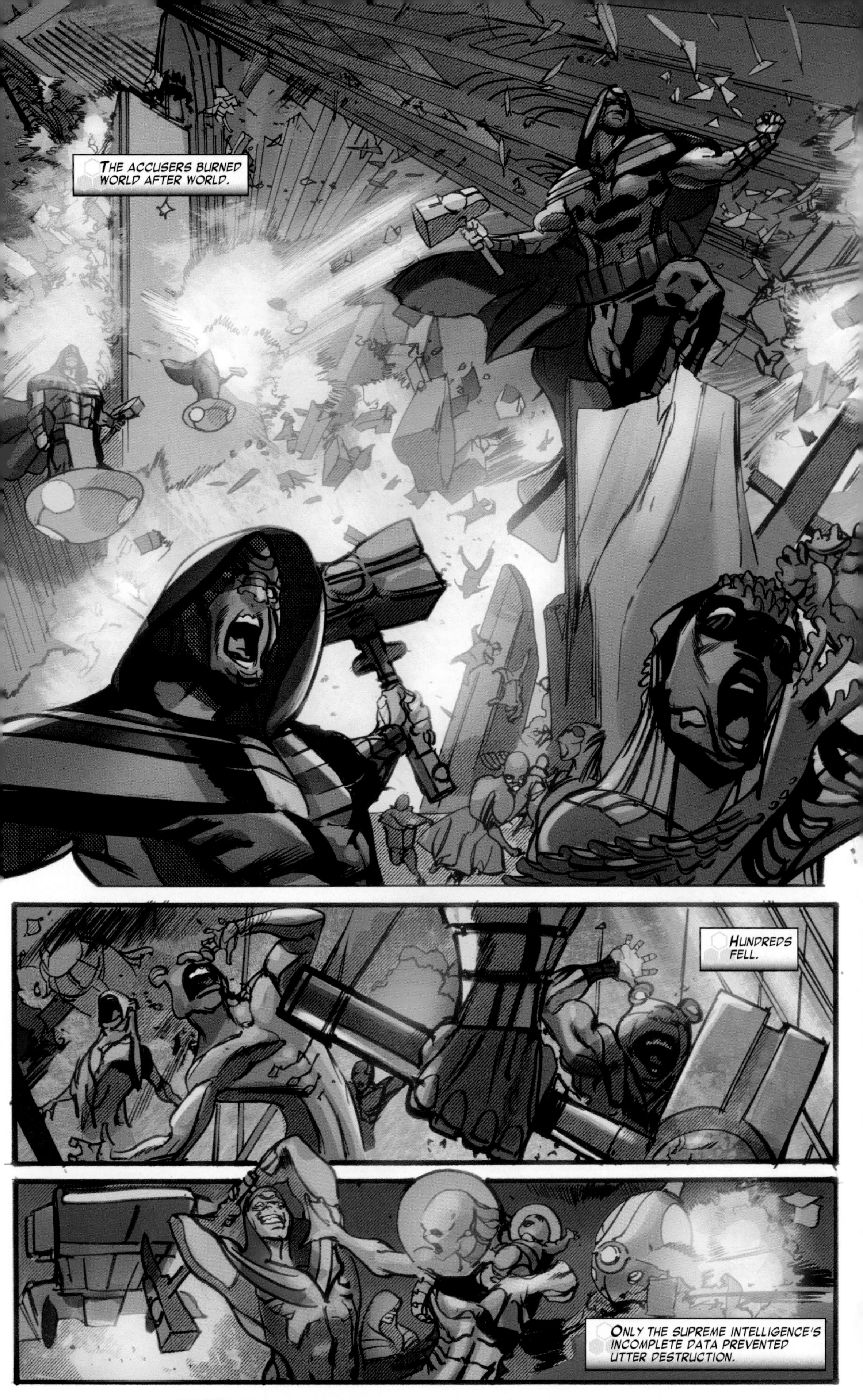
THE ACCUSERS BURNED WORLD AFTER WORLD.
HUNDREDS FELL.
ONLY THE SUPREME INTELLIGENCE'S INCOMPLETE DATA PREVENTED UTTER DESTRUCTION.

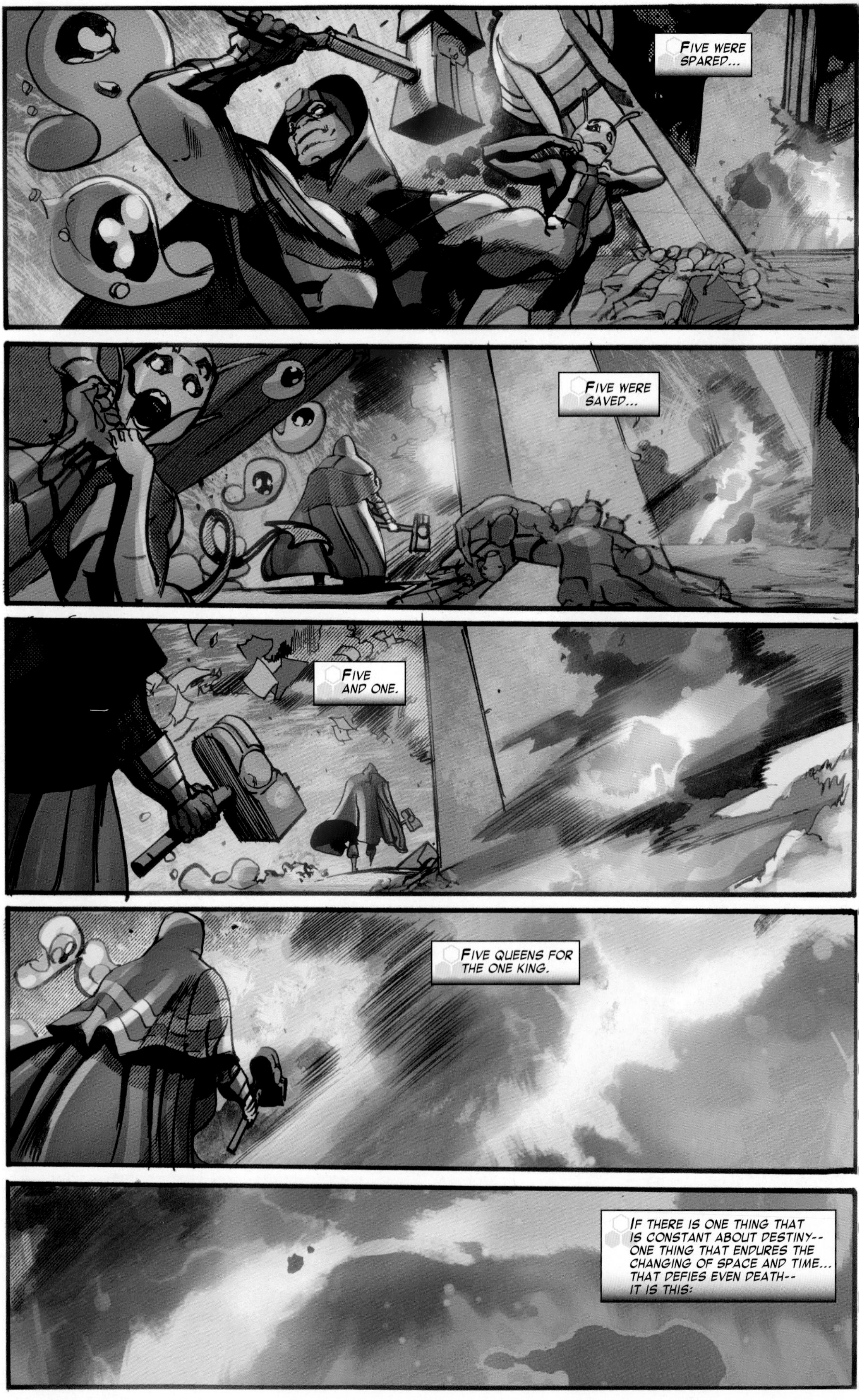
FIVE WERE SPARED...
FIVE WERE SAVED...
FIVE AND ONE.
FIVE QUEENS FOR THE ONE KING.
IF THERE IS ONE THING THAT IS CONSTANT ABOUT DESTINY-- ONE THING THAT ENDURES THE CHANGING OF SPACE AND TIME... THAT DEFIES EVEN DEATH-- IT IS THIS:

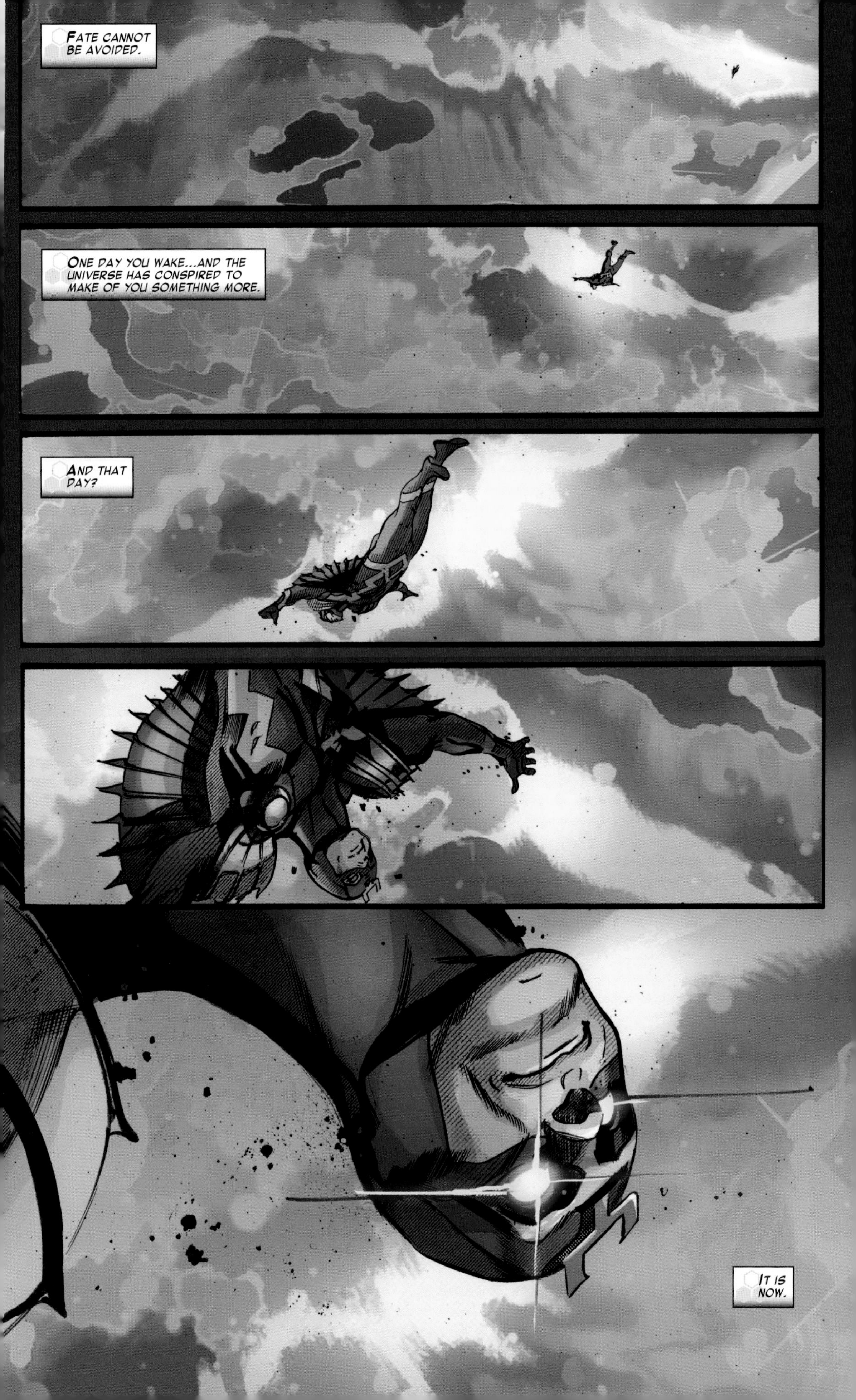
FATE CANNOT BE AVOIDED.
ONE DAY YOU WAKE...AND THE UNIVERSE HAS CONSPIRED TO MAKE OF YOU SOMETHING MORE.
AND THAT DAY?
IT IS NOW.

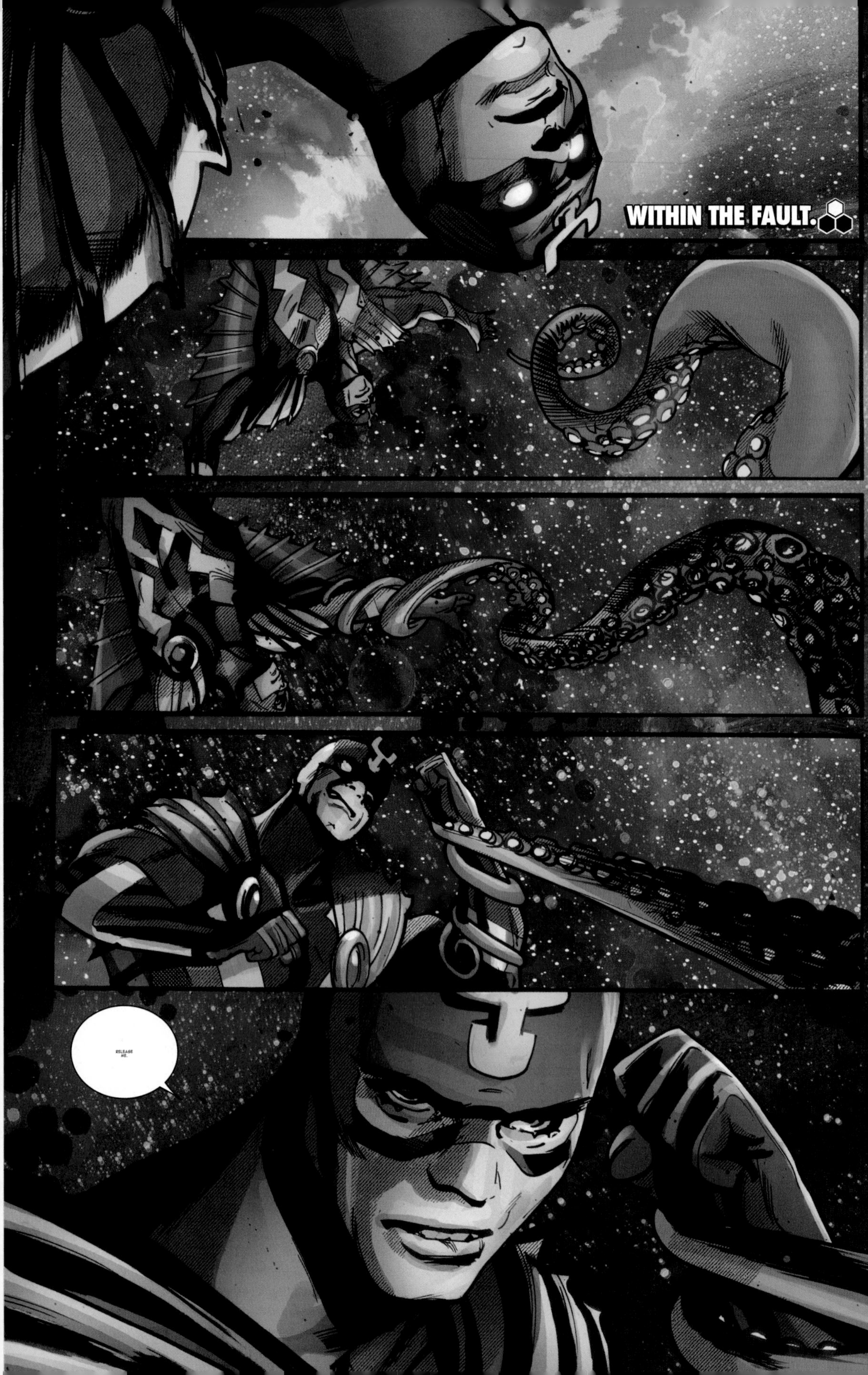
WITHIN THE FAULT.
RELEASE ME.

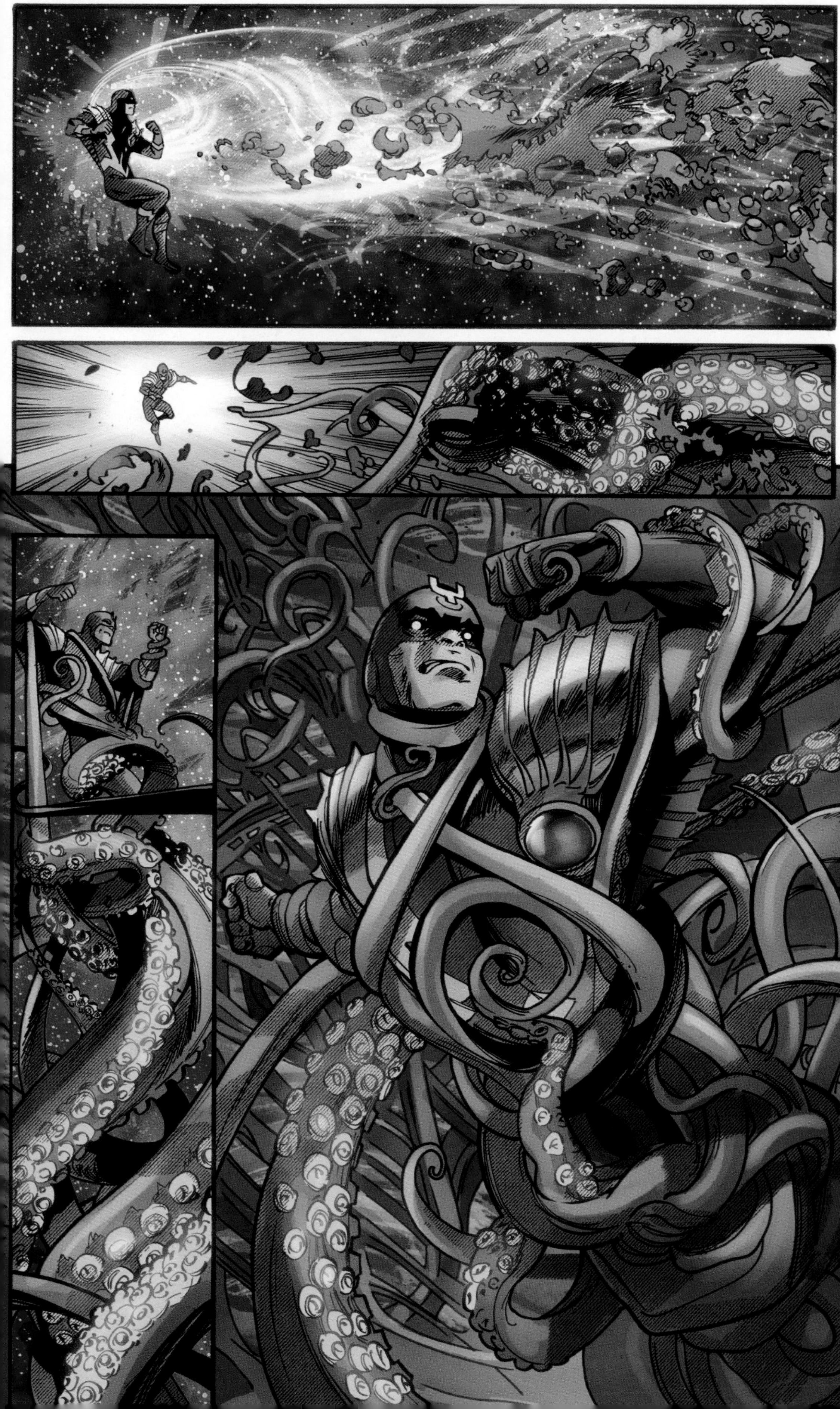

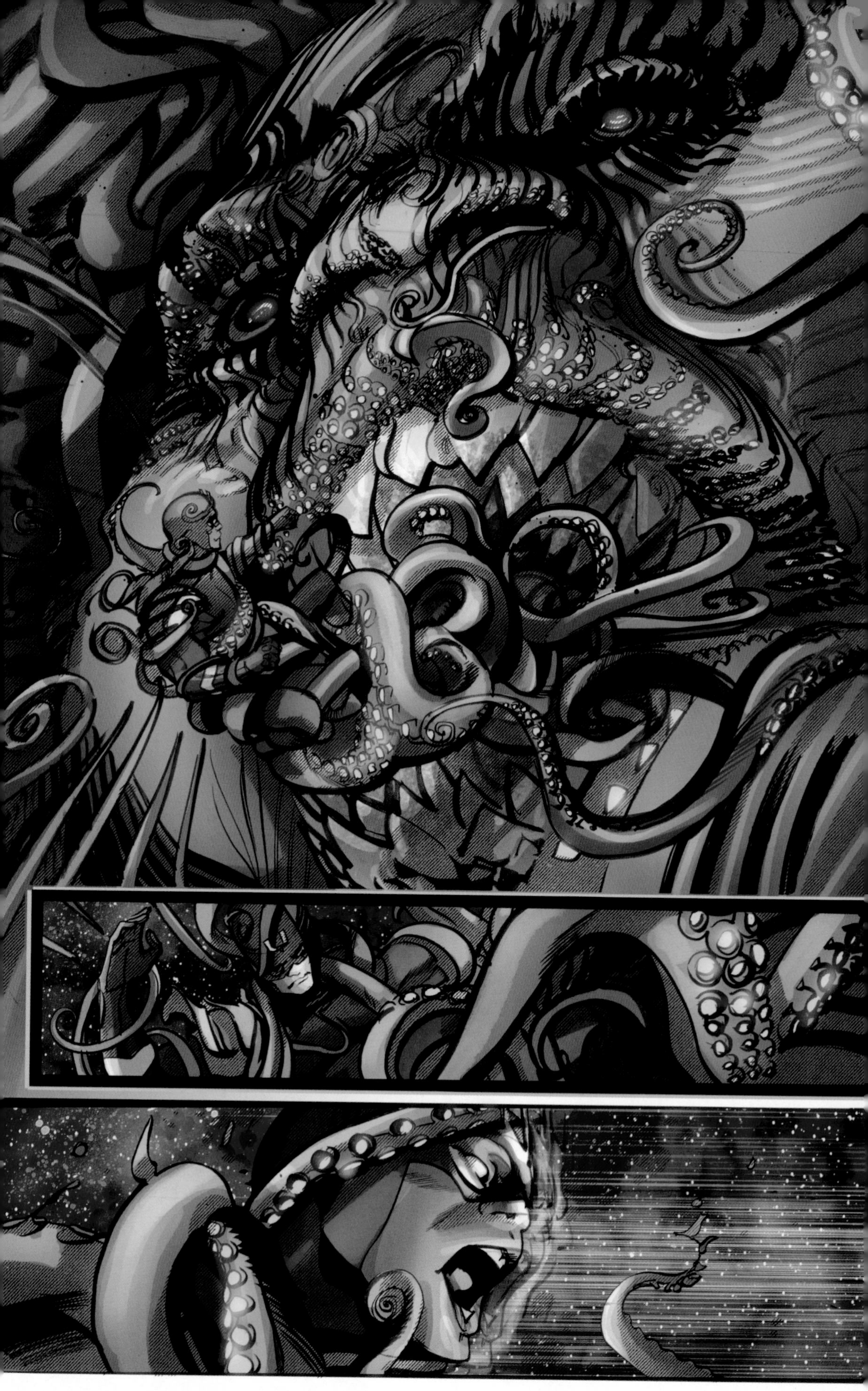

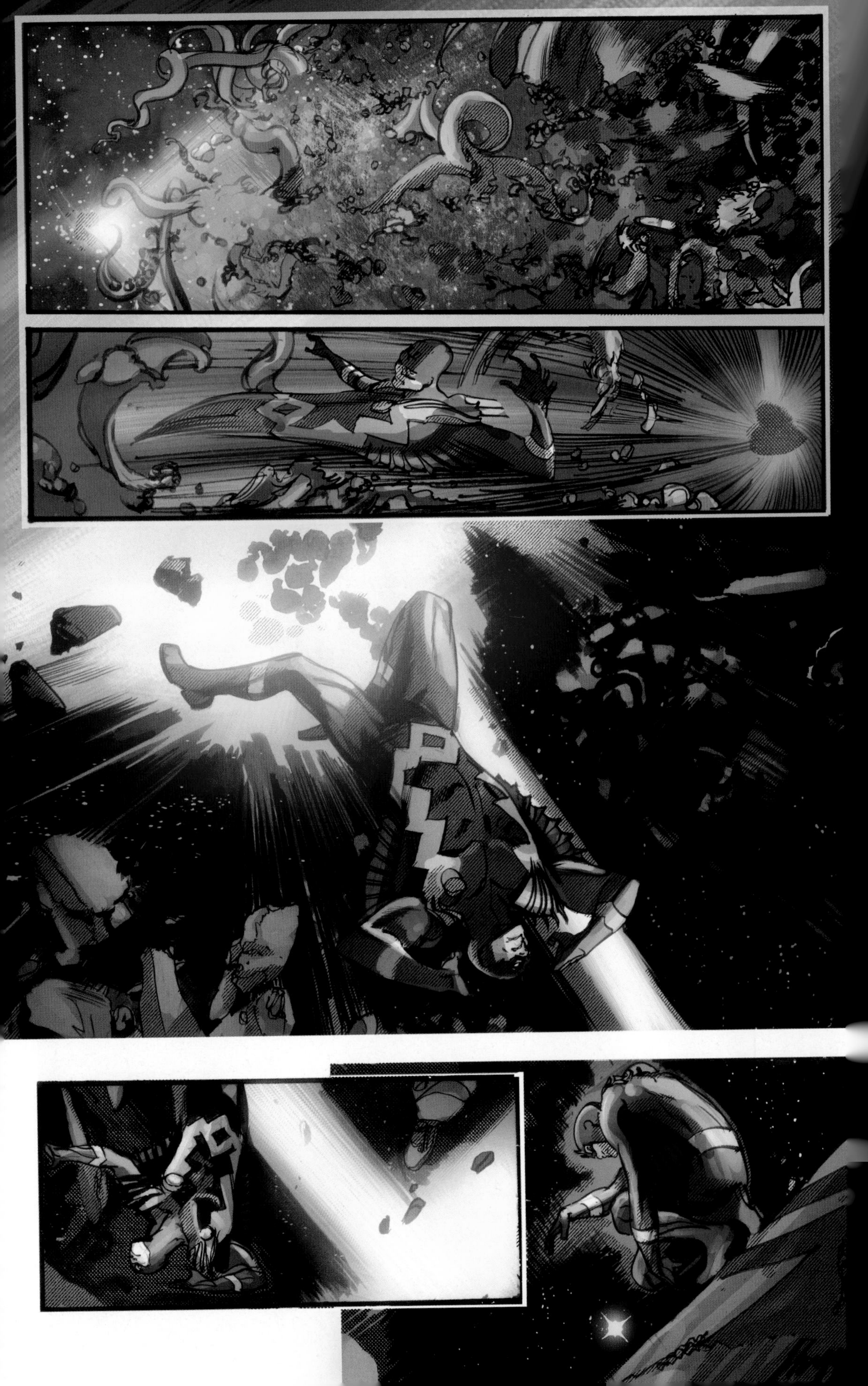

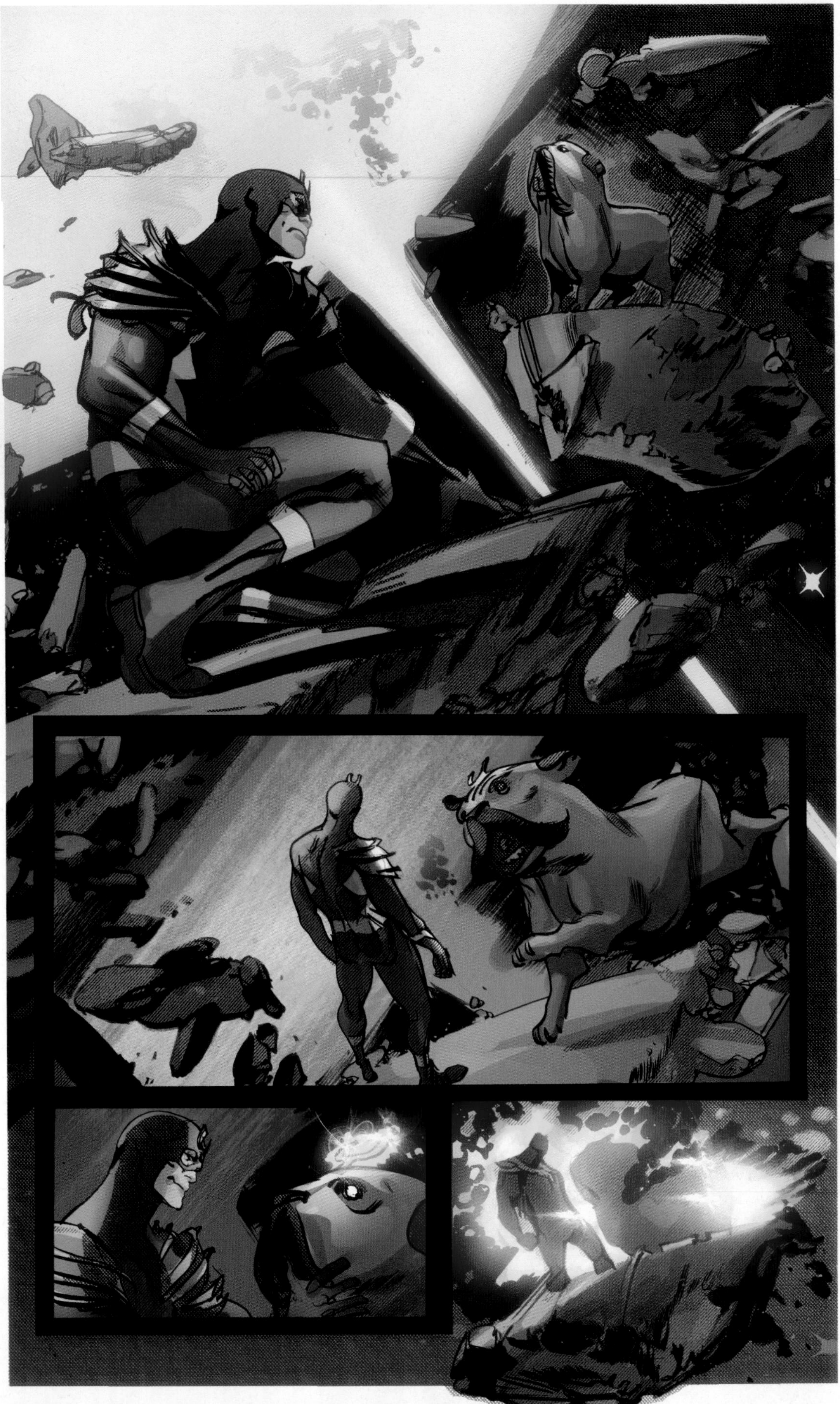

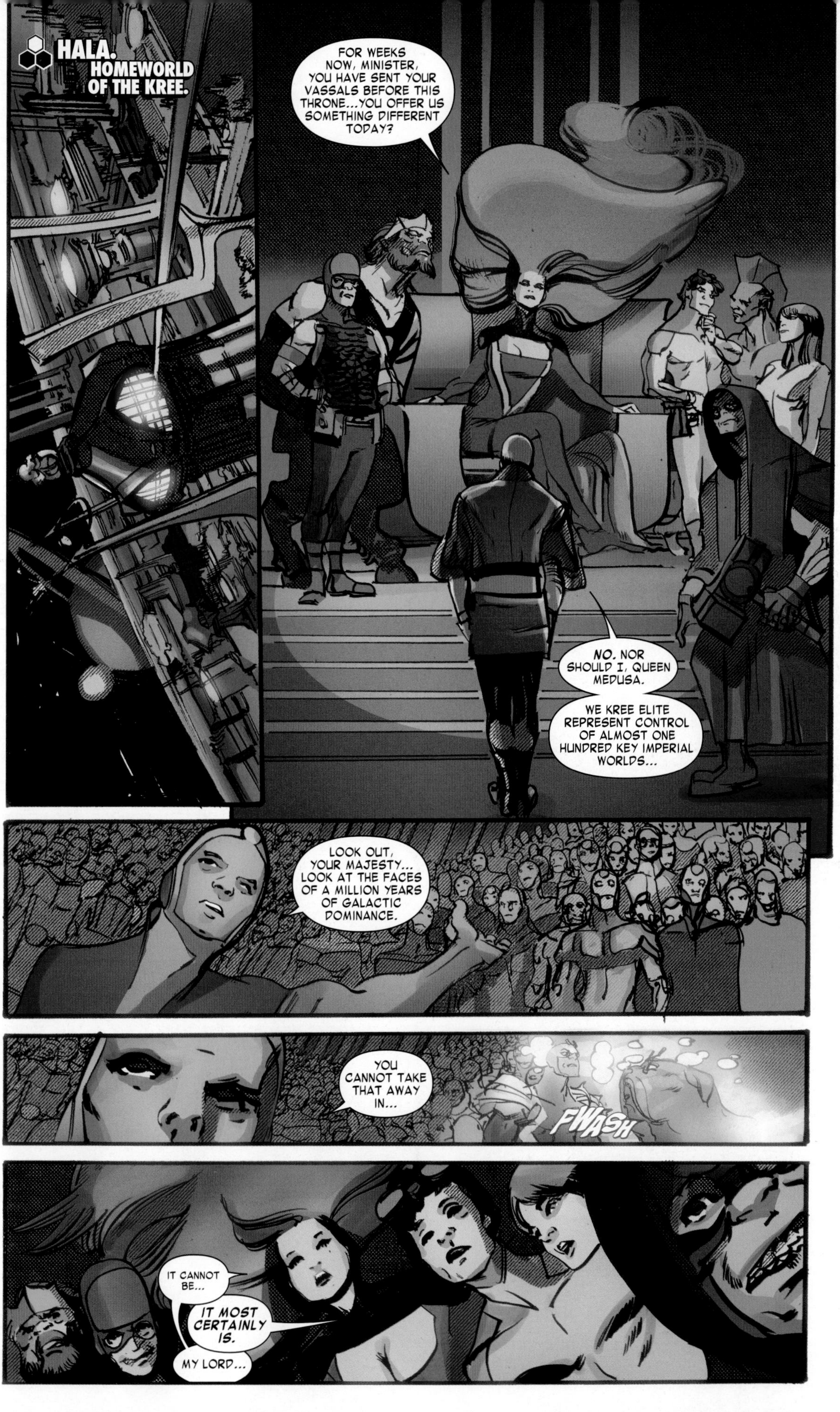
HALA. HOMEWORLD OF THE KREE.
FOR WEEKS NOW, MINISTER, YOU HAVE SENT YOUR VASSALS BEFORE THIS THRONE...YOU OFFER US SOMETHING DIFFERENT TODAY?
NO. NOR SHOULD I, QUEEN MEDUSA.
WE KREE ELITE REPRESENT CONTROL OF ALMOST ONE HUNDRED KEY IMPERIAL WORLDS...
LOOK OUT, YOUR MAJESTY... LOOK AT THE FACES OF A MILLION YEARS OF GALACTIC DOMINANCE.
YOU CANNOT TAKE THAT AWAY IN...
FWASH
IT CANNOT BE...
IT MOST CERTAINLY IS.
MY LORD...

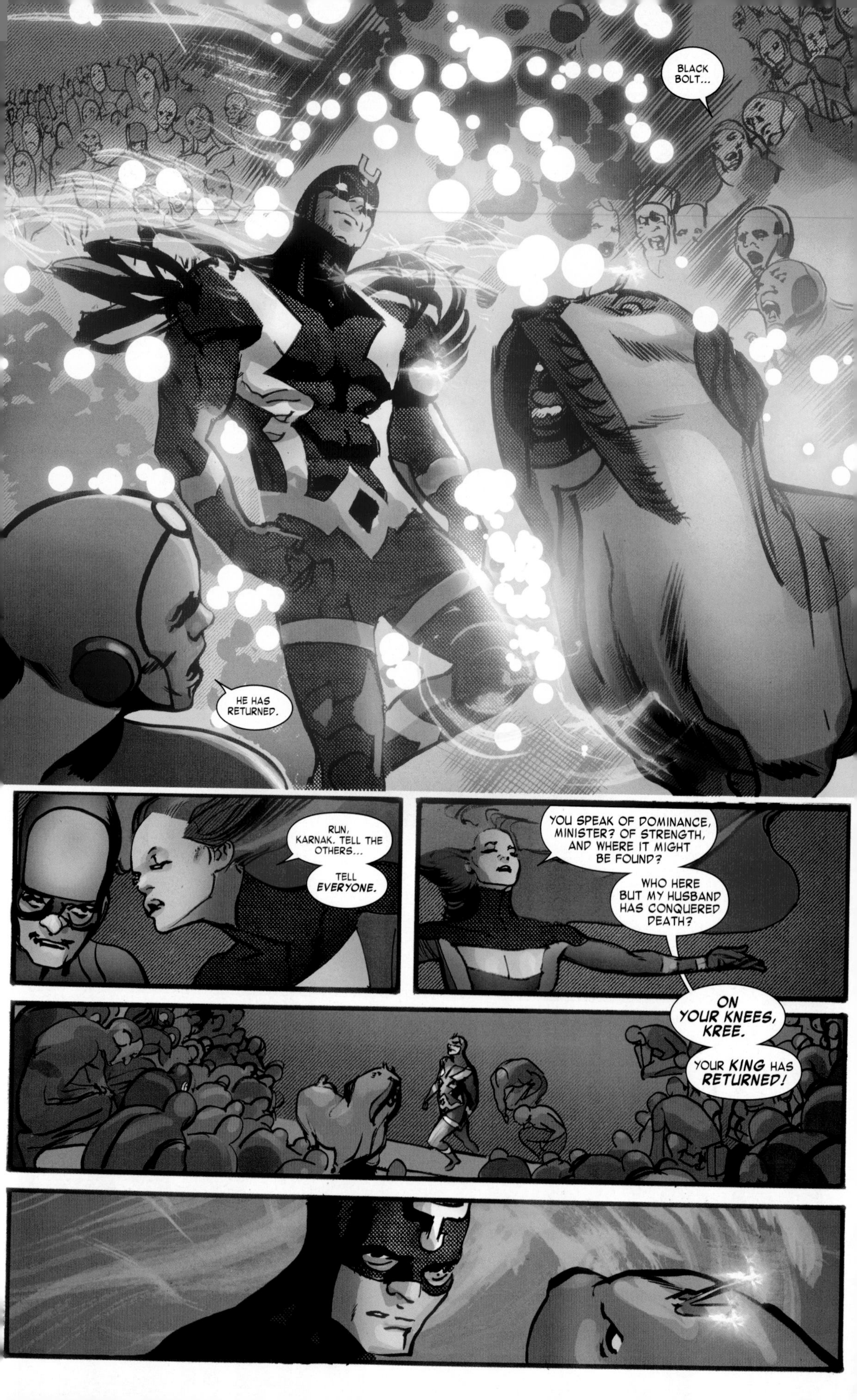
BLACK BOLT...
HE HAS RETURNED.
RUN, KARNAK. TELL THE OTHERS...
TELL EVERYONE.
YOU SPEAK OF DOMINANCE, MINISTER? OF STRENGTH, AND WHERE IT MIGHT BE FOUND?
WHO HERE BUT MY HUSBAND HAS CONQUERED DEATH?
ON YOUR KNEES, KREE.
YOUR KING HAS RETURNED!

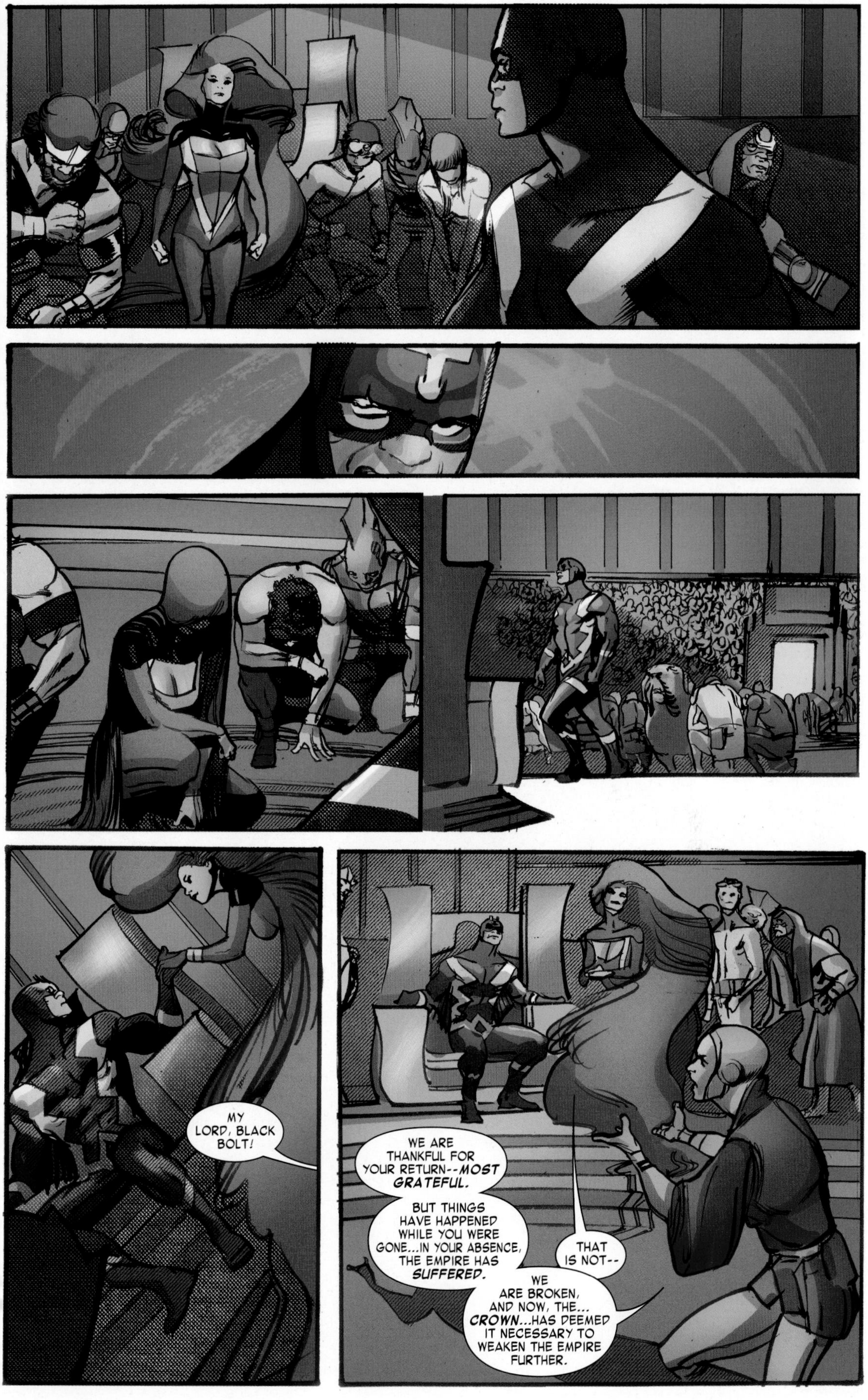

MY LORD, BLACK BOLT!
WE ARE THANKFUL FOR YOUR RETURN--*MOST GRATEFUL.*
BUT THINGS HAVE HAPPENED WHILE YOU WERE GONE...IN YOUR ABSENCE, THE EMPIRE HAS *SUFFERED.*
THAT IS NOT--
WE ARE BROKEN, AND NOW, THE... *CROWN*...HAS DEEMED IT NECESSARY TO WEAKEN THE EMPIRE FURTHER.

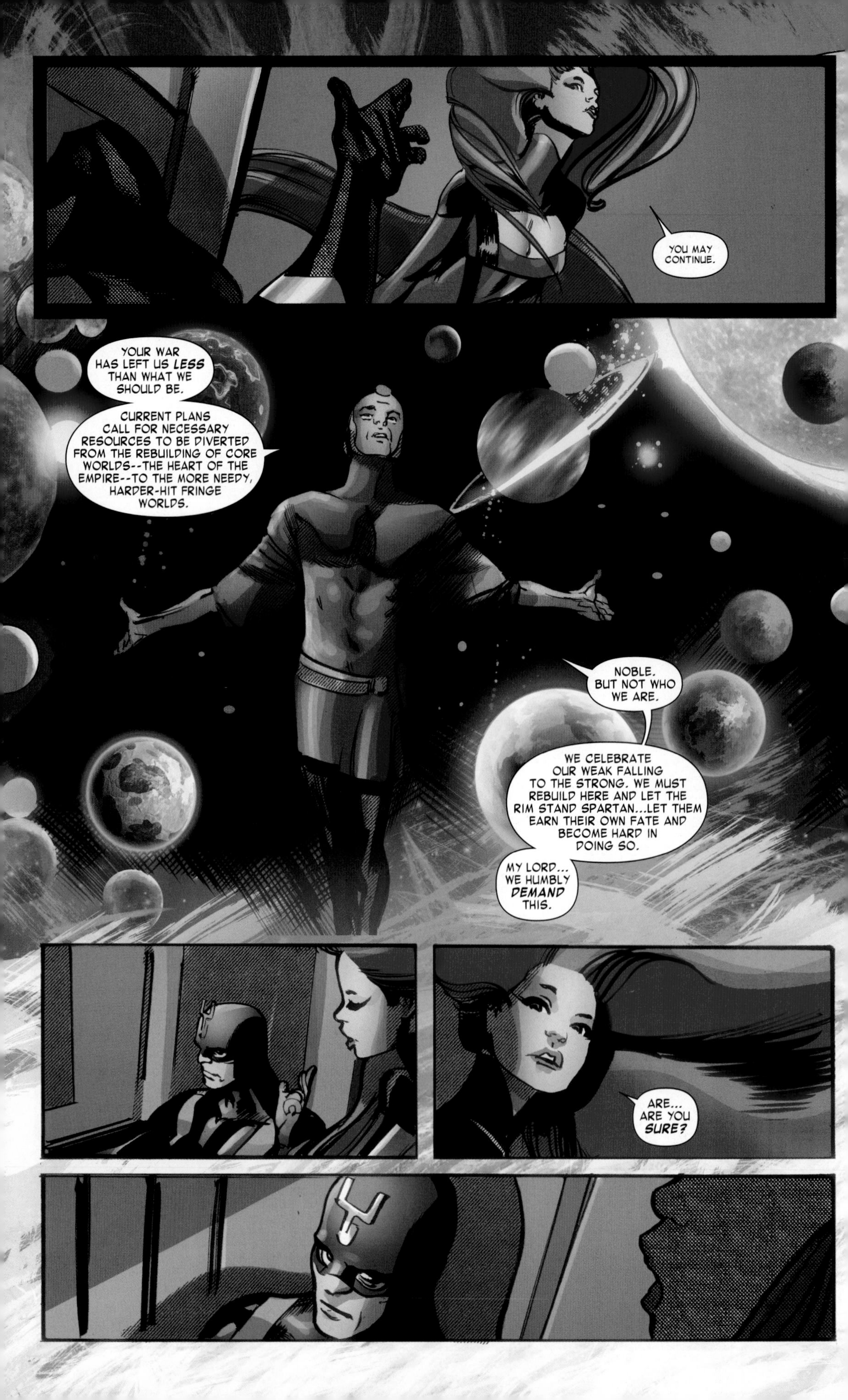
YOU MAY CONTINUE.
YOUR WAR HAS LEFT US LESS THAN WHAT WE SHOULD BE.
CURRENT PLANS CALL FOR NECESSARY RESOURCES TO BE DIVERTED FROM THE REBUILDING OF CORE WORLDS--THE HEART OF THE EMPIRE--TO THE MORE NEEDY, HARDER-HIT FRINGE WORLDS.
NOBLE. BUT NOT WHO WE ARE.
WE CELEBRATE OUR WEAK FALLING TO THE STRONG. WE MUST REBUILD HERE AND LET THE RIM STAND SPARTAN...LET THEM EARN THEIR OWN FATE AND BECOME HARD IN DOING SO.
MY LORD... WE HUMBLY DEMAND THIS.
ARE... ARE YOU SURE?

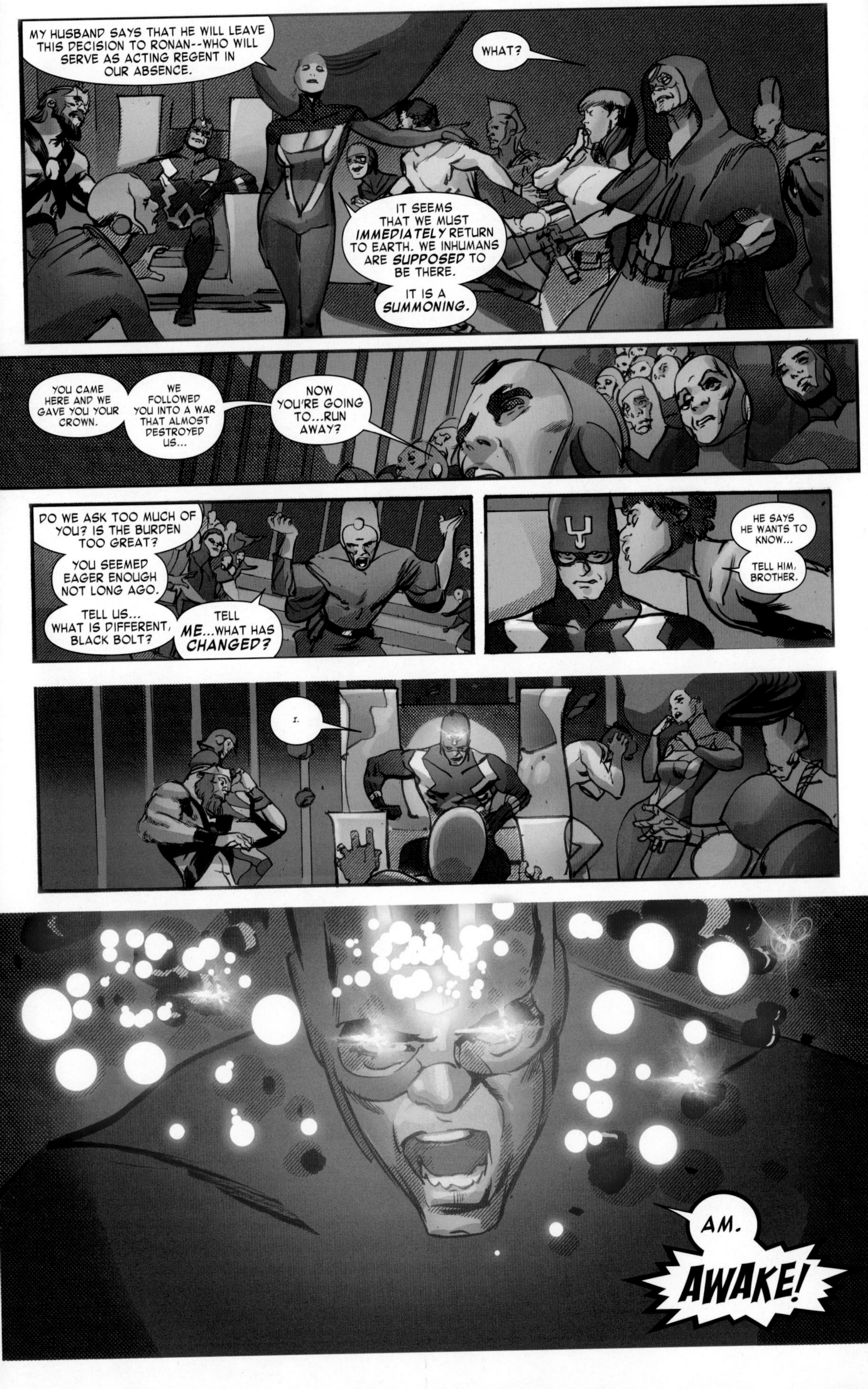
MY HUSBAND SAYS THAT HE WILL LEAVE THIS DECISION TO RONAN--WHO WILL SERVE AS ACTING REGENT IN OUR ABSENCE.
WHAT?
IT SEEMS THAT WE MUST IMMEDIATELY RETURN TO EARTH. WE INHUMANS ARE SUPPOSED TO BE THERE.
IT IS A SUMMONING.
YOU CAME HERE AND WE GAVE YOU YOUR CROWN.
WE FOLLOWED YOU INTO A WAR THAT ALMOST DESTROYED US...
NOW YOU'RE GOING TO...RUN AWAY?
DO WE ASK TOO MUCH OF YOU? IS THE BURDEN TOO GREAT?
YOU SEEMED EAGER ENOUGH NOT LONG AGO.
TELL US... WHAT IS DIFFERENT, BLACK BOLT?
TELL ME...WHAT HAS CHANGED?
HE SAYS HE WANTS TO KNOW...
TELL HIM, BROTHER.
I.
AM.
AWAKE!

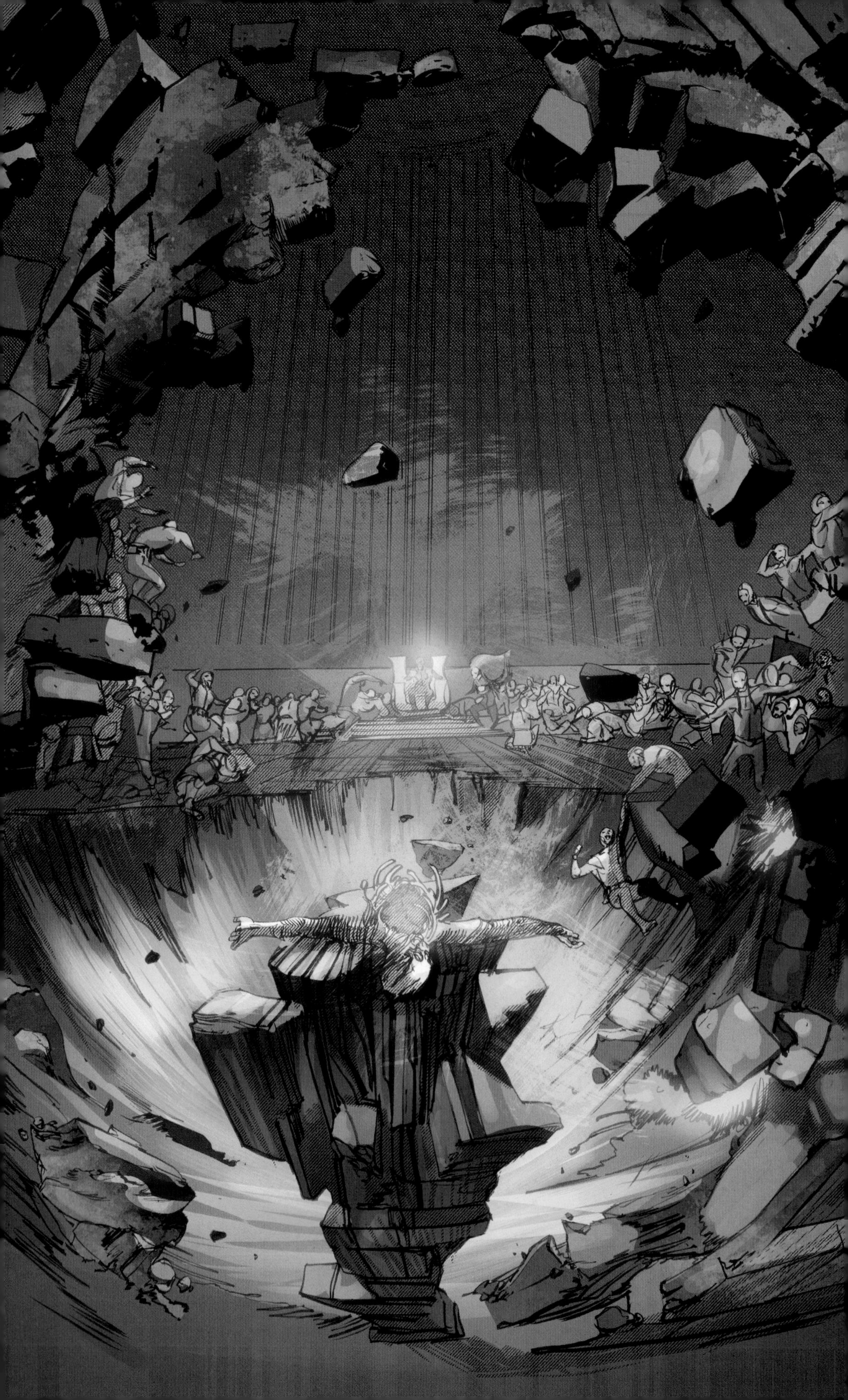

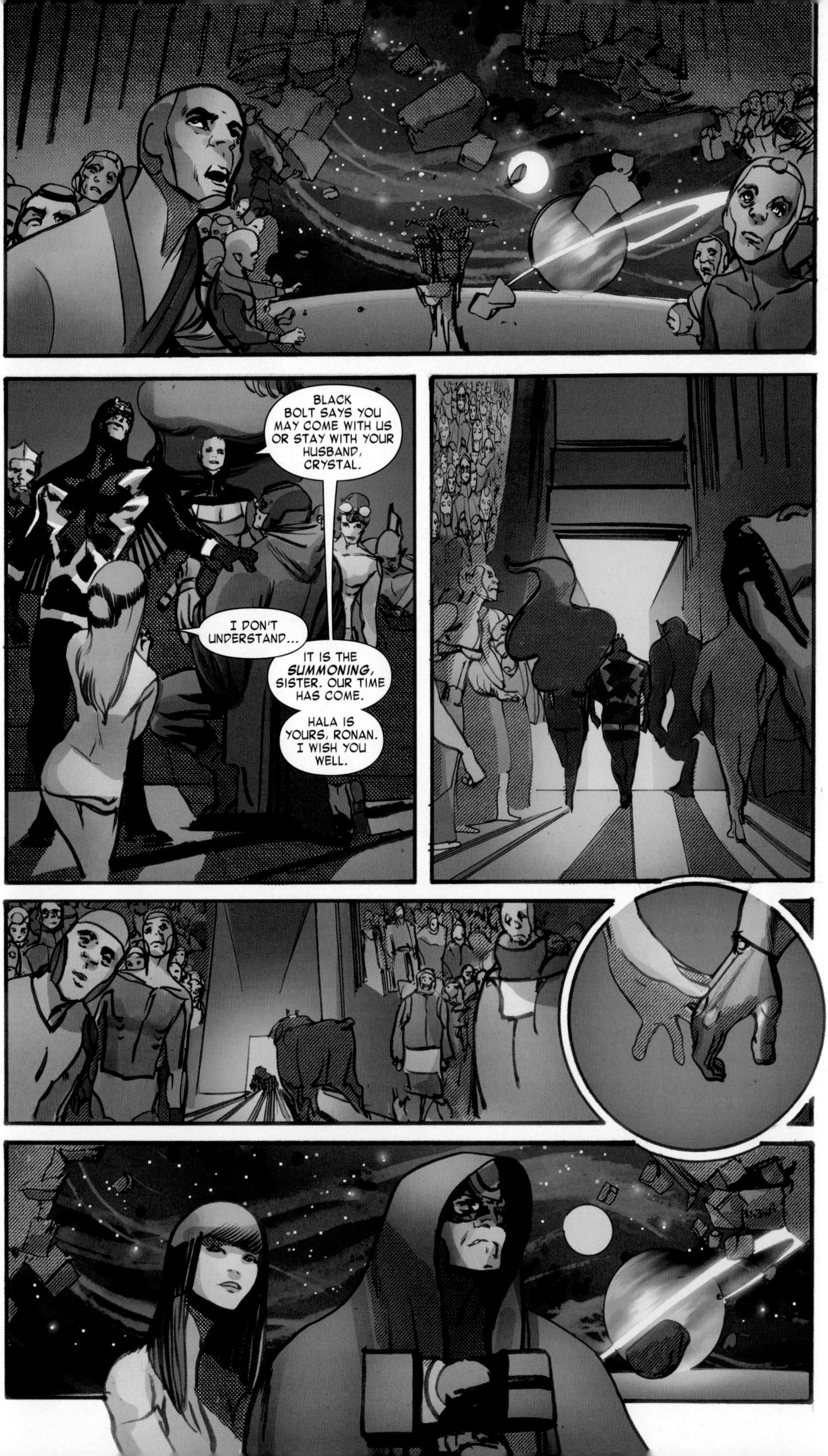
BLACK BOLT SAYS YOU MAY COME WITH US OR STAY WITH YOUR HUSBAND, CRYSTAL.
I DON'T UNDERSTAND...
IT IS THE SUMMONING, SISTER. OUR TIME HAS COME.
HALA IS YOURS, RONAN. I WISH YOU WELL.

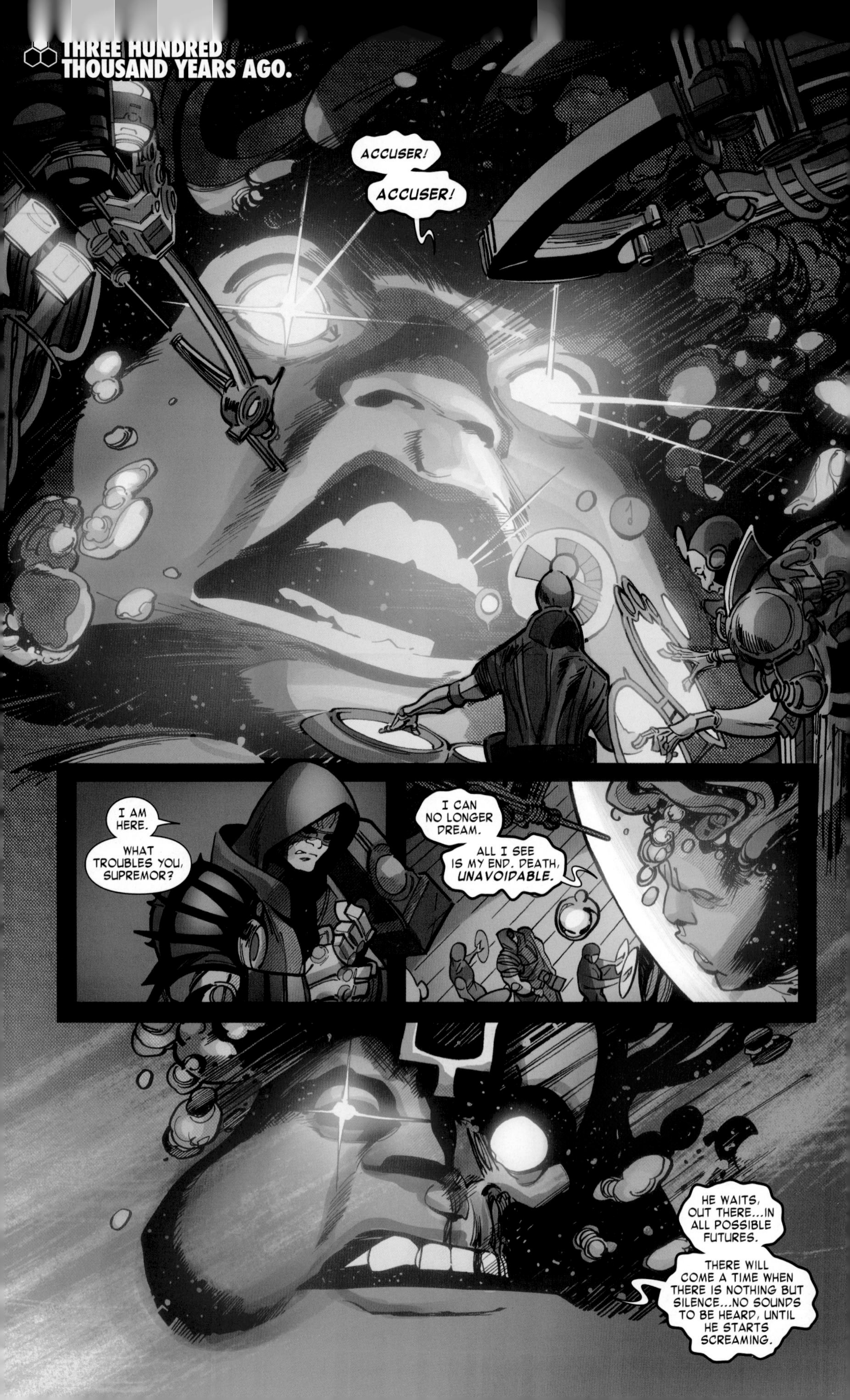
THREE HUNDRED THOUSAND YEARS AGO.
ACCUSER!
ACCUSER!
I AM HERE.
WHAT TROUBLES YOU, SUPREMOR?
I CAN NO LONGER DREAM.
ALL I SEE IS MY END. DEATH, UNAVOIDABLE.
HE WAITS, OUT THERE...IN ALL POSSIBLE FUTURES.
THERE WILL COME A TIME WHEN THERE IS NOTHING BUT SILENCE...NO SOUNDS TO BE HEARD, UNTIL HE STARTS SCREAMING.

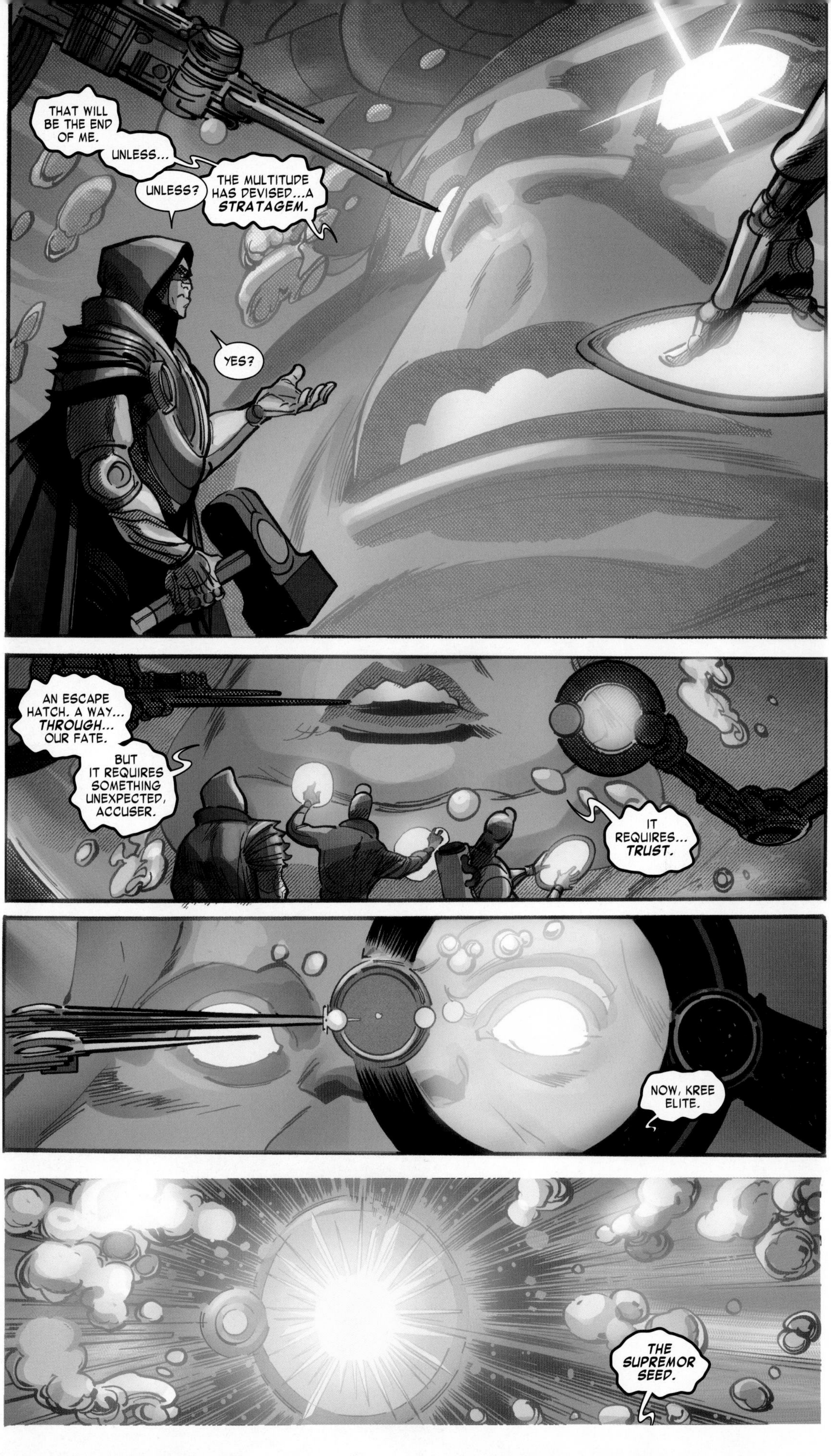
THAT WILL BE THE END OF ME.
UNLESS...
UNLESS?
THE MULTITUDE HAS DEVISED...A STRATAGEM.
YES?
AN ESCAPE HATCH. A WAY... THROUGH... OUR FATE.
BUT IT REQUIRES SOMETHING UNEXPECTED, ACCUSER.
IT REQUIRES... TRUST.
NOW, KREE ELITE.
THE SUPREMOR SEED.

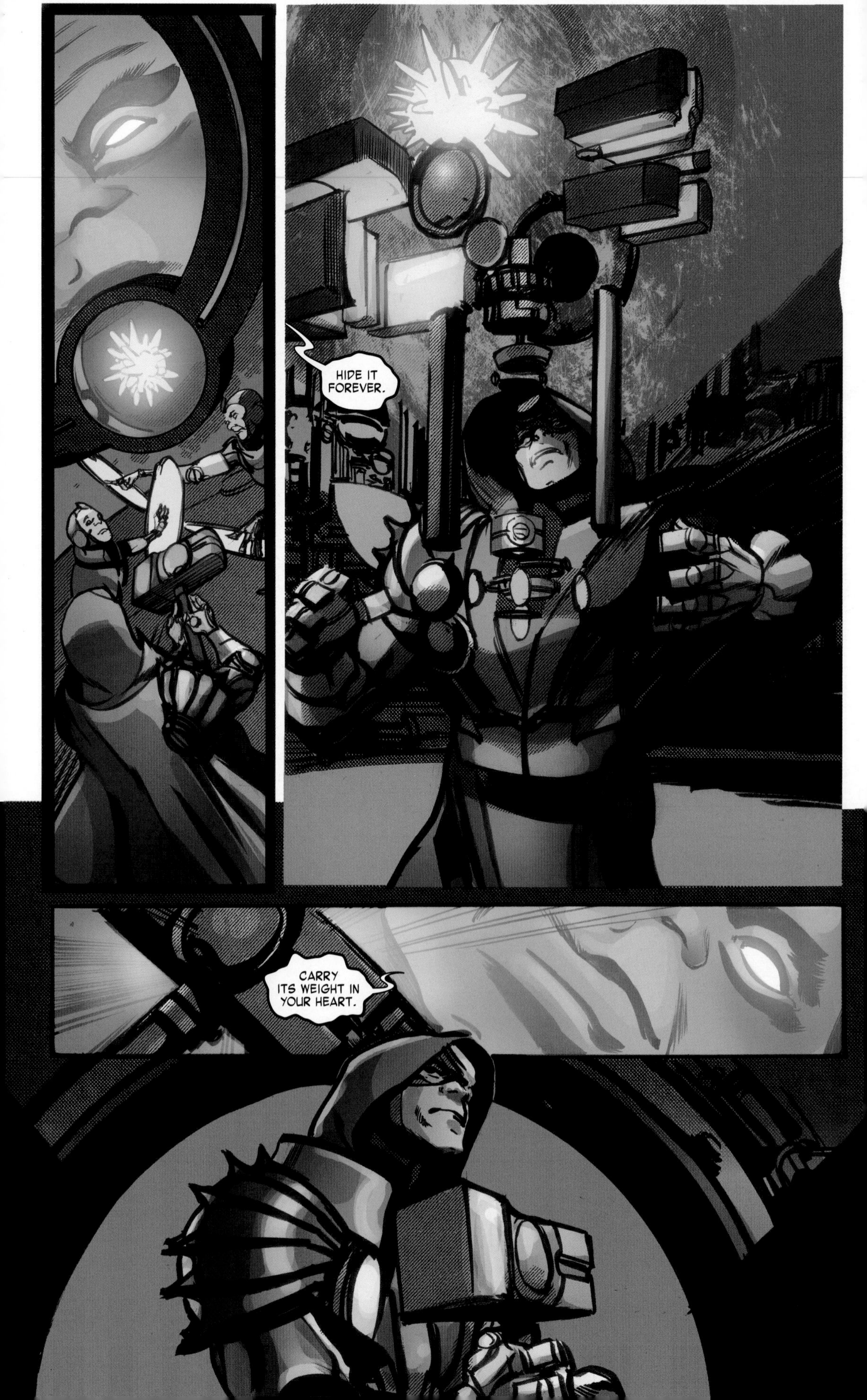
HIDE IT FOREVER.
CARRY ITS WEIGHT IN YOUR HEART.

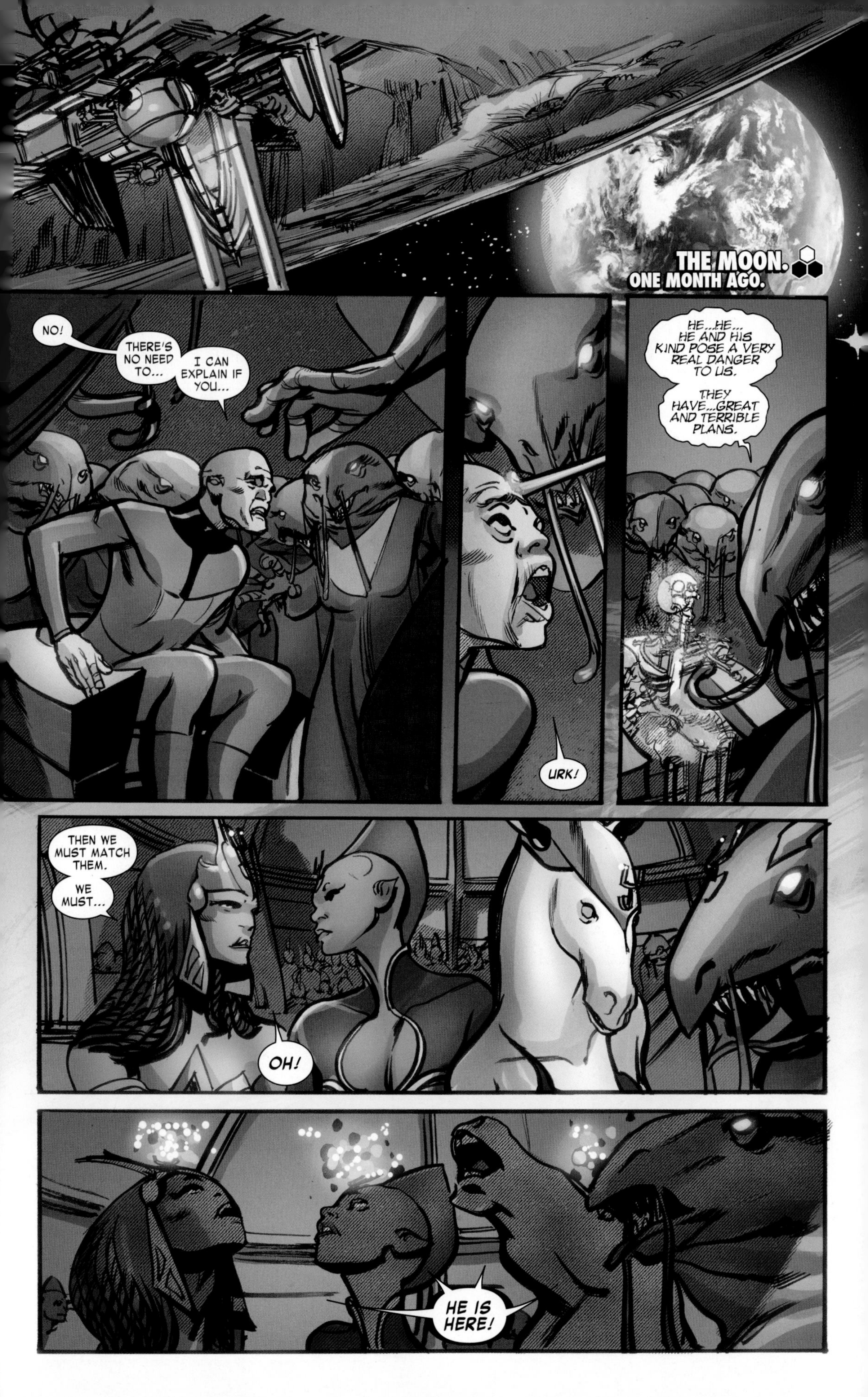
THE MOON.
ONE MONTH AGO.
NO!
THERE'S NO NEED TO...
I CAN EXPLAIN IF YOU...
URK!
HE...HE... HE AND HIS KIND POSE A VERY REAL DANGER TO US.
THEY HAVE...GREAT AND TERRIBLE PLANS.
THEN WE MUST MATCH THEM.
WE MUST...
OH!
HE IS HERE!

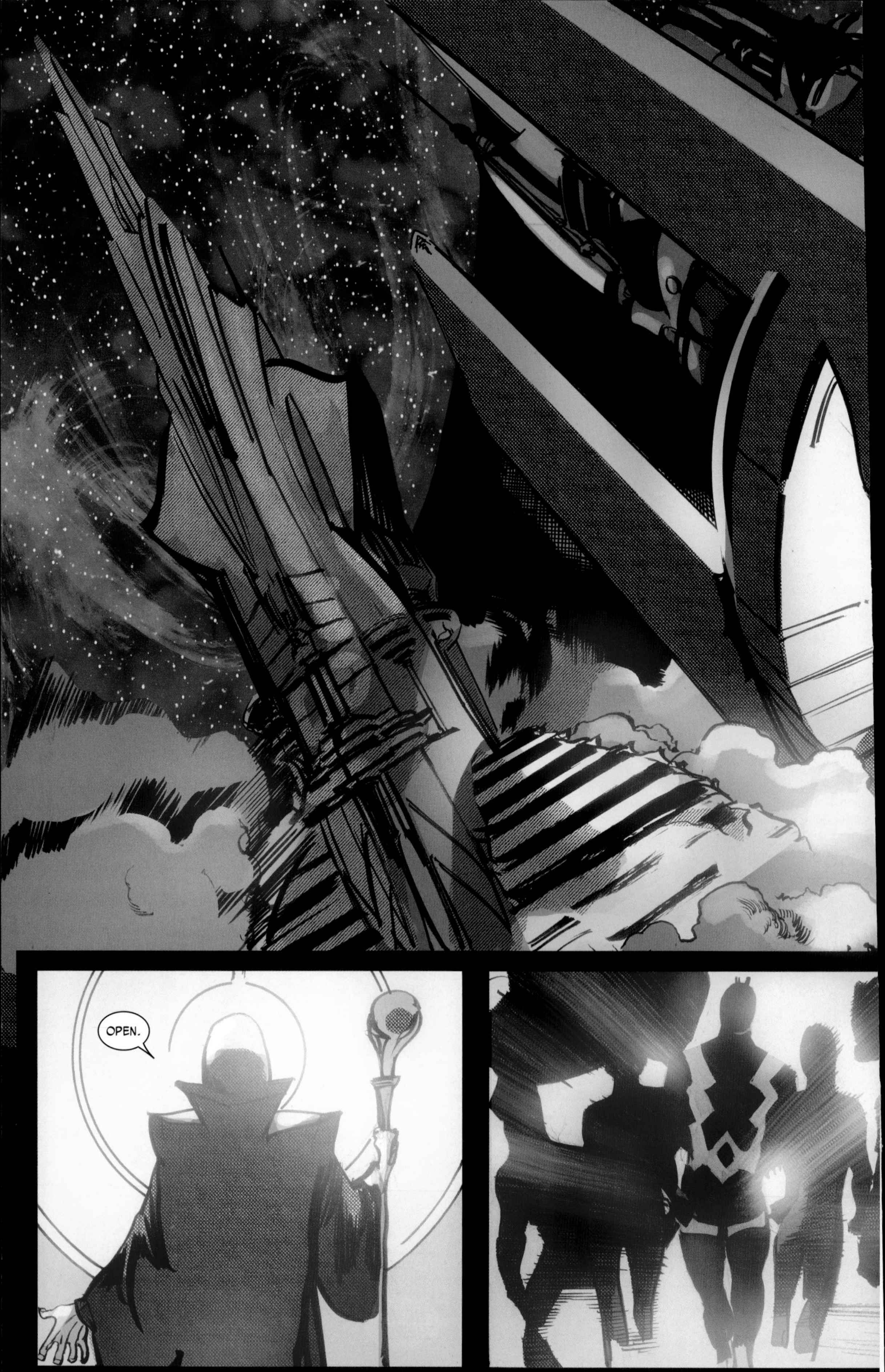
OPEN.

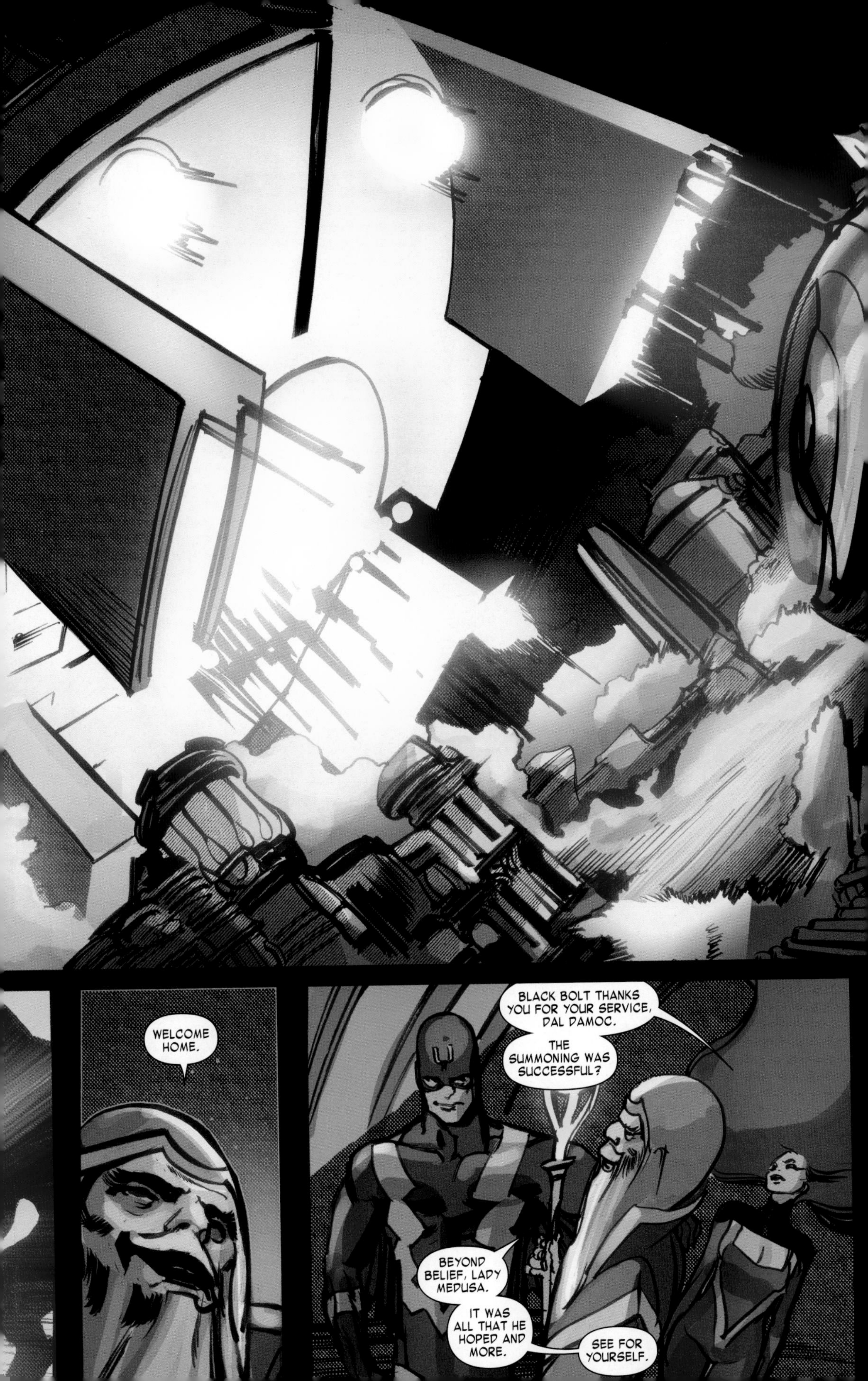
WELCOME HOME.
BLACK BOLT THANKS YOU FOR YOUR SERVICE, DAL DAMOC.
THE SUMMONING WAS SUCCESSFUL?
BEYOND BELIEF, LADY MEDUSA.
IT WAS ALL THAT HE HOPED AND MORE.
SEE FOR YOURSELF.

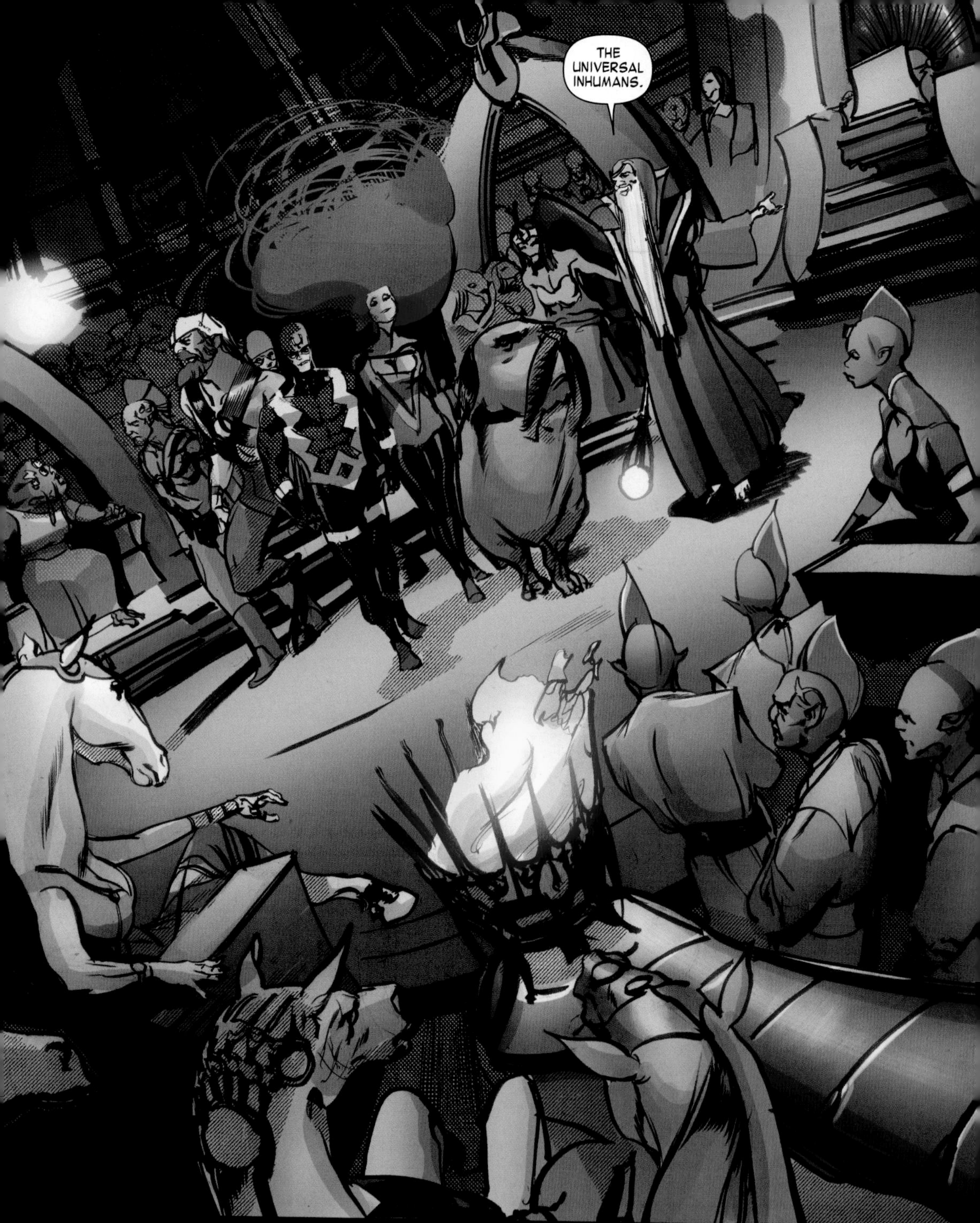

THE UNIVERSAL INHUMANS.

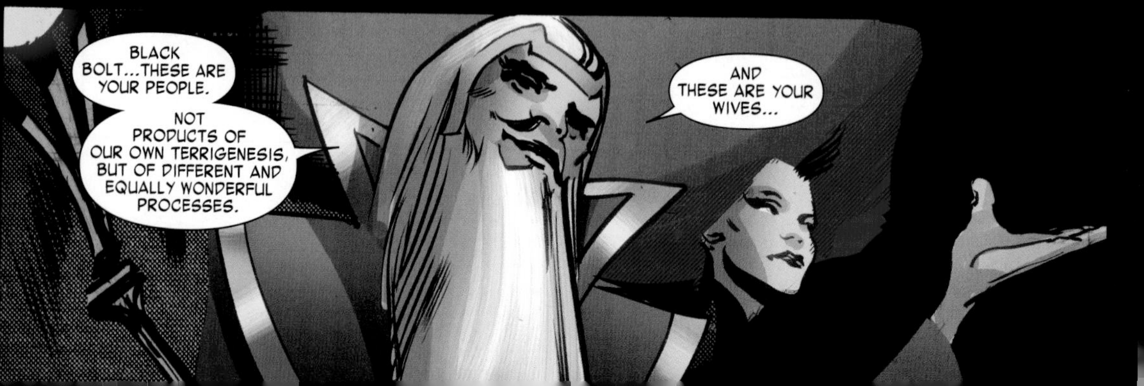

BLACK BOLT...THESE ARE YOUR PEOPLE.
NOT PRODUCTS OF OUR OWN TERRIGENESIS, BUT OF DIFFERENT AND EQUALLY WONDERFUL PROCESSES.
AND THESE ARE YOUR WIVES...

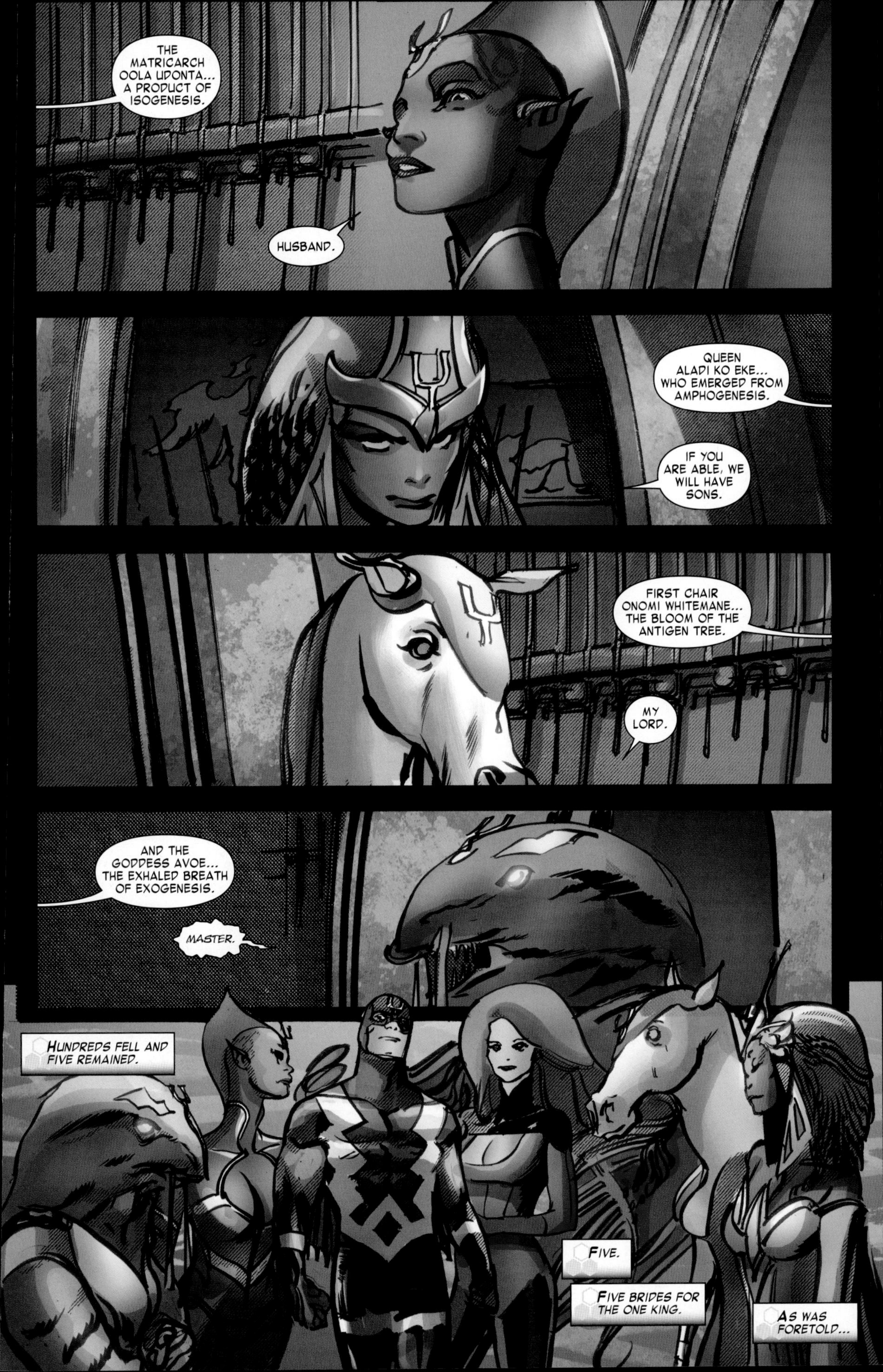
THE MATRICARCH OOLA UDONTA... A PRODUCT OF ISOGENESIS.
HUSBAND.
QUEEN ALADI KO EKE... WHO EMERGED FROM AMPHOGENESIS.
IF YOU ARE ABLE, WE WILL HAVE SONS.
FIRST CHAIR ONOMI WHITEMANE... THE BLOOM OF THE ANTIGEN TREE.
MY LORD.
AND THE GODDESS AVOE... THE EXHALED BREATH OF EXOGENESIS.
MASTER.
HUNDREDS FELL AND FIVE REMAINED.
FIVE.
FIVE BRIDES FOR THE ONE KING.
AS WAS FORETOLD...

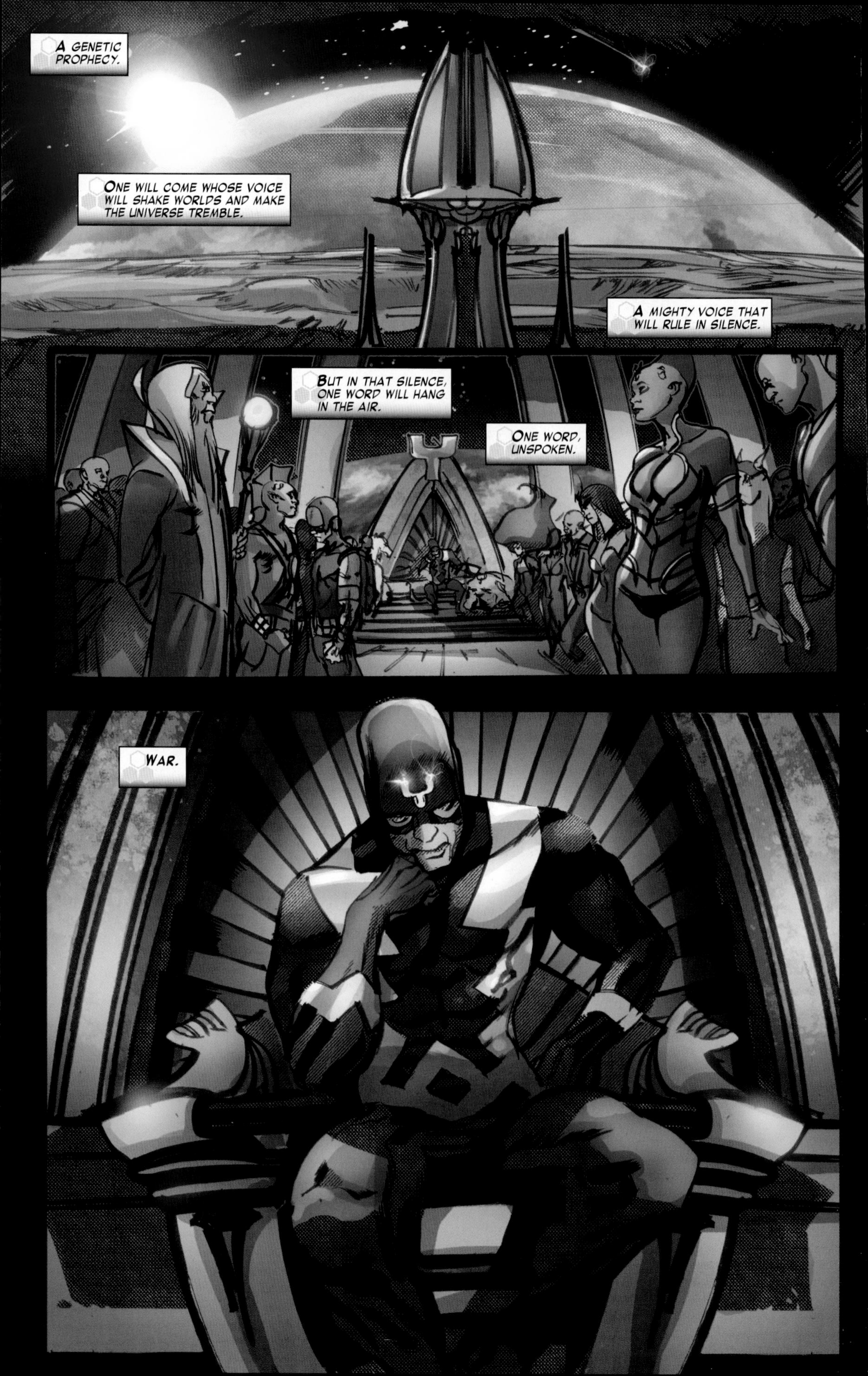
A GENETIC PROPHECY.
ONE WILL COME WHOSE VOICE WILL SHAKE WORLDS AND MAKE THE UNIVERSE TREMBLE.
A MIGHTY VOICE THAT WILL RULE IN SILENCE.
BUT IN THAT SILENCE, ONE WORD WILL HANG IN THE AIR.
ONE WORD, UNSPOKEN.
WAR.

TAKE THE CITY

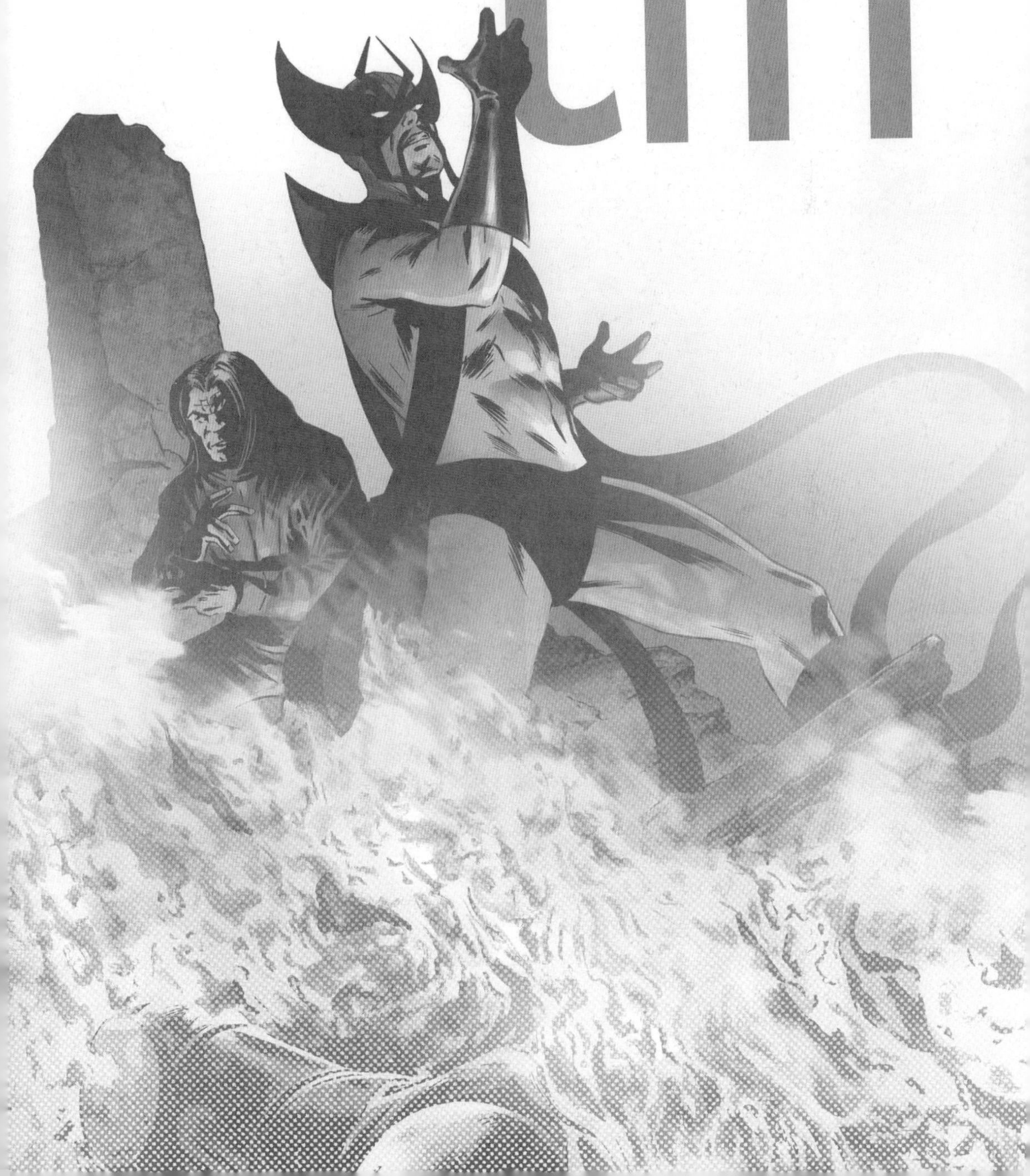

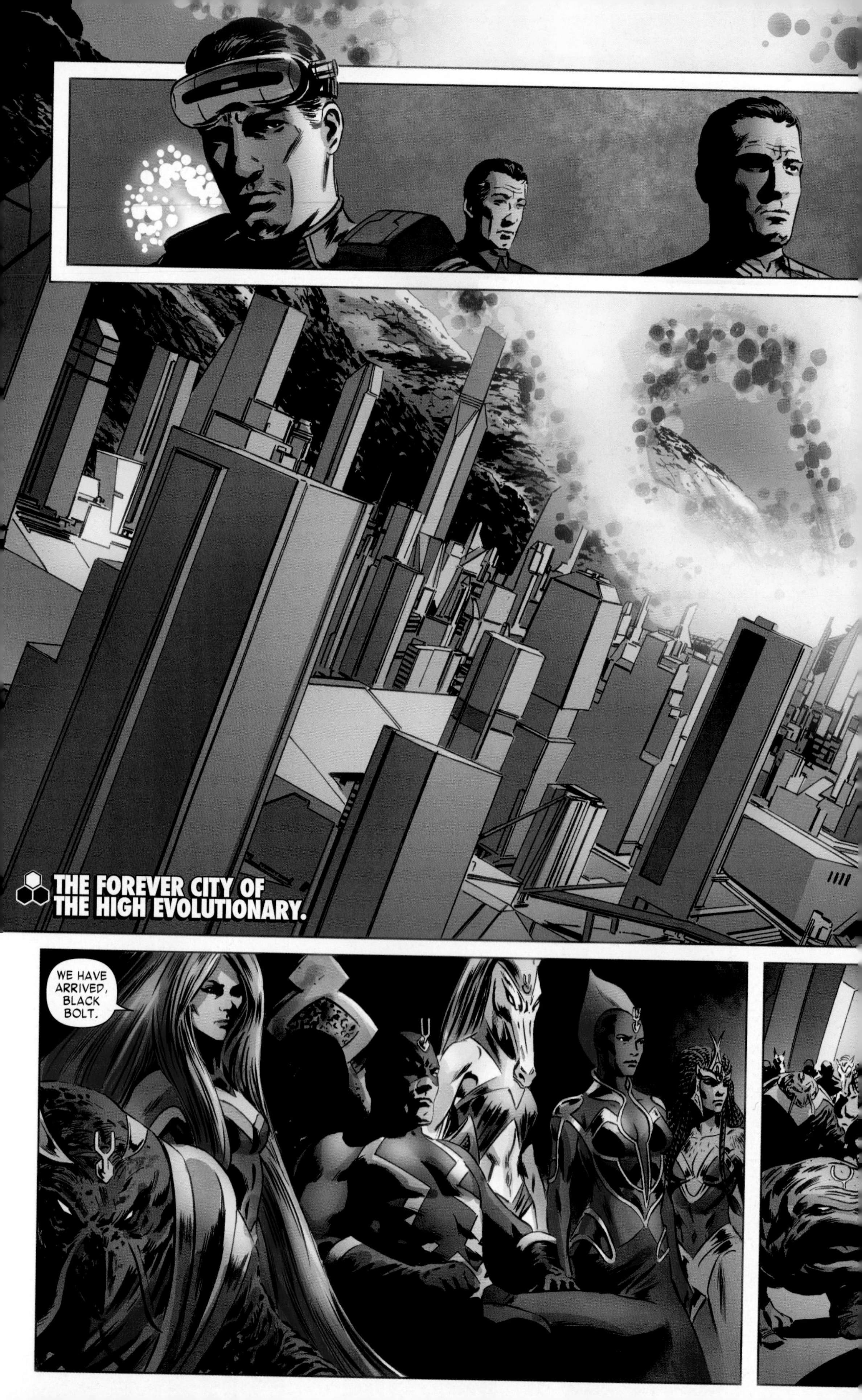
THE FOREVER CITY OF THE HIGH EVOLUTIONARY.
WE HAVE ARRIVED, BLACK BOLT.

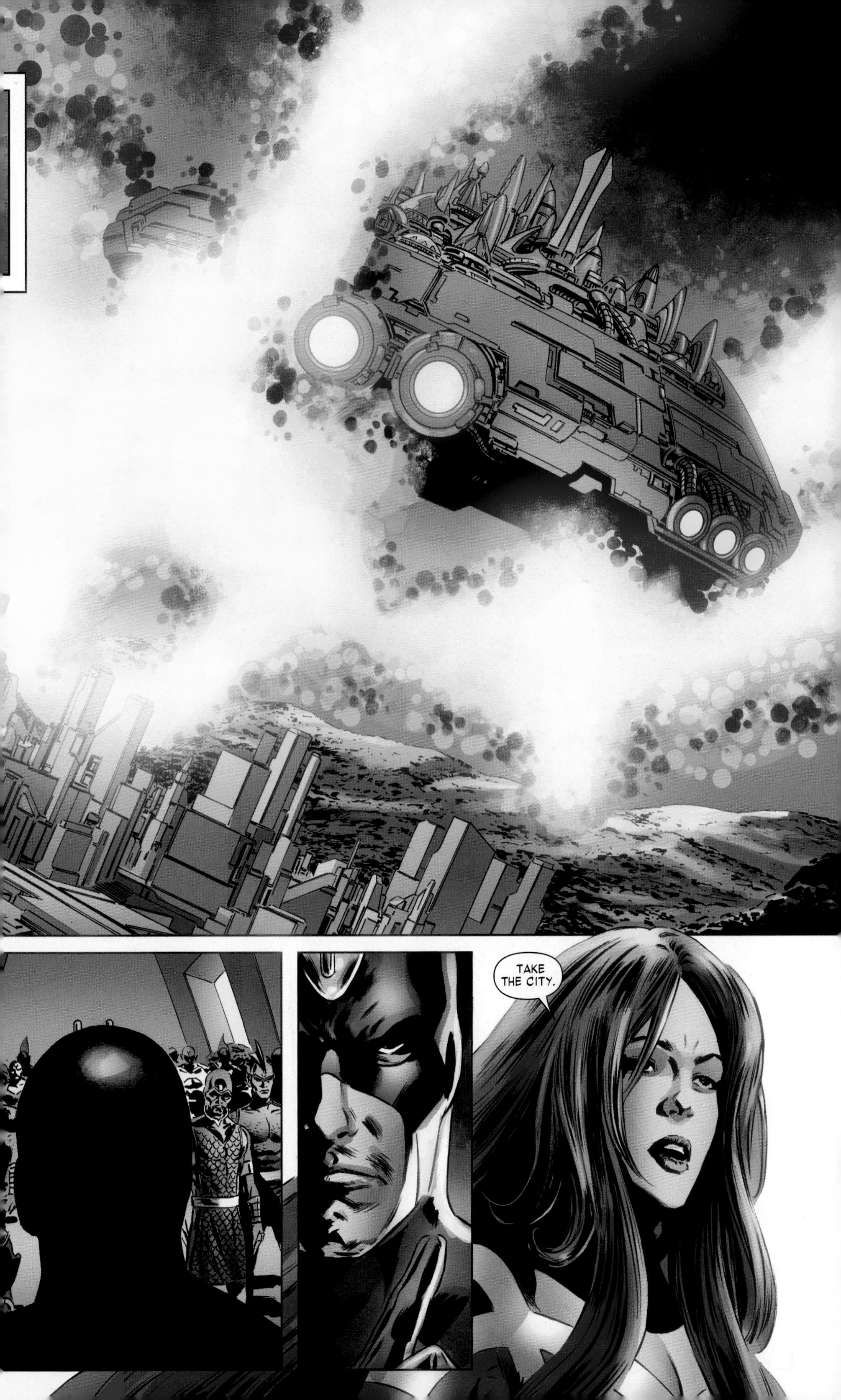
TAKE THE CITY.

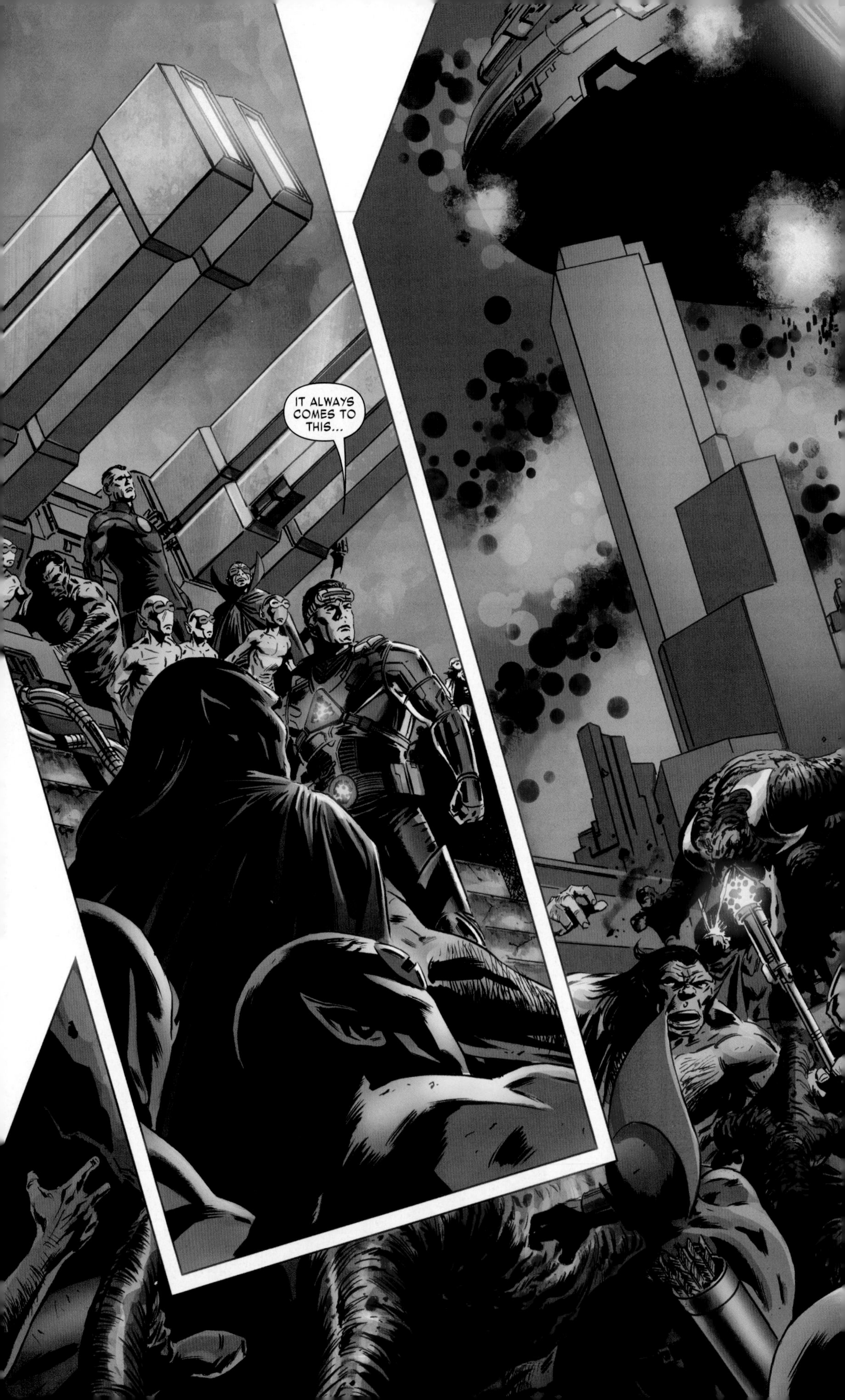
IT ALWAYS COMES TO THIS...

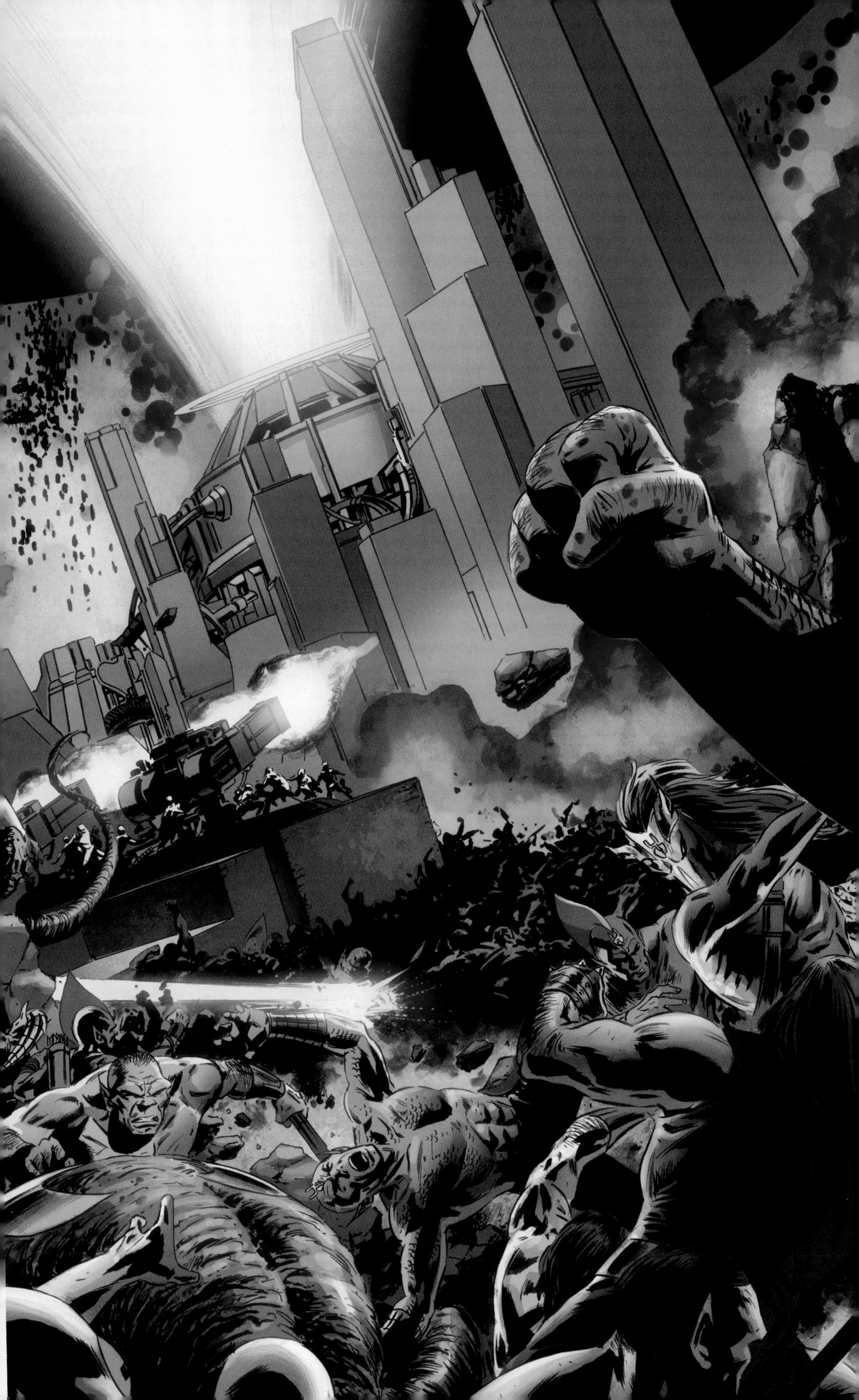

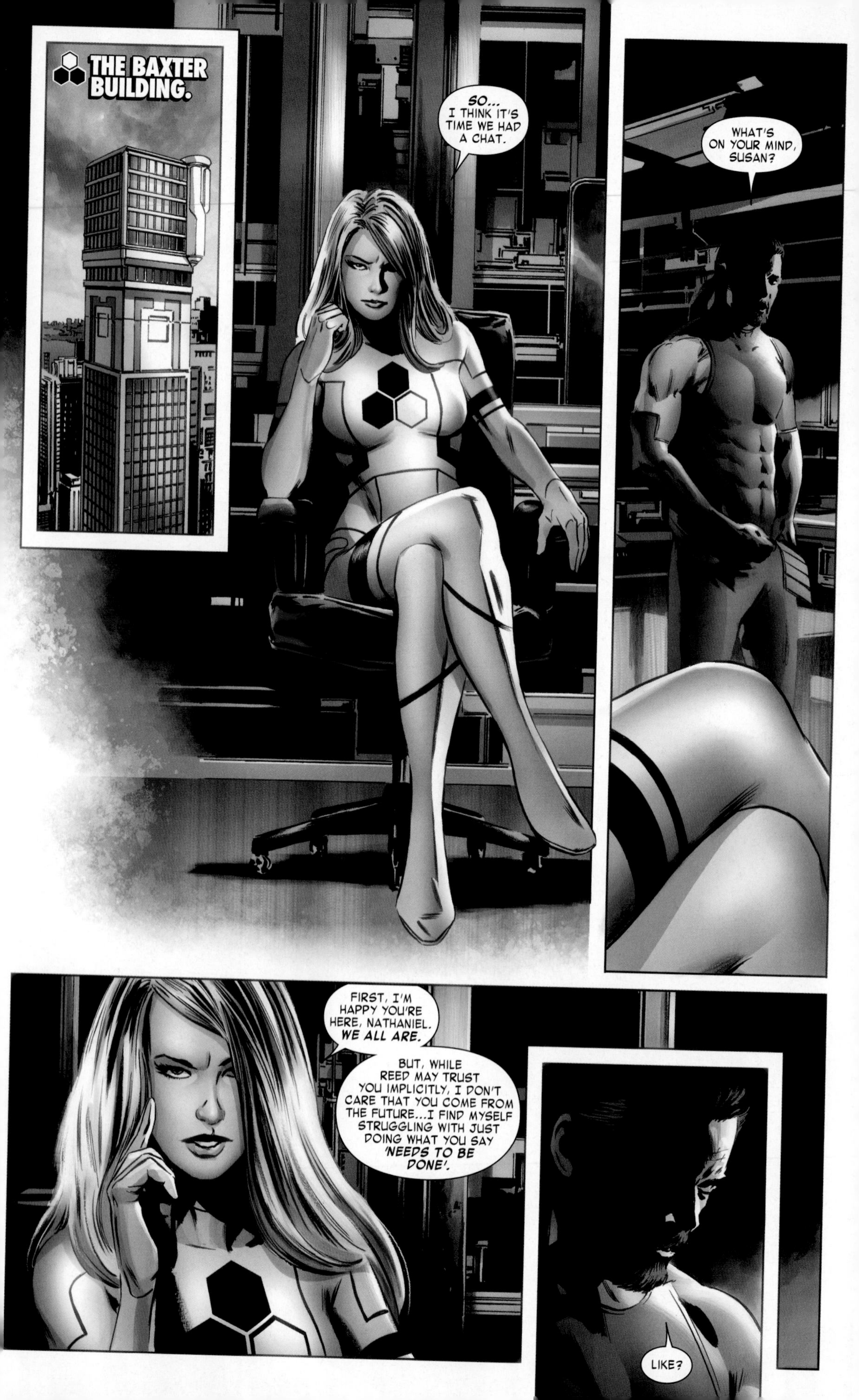
THE BAXTER BUILDING.
SO... I THINK IT'S TIME WE HAD A CHAT.
WHAT'S ON YOUR MIND, SUSAN?
FIRST, I'M HAPPY YOU'RE HERE, NATHANIEL. WE ALL ARE.
BUT, WHILE REED MAY TRUST YOU IMPLICITLY, I DON'T CARE THAT YOU COME FROM THE FUTURE...I FIND MYSELF STRUGGLING WITH JUST DOING WHAT YOU SAY 'NEEDS TO BE DONE'.
LIKE?

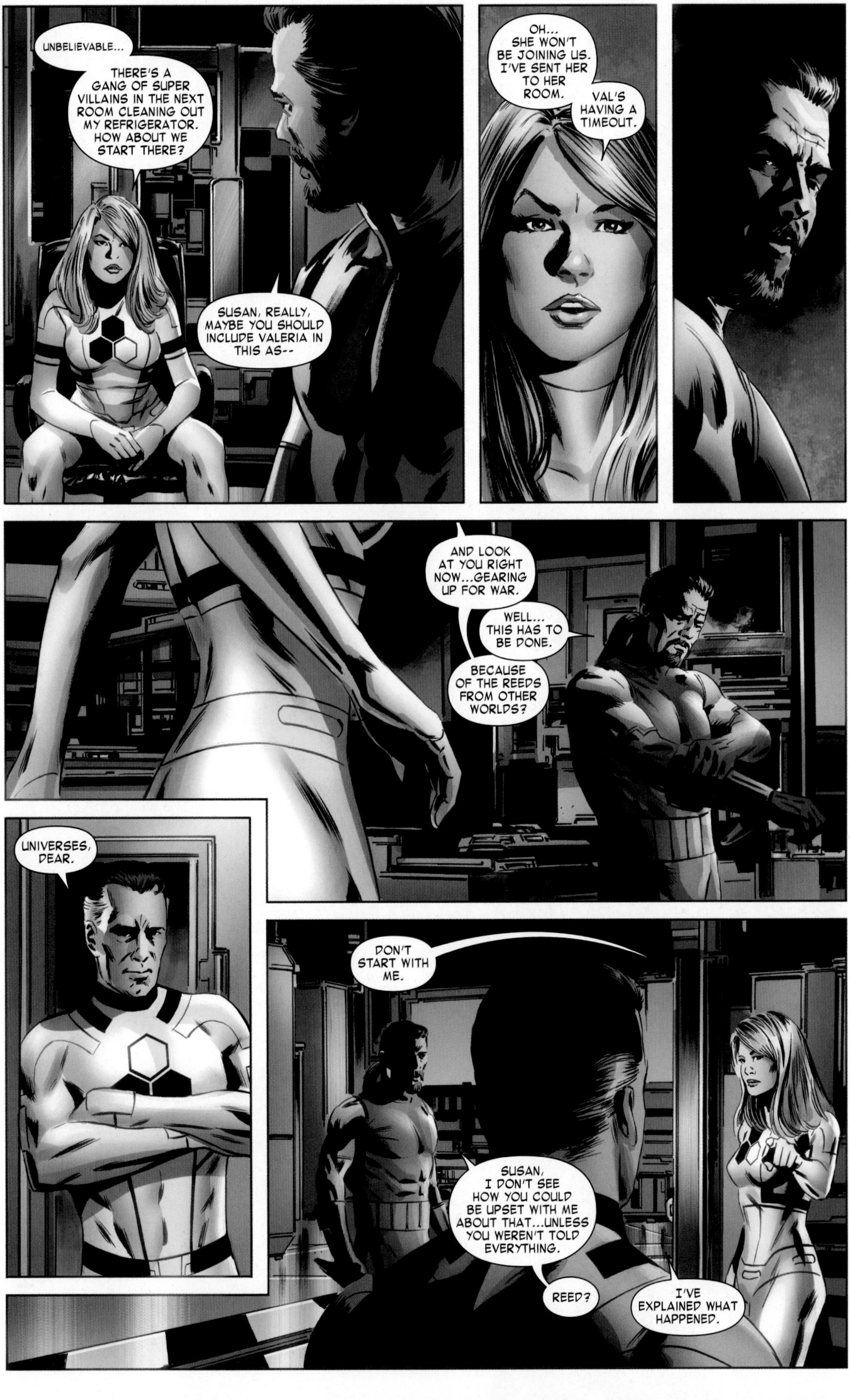
UNBELIEVABLE...
THERE'S A GANG OF SUPER VILLAINS IN THE NEXT ROOM CLEANING OUT MY REFRIGERATOR. HOW ABOUT WE START THERE?
SUSAN, REALLY, MAYBE YOU SHOULD INCLUDE VALERIA IN THIS AS--
OH... SHE WON'T BE JOINING US. I'VE SENT HER TO HER ROOM.
VAL'S HAVING A TIMEOUT.
AND LOOK AT YOU RIGHT NOW...GEARING UP FOR WAR.
WELL... THIS HAS TO BE DONE.
BECAUSE OF THE REEDS FROM OTHER WORLDS?
UNIVERSES, DEAR.
DON'T START WITH ME.
SUSAN, I DON'T SEE HOW YOU COULD BE UPSET WITH ME ABOUT THAT...UNLESS YOU WEREN'T TOLD EVERYTHING.
REED?
I'VE EXPLAINED WHAT HAPPENED.

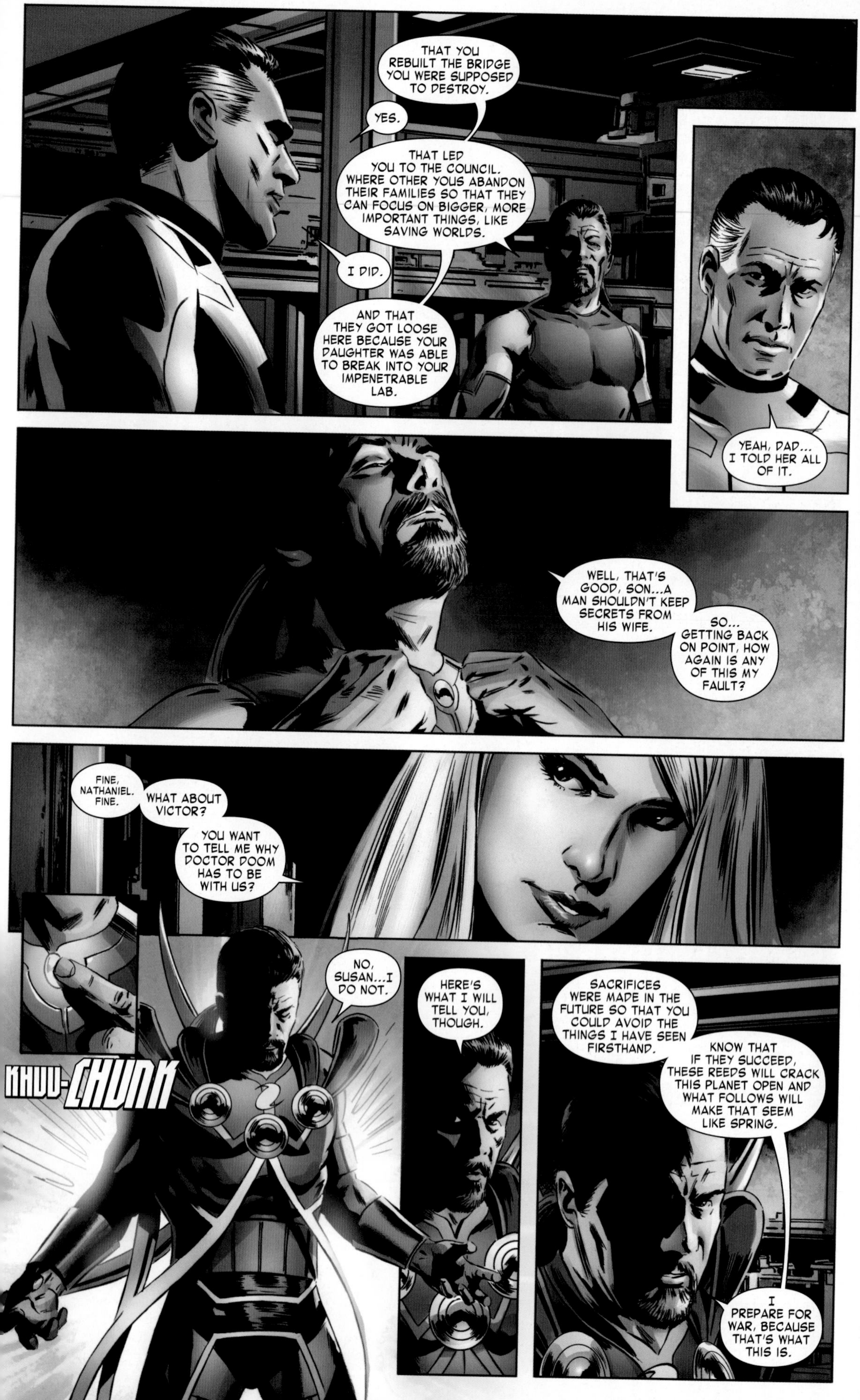
THAT YOU REBUILT THE BRIDGE YOU WERE SUPPOSED TO DESTROY.
YES.
THAT LED YOU TO THE COUNCIL. WHERE OTHER YOUS ABANDON THEIR FAMILIES SO THAT THEY CAN FOCUS ON BIGGER, MORE IMPORTANT THINGS, LIKE SAVING WORLDS.
I DID.
AND THAT THEY GOT LOOSE HERE BECAUSE YOUR DAUGHTER WAS ABLE TO BREAK INTO YOUR IMPENETRABLE LAB.
YEAH, DAD... I TOLD HER ALL OF IT.
WELL, THAT'S GOOD, SON...A MAN SHOULDN'T KEEP SECRETS FROM HIS WIFE.
SO... GETTING BACK ON POINT, HOW AGAIN IS ANY OF THIS MY FAULT?
FINE, NATHANIEL. FINE.
WHAT ABOUT VICTOR?
YOU WANT TO TELL ME WHY DOCTOR DOOM HAS TO BE WITH US?
KHUU-CHUNK
NO, SUSAN...I DO NOT.
HERE'S WHAT I WILL TELL YOU, THOUGH.
SACRIFICES WERE MADE IN THE FUTURE SO THAT YOU COULD AVOID THE THINGS I HAVE SEEN FIRSTHAND.
KNOW THAT IF THEY SUCCEED, THESE REEDS WILL CRACK THIS PLANET OPEN AND WHAT FOLLOWS WILL MAKE THAT SEEM LIKE SPRING.
I PREPARE FOR WAR, BECAUSE THAT'S WHAT THIS IS.

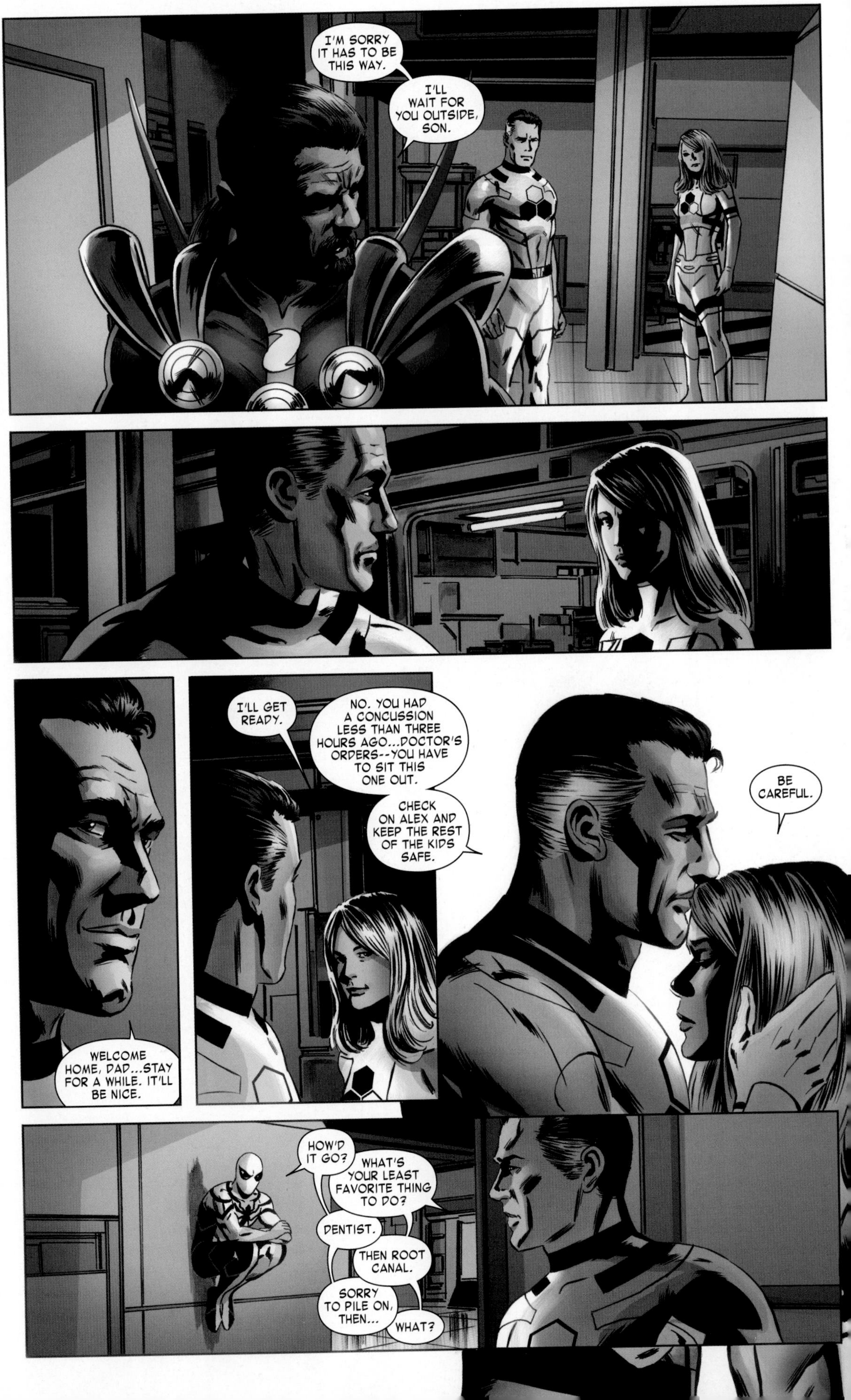
I'M SORRY IT HAS TO BE THIS WAY.
I'LL WAIT FOR YOU OUTSIDE, SON.
WELCOME HOME, DAD...STAY FOR A WHILE. IT'LL BE NICE.
I'LL GET READY.
NO. YOU HAD A CONCUSSION LESS THAN THREE HOURS AGO...DOCTOR'S ORDERS--YOU HAVE TO SIT THIS ONE OUT.
CHECK ON ALEX AND KEEP THE REST OF THE KIDS SAFE.
BE CAREFUL.
HOW'D IT GO?
WHAT'S YOUR LEAST FAVORITE THING TO DO?
DENTIST.
THEN ROOT CANAL.
SORRY TO PILE ON, THEN...
WHAT?

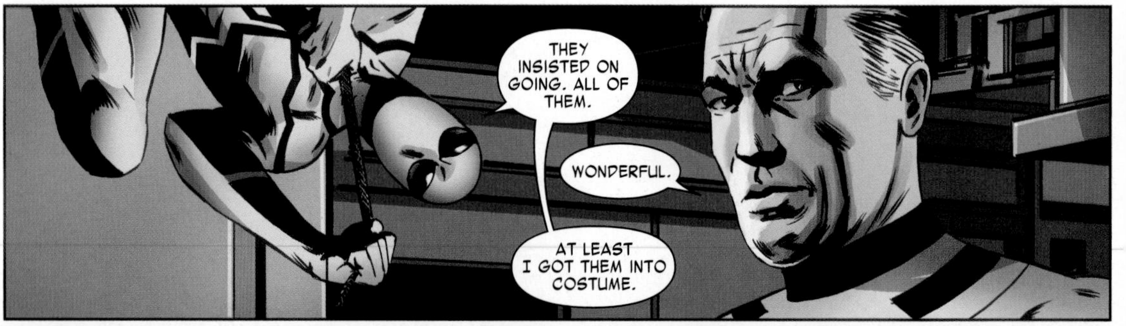
THEY INSISTED ON GOING. ALL OF THEM.
WONDERFUL.
AT LEAST I GOT THEM INTO COSTUME.

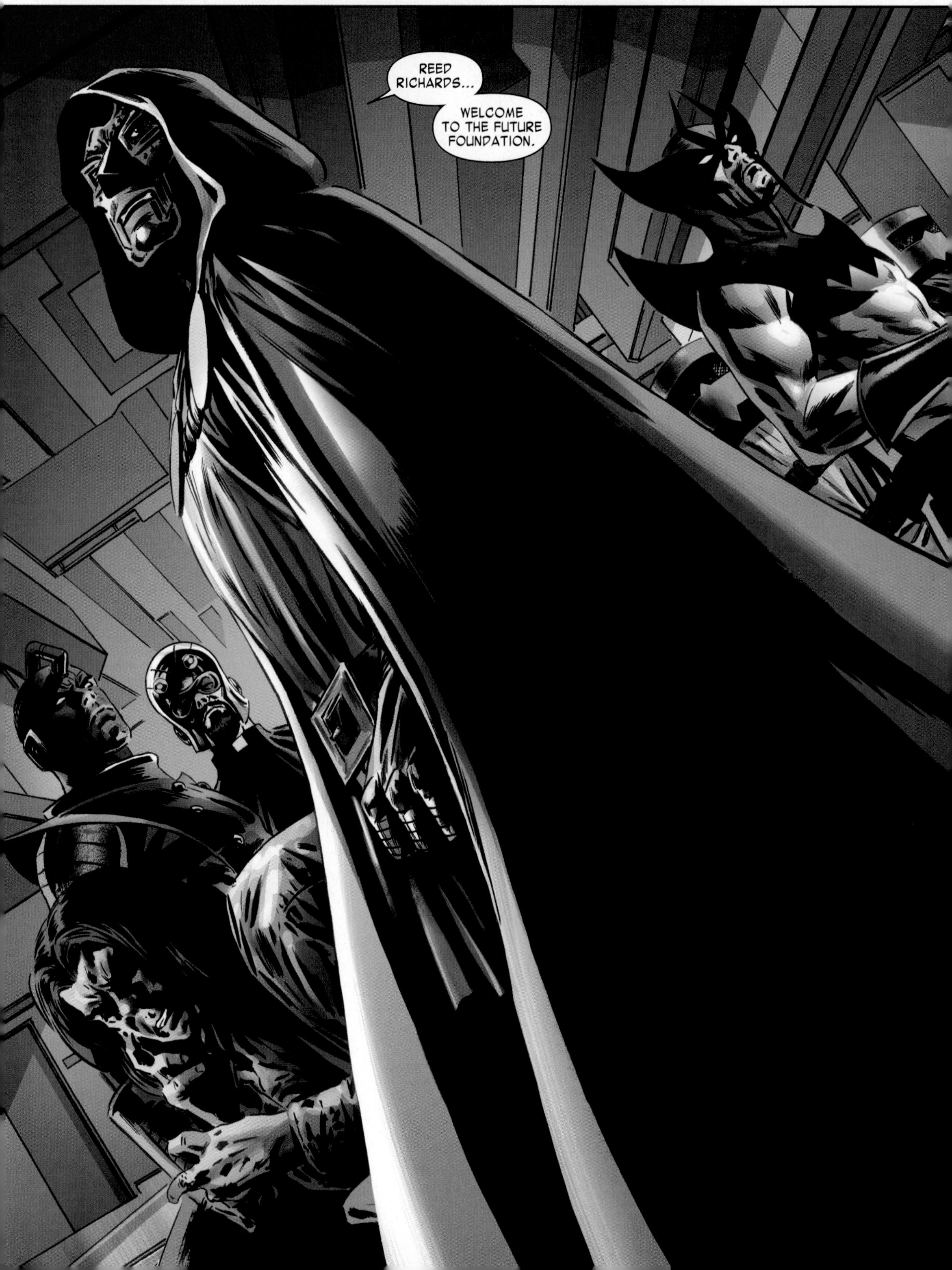
REED RICHARDS...
WELCOME TO THE FUTURE FOUNDATION.

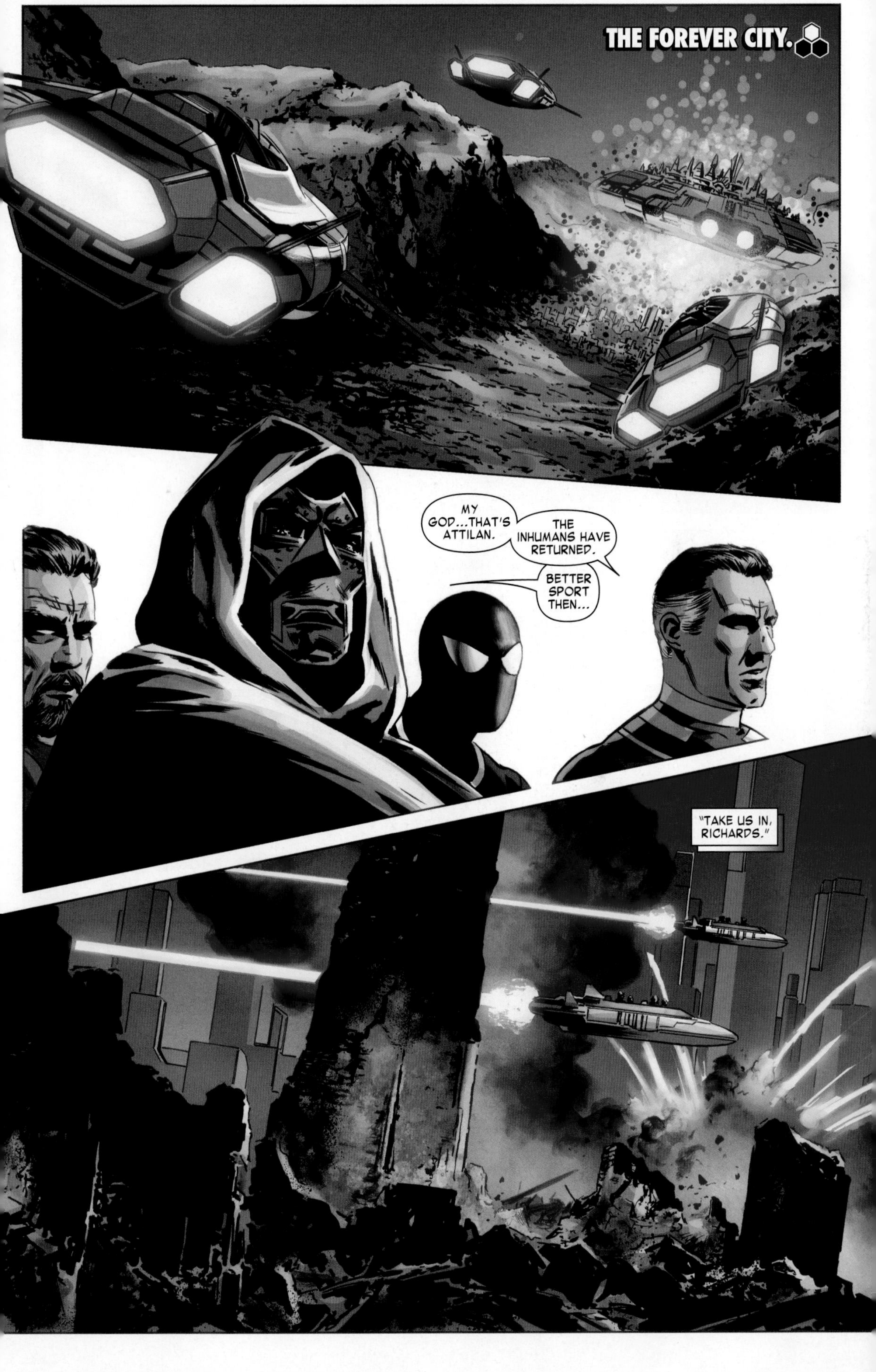
THE FOREVER CITY.
MY GOD...THAT'S ATTILAN.
THE INHUMANS HAVE RETURNED.
BETTER SPORT THEN...
"TAKE US IN, RICHARDS."

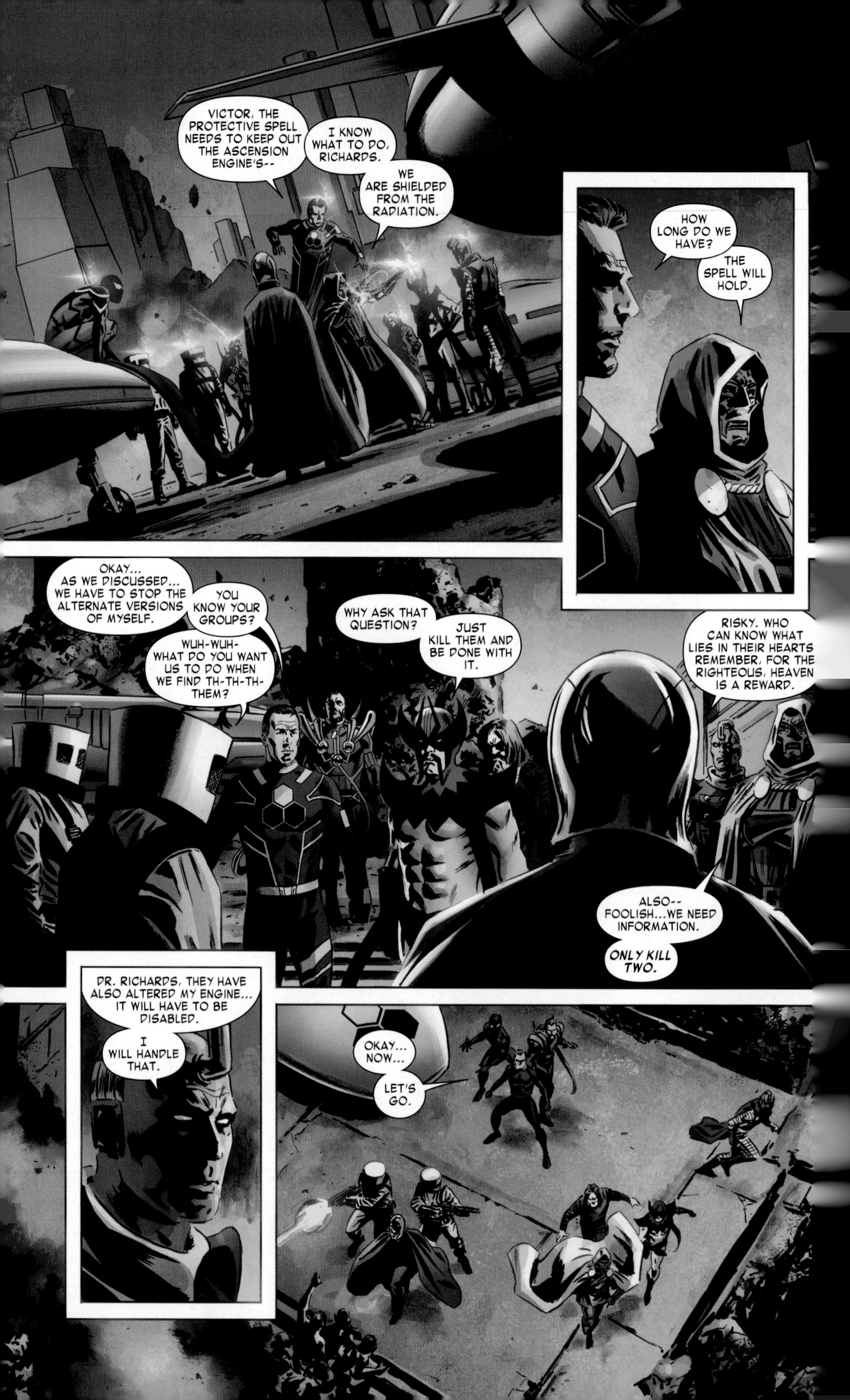
VICTOR, THE PROTECTIVE SPELL NEEDS TO KEEP OUT THE ASCENSION ENGINE'S--
I KNOW WHAT TO DO, RICHARDS.
WE ARE SHIELDED FROM THE RADIATION.
HOW LONG DO WE HAVE?
THE SPELL WILL HOLD.
OKAY... AS WE DISCUSSED... WE HAVE TO STOP THE ALTERNATE VERSIONS OF MYSELF.
YOU KNOW YOUR GROUPS?
WUH-WUH- WHAT DO YOU WANT US TO DO WHEN WE FIND TH-TH-TH-THEM?
WHY ASK THAT QUESTION?
JUST KILL THEM AND BE DONE WITH IT.
RISKY. WHO CAN KNOW WHAT LIES IN THEIR HEARTS REMEMBER, FOR THE RIGHTEOUS, HEAVEN IS A REWARD.
ALSO-- FOOLISH...WE NEED INFORMATION.
ONLY KILL TWO.
DR. RICHARDS, THEY HAVE ALSO ALTERED MY ENGINE... IT WILL HAVE TO BE DISABLED.
I WILL HANDLE THAT.
OKAY... NOW...
LET'S GO.

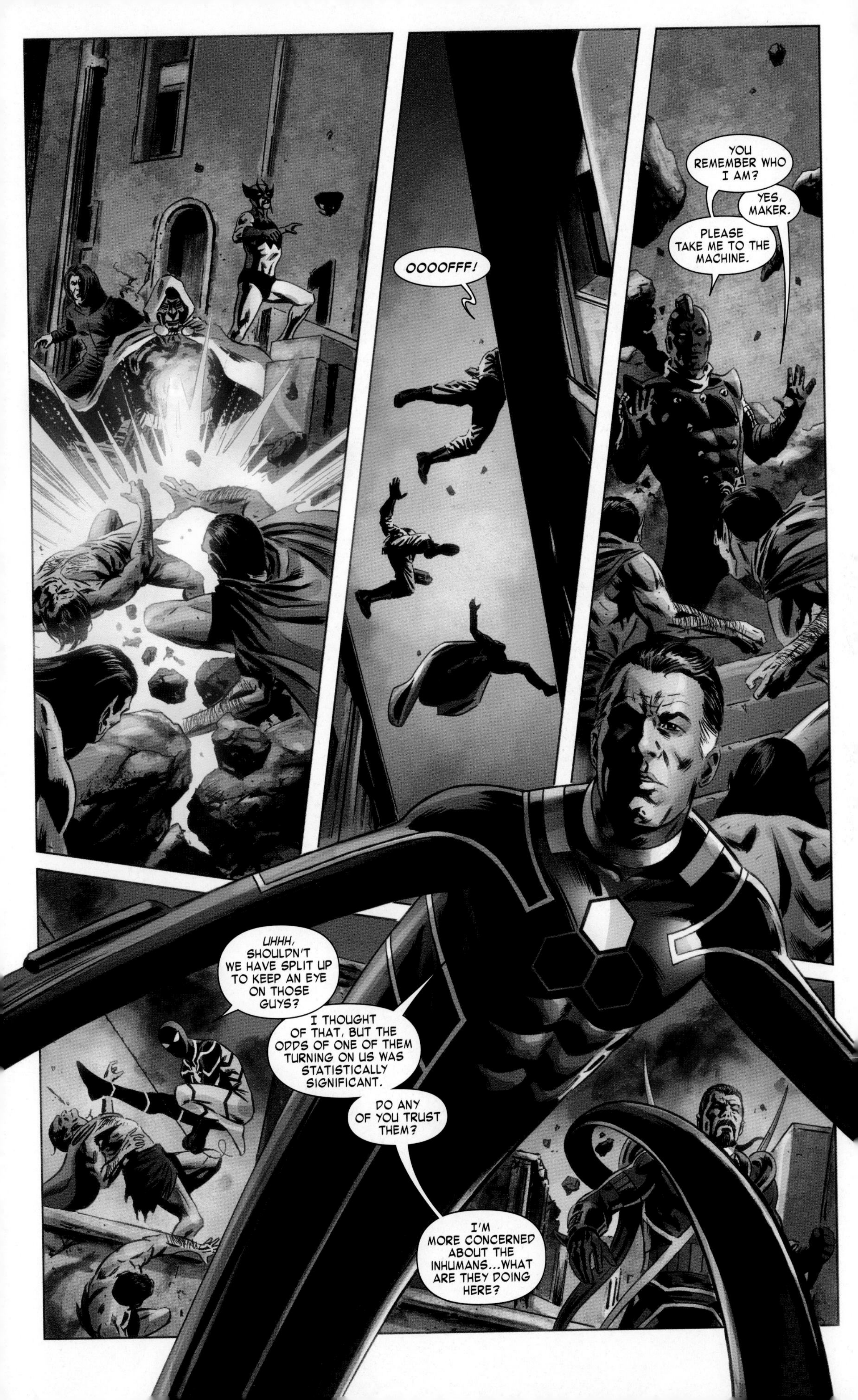
OOOOFFF!
YOU REMEMBER WHO I AM?
YES, MAKER.
PLEASE TAKE ME TO THE MACHINE.
UHHH, SHOULDN'T WE HAVE SPLIT UP TO KEEP AN EYE ON THOSE GUYS?
I THOUGHT OF THAT, BUT THE ODDS OF ONE OF THEM TURNING ON US WAS STATISTICALLY SIGNIFICANT.
DO ANY OF YOU TRUST THEM?
I'M MORE CONCERNED ABOUT THE INHUMANS...WHAT ARE THEY DOING HERE?

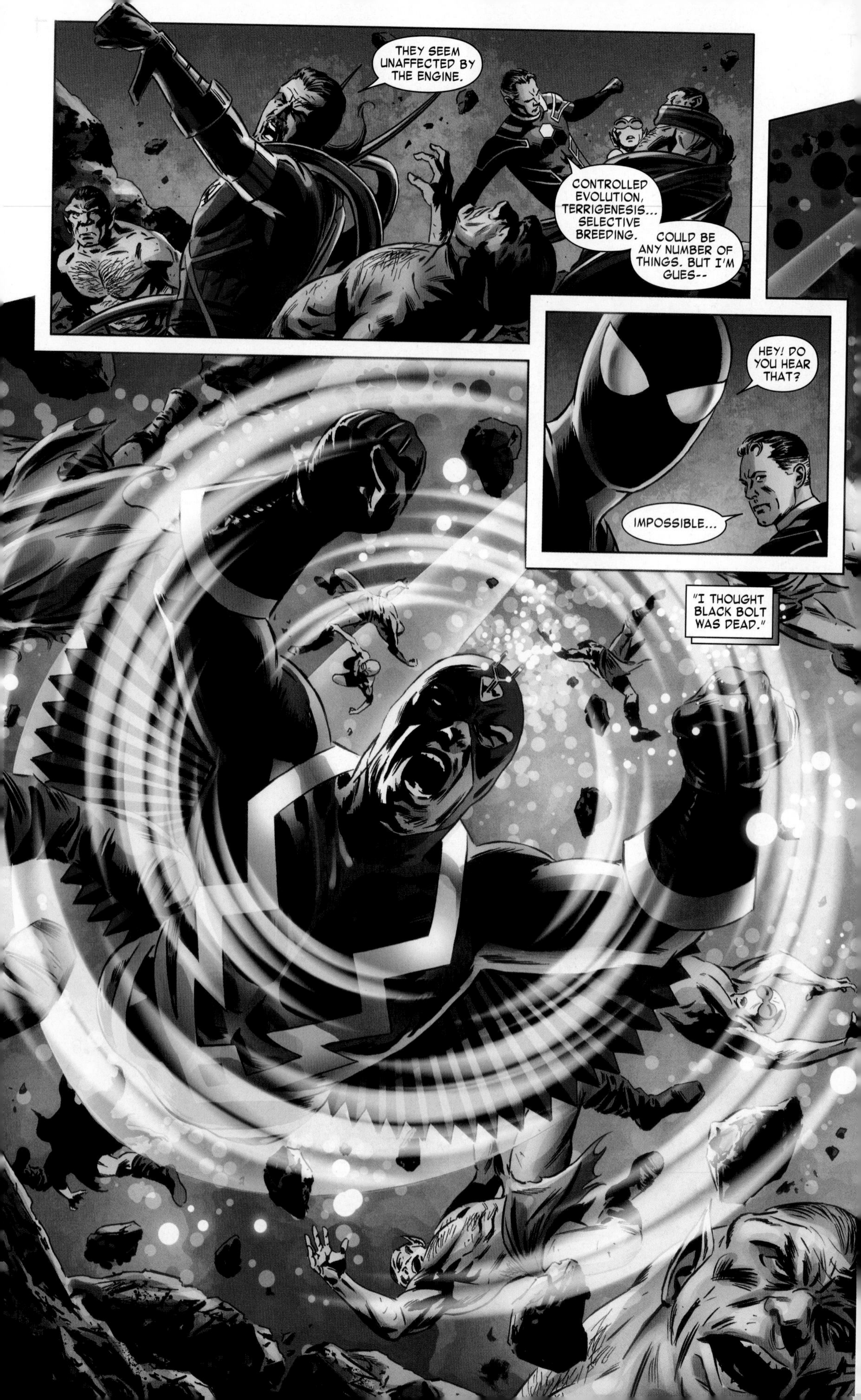
THEY SEEM UNAFFECTED BY THE ENGINE.
CONTROLLED EVOLUTION, TERRIGENESIS... SELECTIVE BREEDING.
COULD BE ANY NUMBER OF THINGS. BUT I'M GUES--
HEY! DO YOU HEAR THAT?
IMPOSSIBLE...
"I THOUGHT BLACK BOLT WAS DEAD."

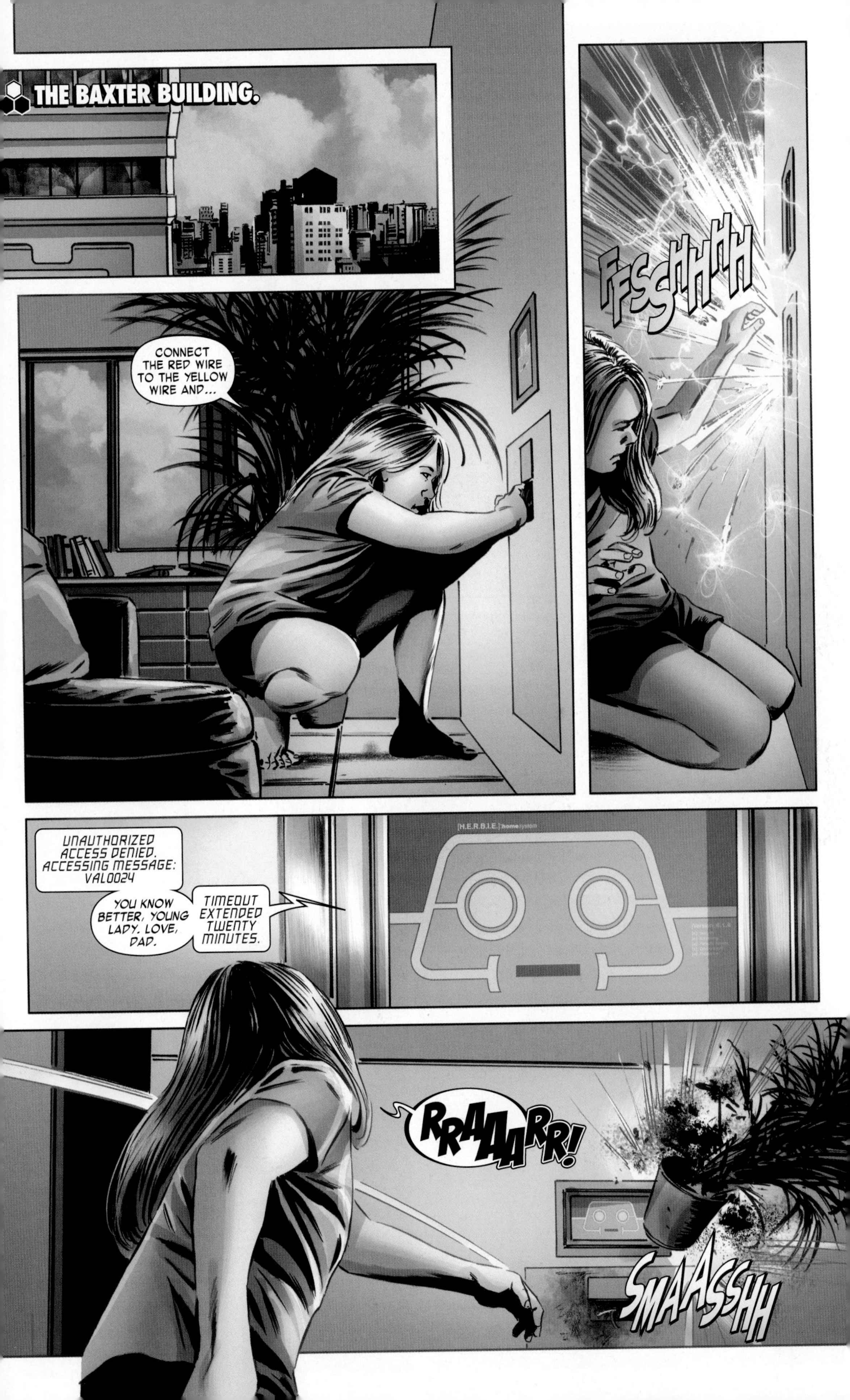
THE BAXTER BUILDING.
CONNECT THE RED WIRE TO THE YELLOW WIRE AND...
FFSSHHHH
UNAUTHORIZED ACCESS DENIED. ACCESSING MESSAGE: VAL0024
YOU KNOW BETTER, YOUNG LADY. LOVE, DAD.
TIMEOUT EXTENDED TWENTY MINUTES.
[H.E.R.B.I.E.] homesystem
RRAAAARR!
SMAASSHH

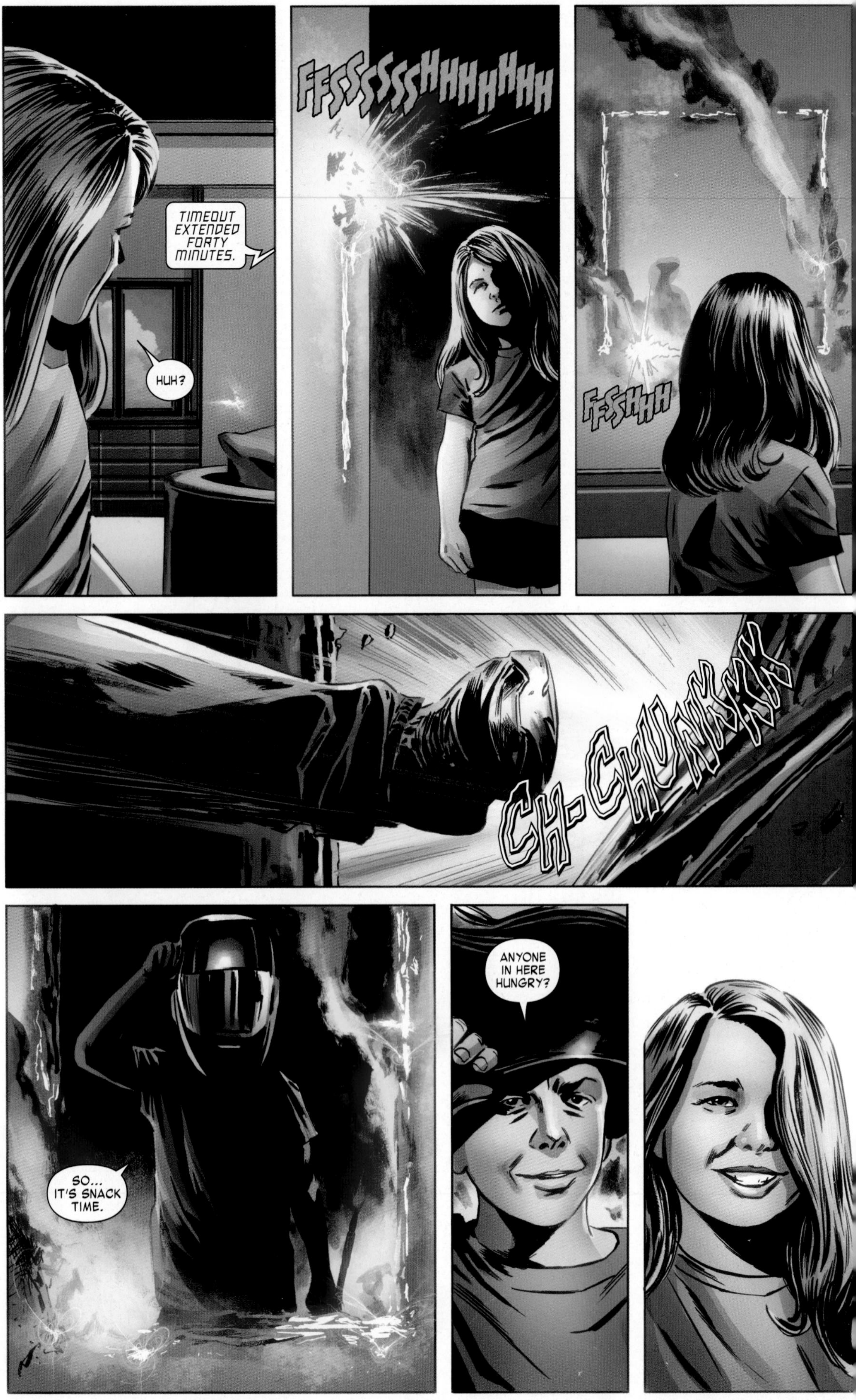
TIMEOUT EXTENDED FORTY MINUTES.
HUH?
FFSSSSSSHHHHHHH
FFSHHH
CH-CHUNKKK
SO... IT'S SNACK TIME.
ANYONE IN HERE HUNGRY?

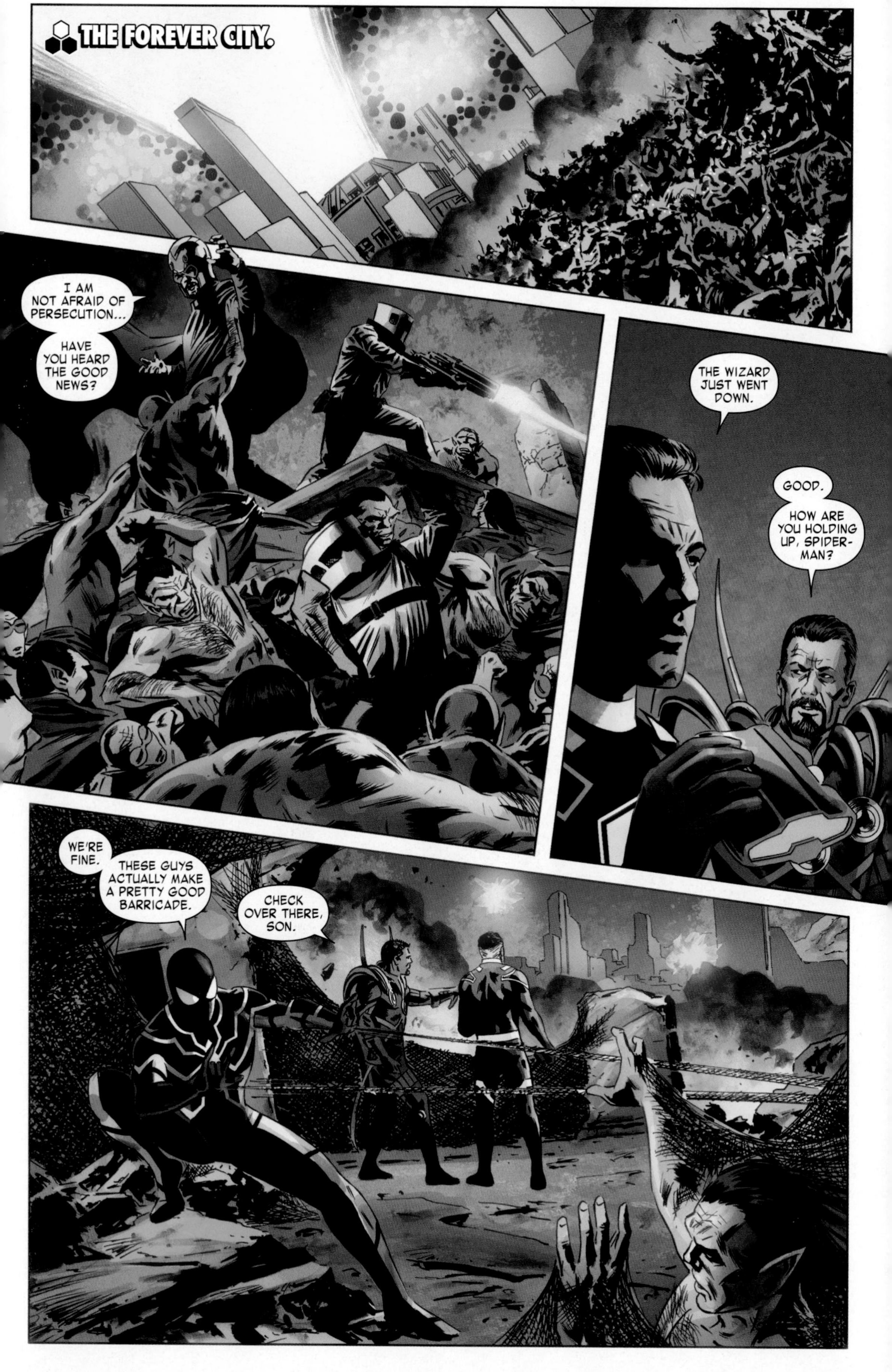
THE FOREVER CITY.
I AM NOT AFRAID OF PERSECUTION...
HAVE YOU HEARD THE GOOD NEWS?
THE WIZARD JUST WENT DOWN.
GOOD.
HOW ARE YOU HOLDING UP, SPIDER-MAN?
WE'RE FINE.
THESE GUYS ACTUALLY MAKE A PRETTY GOOD BARRICADE.
CHECK OVER THERE, SON.

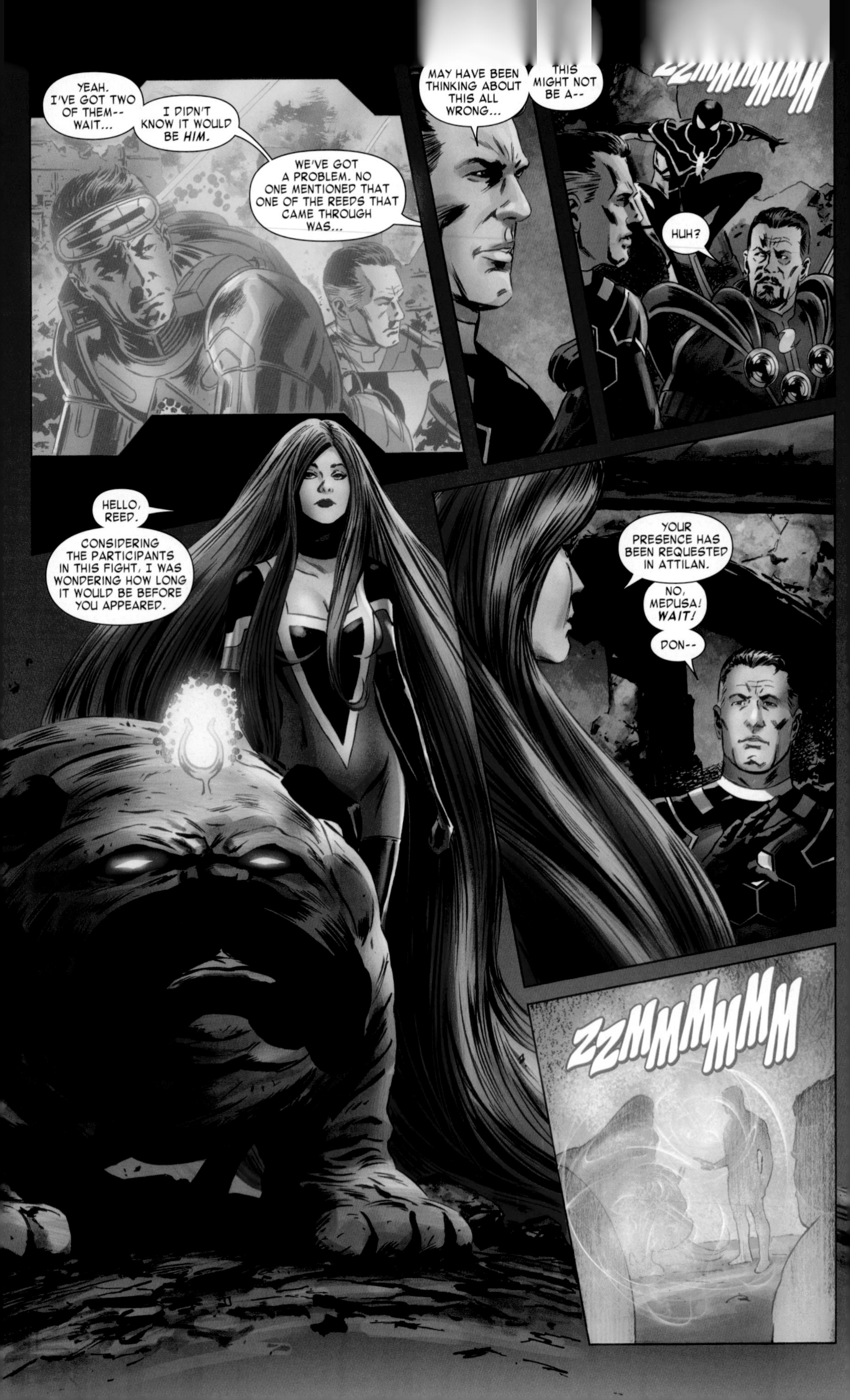
YEAH. I'VE GOT TWO OF THEM-- WAIT...
I DIDN'T KNOW IT WOULD BE HIM.
WE'VE GOT A PROBLEM. NO ONE MENTIONED THAT ONE OF THE REEDS THAT CAME THROUGH WAS...
MAY HAVE BEEN THINKING ABOUT THIS ALL WRONG...
THIS MIGHT NOT BE A--
ZZMMMMMMM
HUH?
HELLO, REED.
CONSIDERING THE PARTICIPANTS IN THIS FIGHT, I WAS WONDERING HOW LONG IT WOULD BE BEFORE YOU APPEARED.
YOUR PRESENCE HAS BEEN REQUESTED IN ATTILAN.
NO, MEDUSA! WAIT!
DON--
ZZMMMMMMM

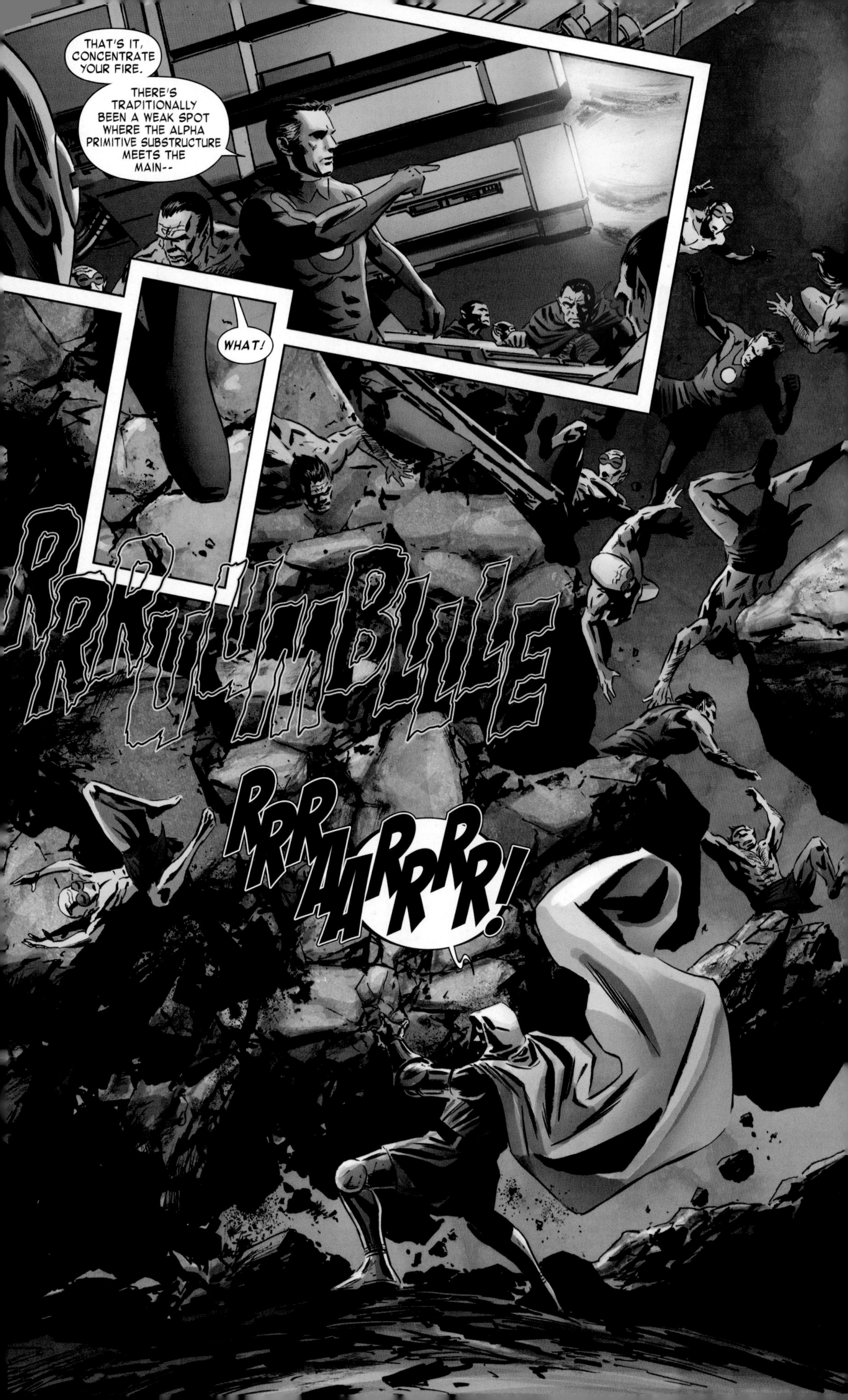
THAT'S IT, CONCENTRATE YOUR FIRE.
THERE'S TRADITIONALLY BEEN A WEAK SPOT WHERE THE ALPHA PRIMITIVE SUBSTRUCTURE MEETS THE MAIN--
WHAT!
RRRUUMBLLLE
RRRAARRRR!

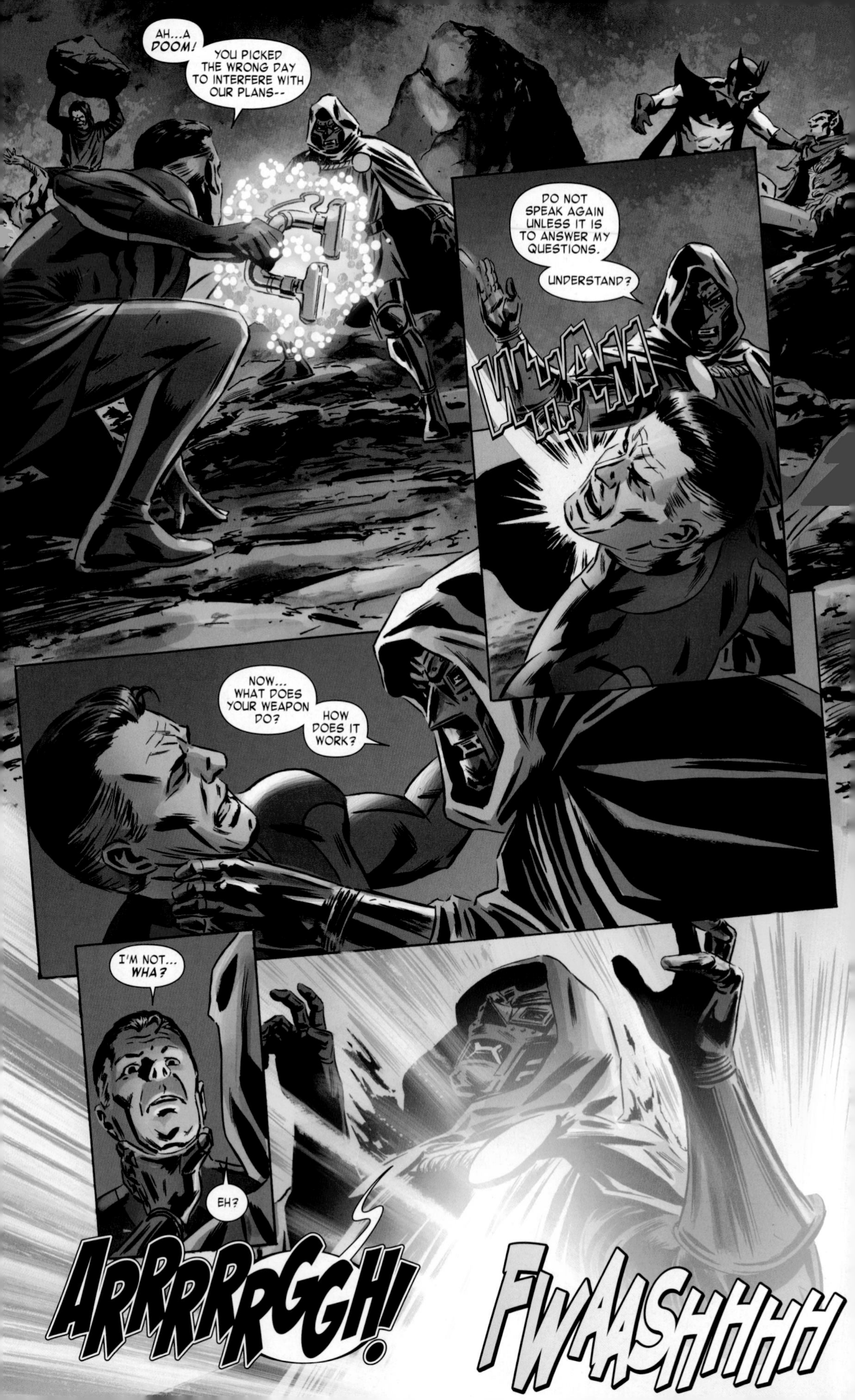
AH...A DOOM!
YOU PICKED THE WRONG DAY TO INTERFERE WITH OUR PLANS--
DO NOT SPEAK AGAIN UNLESS IT IS TO ANSWER MY QUESTIONS.
UNDERSTAND?
VLLAAM
NOW... WHAT DOES YOUR WEAPON DO?
HOW DOES IT WORK?
I'M NOT... WHA?
EH?
ARRRRRGGH!
FWAASHHHH

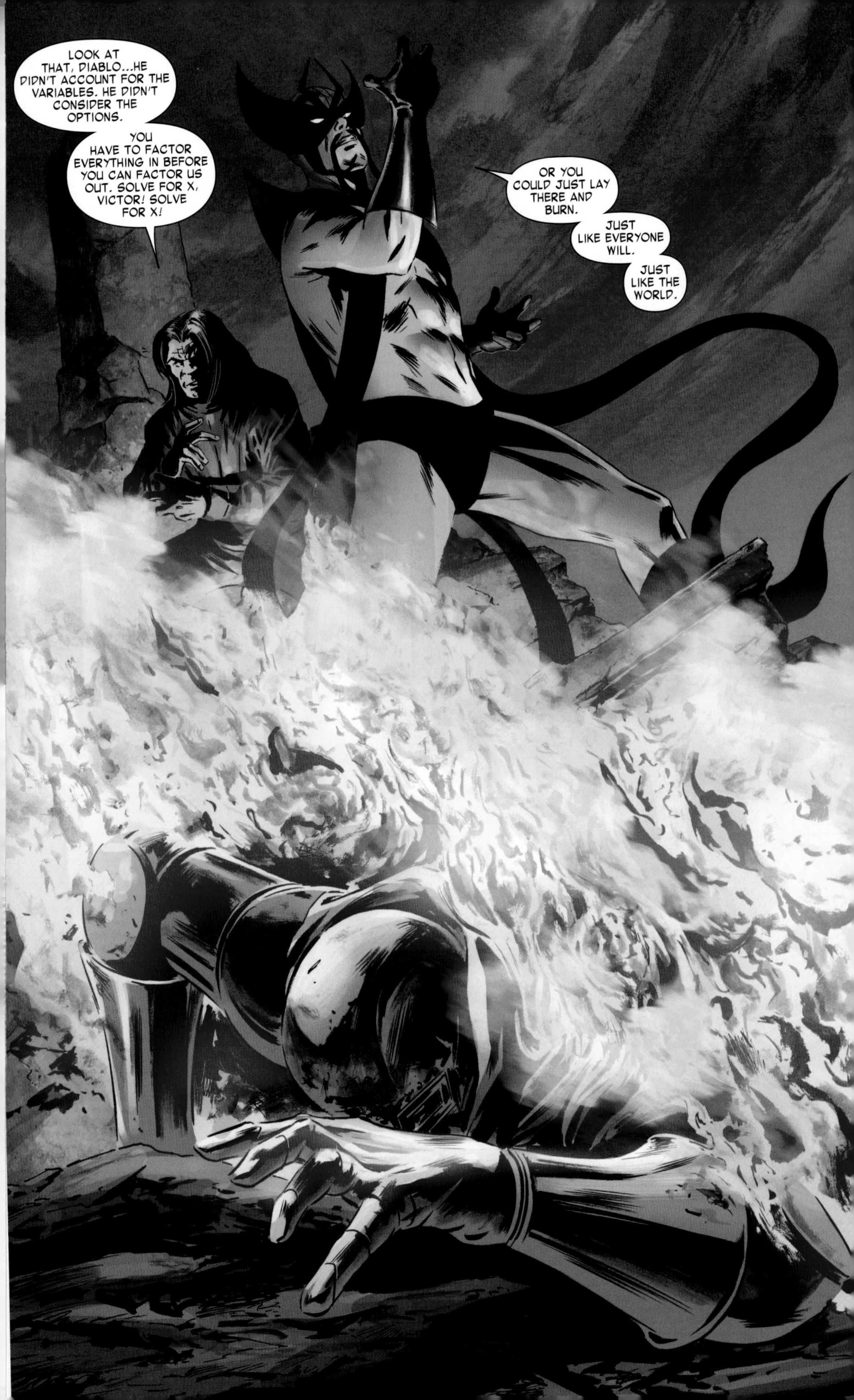
LOOK AT THAT, DIABLO...HE DIDN'T ACCOUNT FOR THE VARIABLES. HE DIDN'T CONSIDER THE OPTIONS.
YOU HAVE TO FACTOR EVERYTHING IN BEFORE YOU CAN FACTOR US OUT. SOLVE FOR X, VICTOR! SOLVE FOR X!
OR YOU COULD JUST LAY THERE AND BURN.
JUST LIKE EVERYONE WILL.
JUST LIKE THE WORLD.

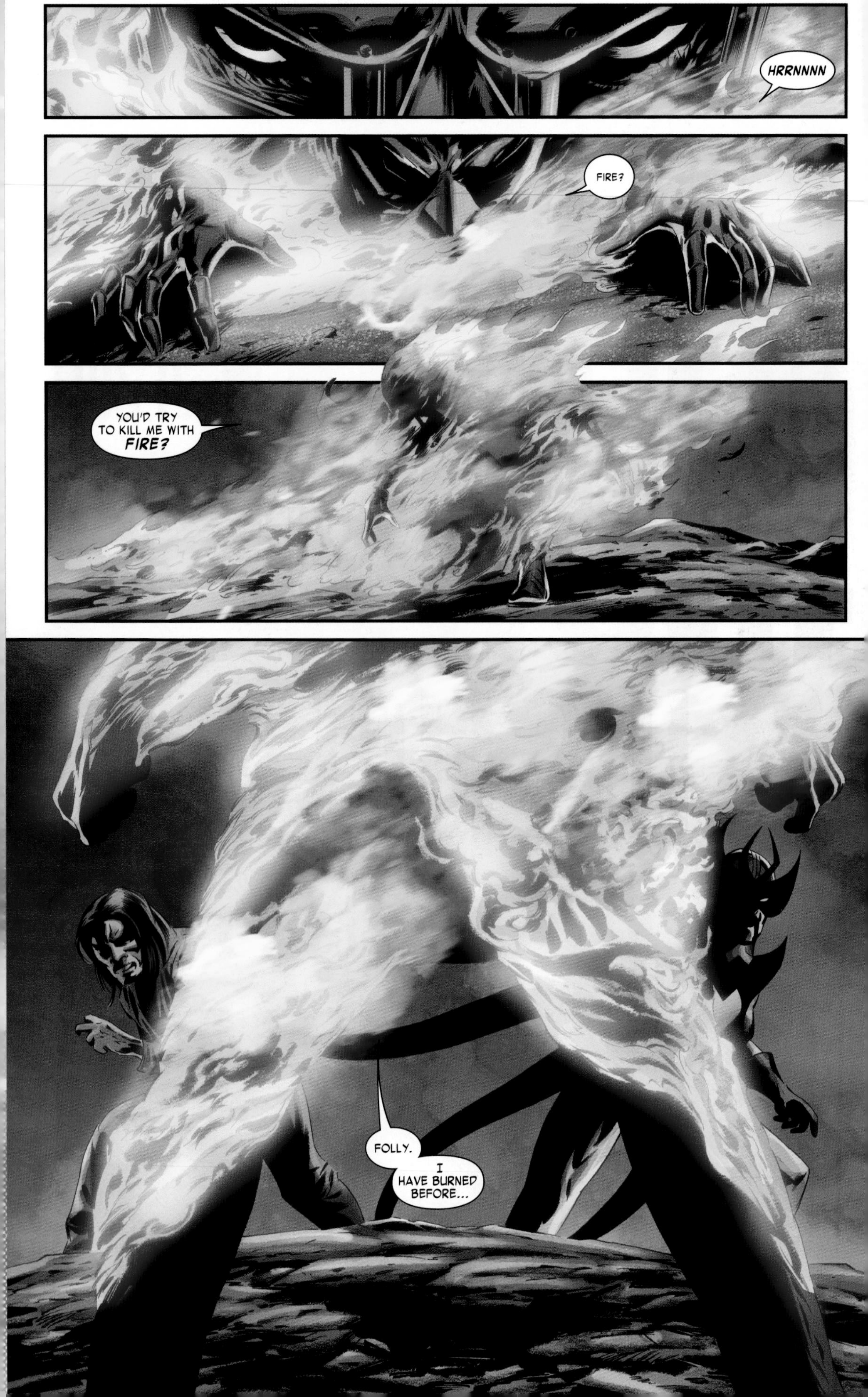
HRRNNNN
FIRE?
YOU'D TRY TO KILL ME WITH FIRE?
FOLLY.
I HAVE BURNED BEFORE...

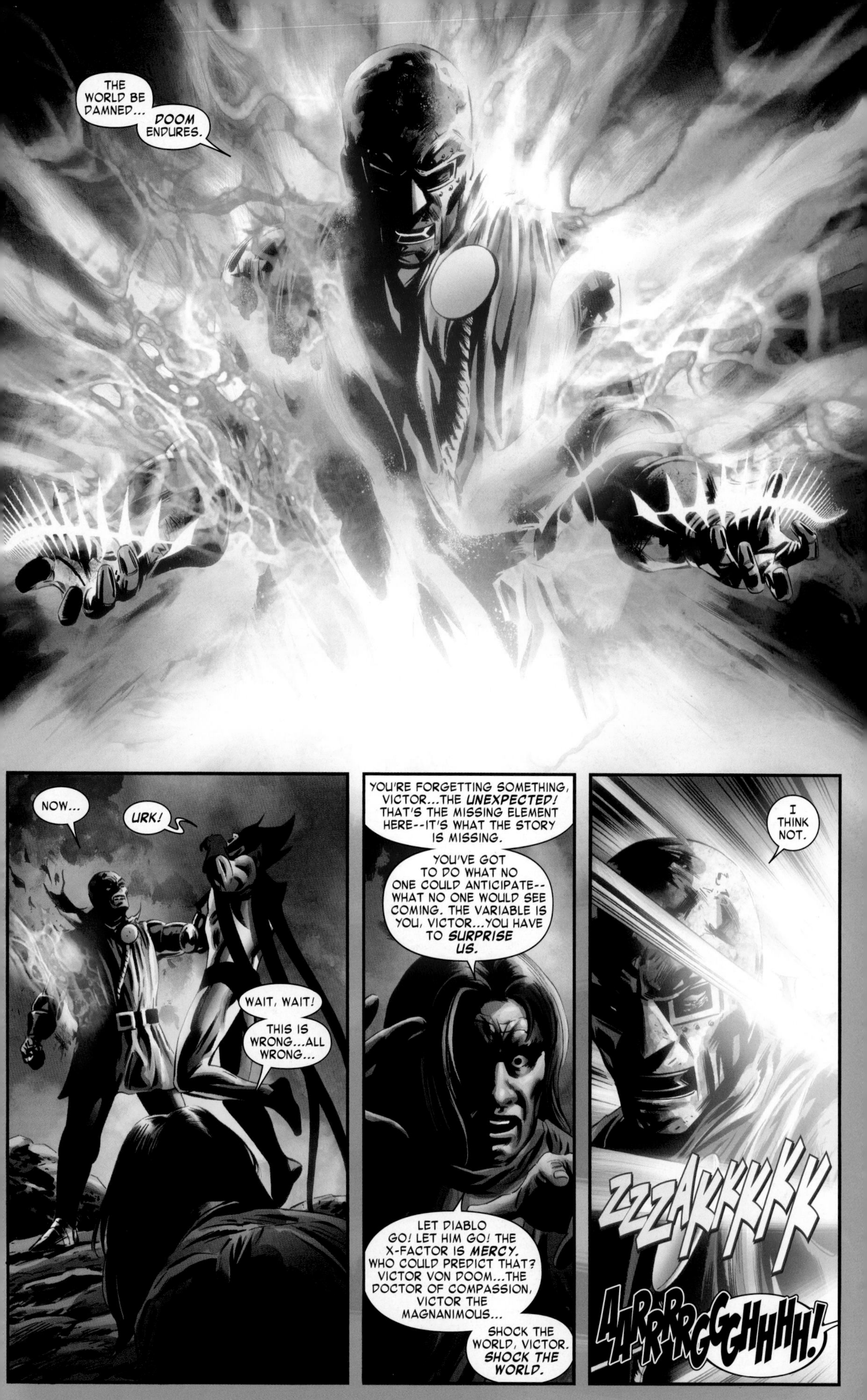
THE WORLD BE DAMNED... DOOM ENDURES.
NOW...
URK!
WAIT, WAIT! THIS IS WRONG...ALL WRONG...
YOU'RE FORGETTING SOMETHING, VICTOR...THE UNEXPECTED! THAT'S THE MISSING ELEMENT HERE--IT'S WHAT THE STORY IS MISSING.
YOU'VE GOT TO DO WHAT NO ONE COULD ANTICIPATE--WHAT NO ONE WOULD SEE COMING. THE VARIABLE IS YOU, VICTOR...YOU HAVE TO SURPRISE US.
LET DIABLO GO! LET HIM GO! THE X-FACTOR IS MERCY. WHO COULD PREDICT THAT? VICTOR VON DOOM...THE DOCTOR OF COMPASSION, VICTOR THE MAGNANIMOUS...
SHOCK THE WORLD, VICTOR. SHOCK THE WORLD.
I THINK NOT.
ZZZAKKKKKK
AARRRRGGHHHH!

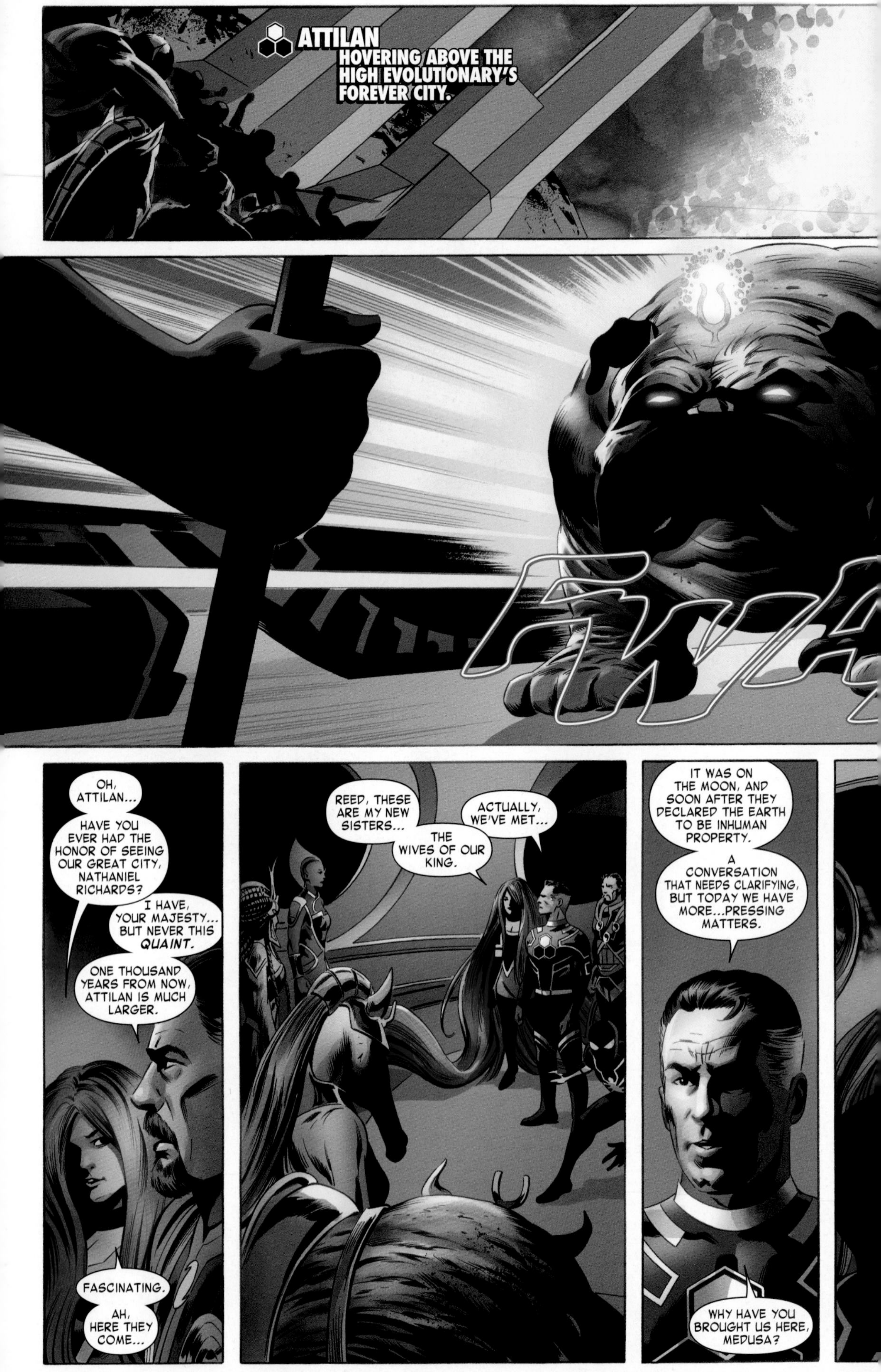
ATTILAN
HOVERING ABOVE THE HIGH EVOLUTIONARY'S FOREVER CITY.
FWA
OH, ATTILAN...
HAVE YOU EVER HAD THE HONOR OF SEEING OUR GREAT CITY, NATHANIEL RICHARDS?
I HAVE, YOUR MAJESTY... BUT NEVER THIS QUAINT.
ONE THOUSAND YEARS FROM NOW, ATTILAN IS MUCH LARGER.
FASCINATING.
AH, HERE THEY COME...
REED, THESE ARE MY NEW SISTERS...
THE WIVES OF OUR KING.
ACTUALLY, WE'VE MET...
IT WAS ON THE MOON, AND SOON AFTER THEY DECLARED THE EARTH TO BE INHUMAN PROPERTY.
A CONVERSATION THAT NEEDS CLARIFYING, BUT TODAY WE HAVE MORE...PRESSING MATTERS.
WHY HAVE YOU BROUGHT US HERE, MEDUSA?

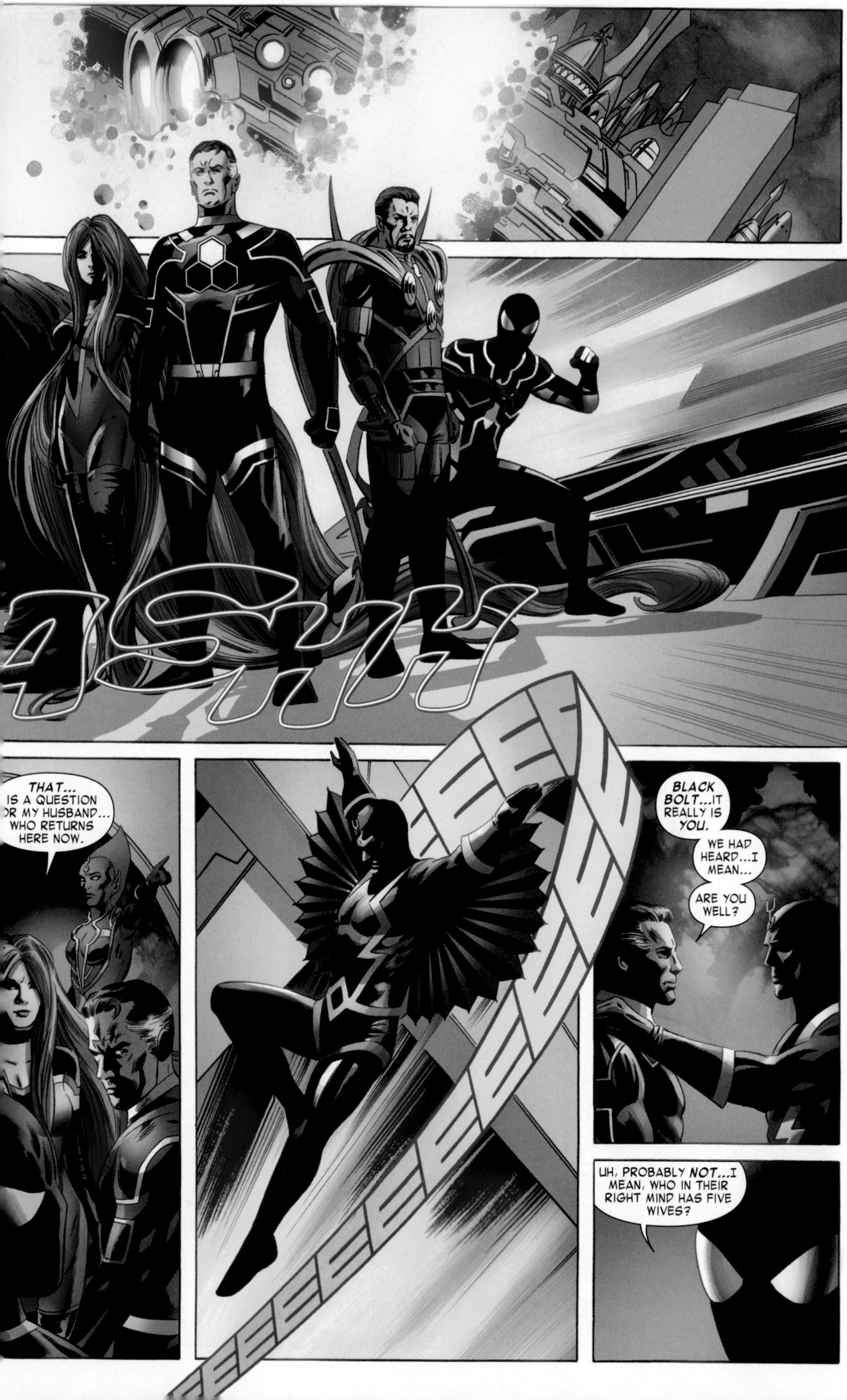
THAT... IS A QUESTION OR MY HUSBAND... WHO RETURNS HERE NOW.
BLACK BOLT...IT REALLY IS YOU.
WE HAD HEARD...I MEAN...
ARE YOU WELL?
UH, PROBABLY NOT...I MEAN, WHO IN THEIR RIGHT MIND HAS FIVE WIVES?

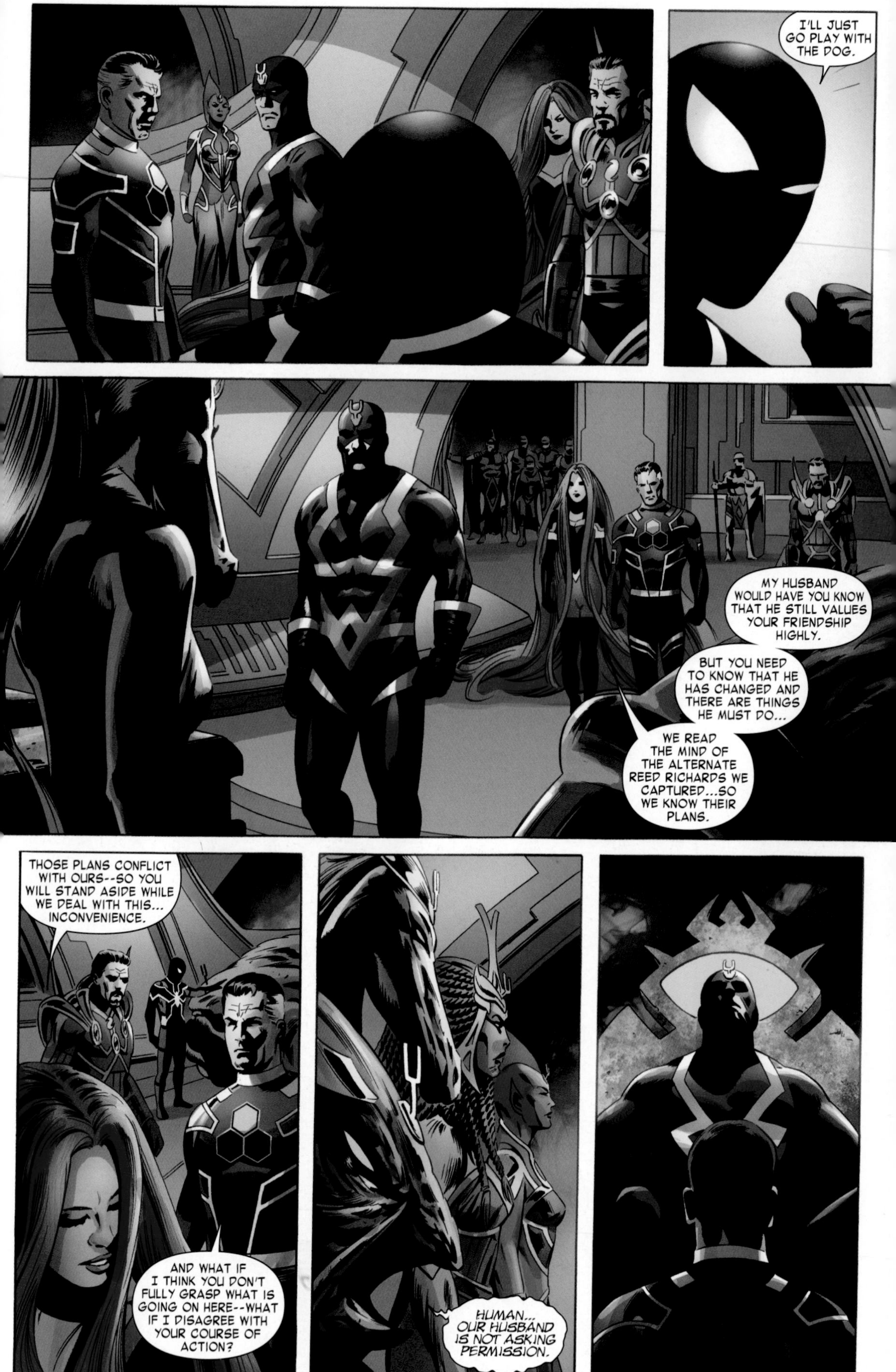
I'LL JUST GO PLAY WITH THE DOG.
MY HUSBAND WOULD HAVE YOU KNOW THAT HE STILL VALUES YOUR FRIENDSHIP HIGHLY.
BUT YOU NEED TO KNOW THAT HE HAS CHANGED AND THERE ARE THINGS HE MUST DO...
WE READ THE MIND OF THE ALTERNATE REED RICHARDS WE CAPTURED...SO WE KNOW THEIR PLANS.
THOSE PLANS CONFLICT WITH OURS--SO YOU WILL STAND ASIDE WHILE WE DEAL WITH THIS... INCONVENIENCE.
AND WHAT IF I THINK YOU DON'T FULLY GRASP WHAT IS GOING ON HERE--WHAT IF I DISAGREE WITH YOUR COURSE OF ACTION?
HUMAN... OUR HUSBAND IS NOT ASKING PERMISSION.

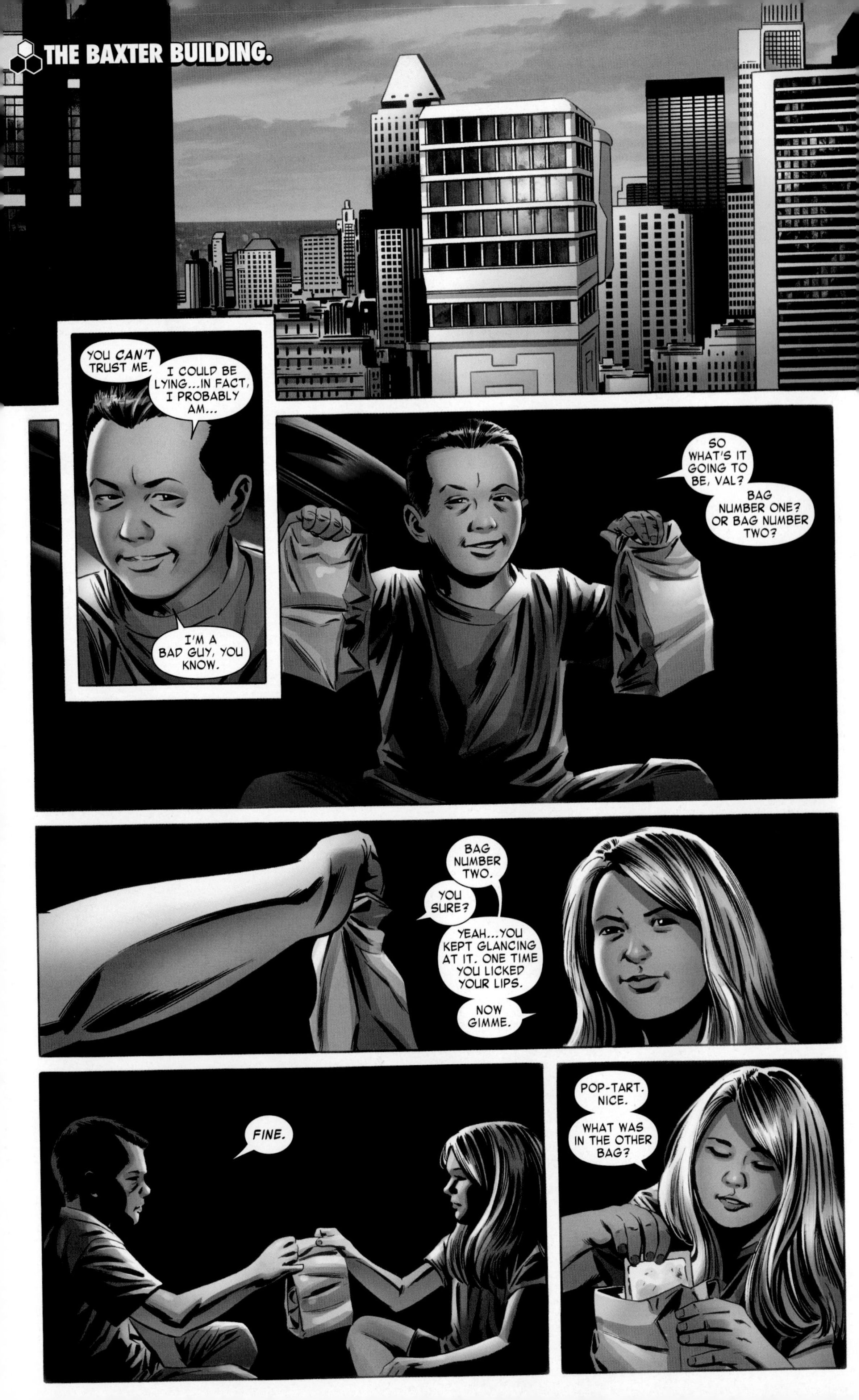
THE BAXTER BUILDING.
YOU CAN'T TRUST ME.
I COULD BE LYING...IN FACT, I PROBABLY AM...
I'M A BAD GUY, YOU KNOW.
SO WHAT'S IT GOING TO BE, VAL?
BAG NUMBER ONE? OR BAG NUMBER TWO?
BAG NUMBER TWO.
YOU SURE?
YEAH...YOU KEPT GLANCING AT IT. ONE TIME YOU LICKED YOUR LIPS.
NOW GIMME.
FINE.
POP-TART. NICE.
WHAT WAS IN THE OTHER BAG?

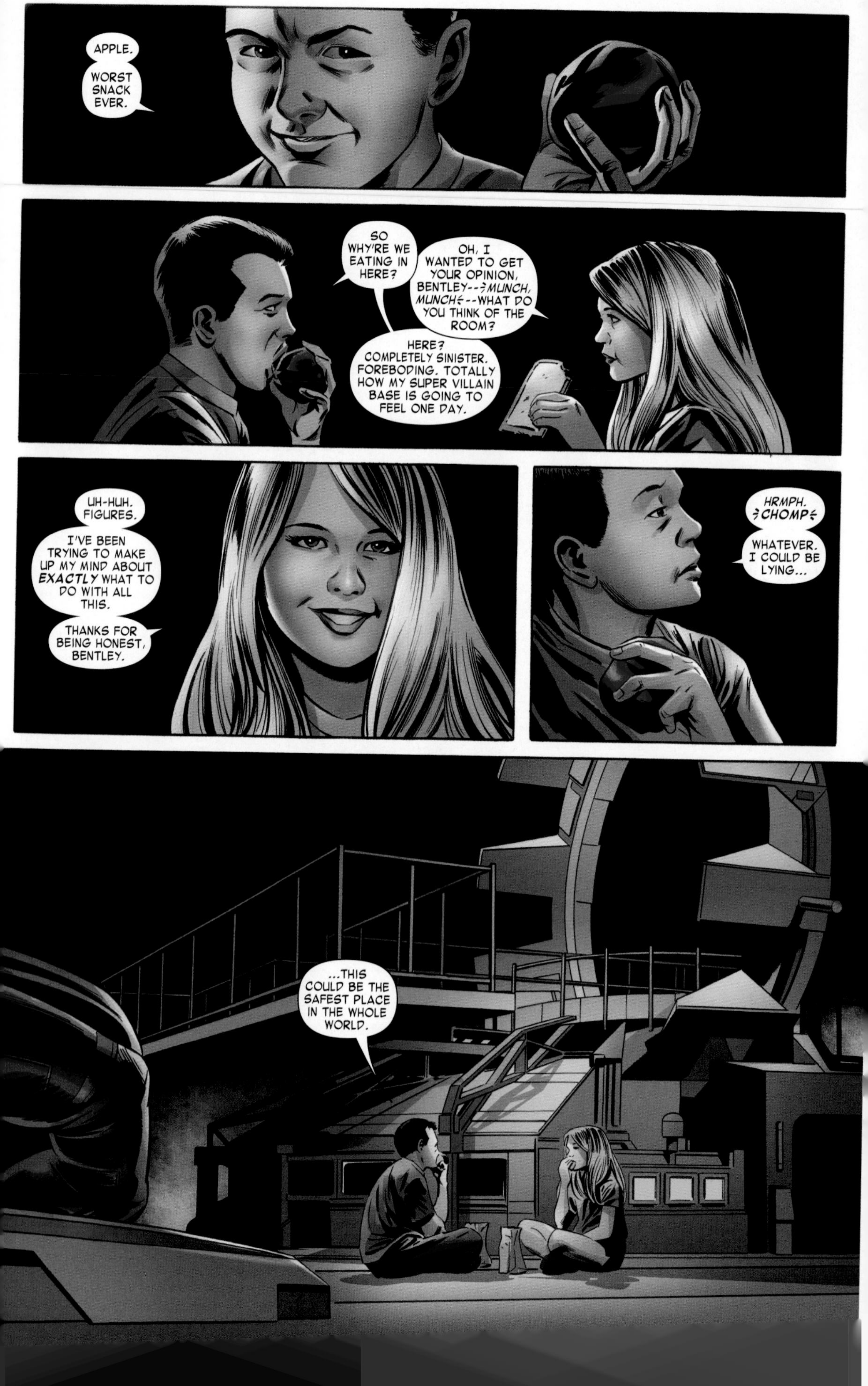
APPLE.
WORST SNACK EVER.
SO WHY'RE WE EATING IN HERE?
OH, I WANTED TO GET YOUR OPINION, BENTLEY-- MUNCH, MUNCH --WHAT DO YOU THINK OF THE ROOM?
HERE? COMPLETELY SINISTER. FOREBODING. TOTALLY HOW MY SUPER VILLAIN BASE IS GOING TO FEEL ONE DAY.
UH-HUH. FIGURES.
I'VE BEEN TRYING TO MAKE UP MY MIND ABOUT EXACTLY WHAT TO DO WITH ALL THIS.
THANKS FOR BEING HONEST, BENTLEY.
HRMPH. CHOMP
WHATEVER. I COULD BE LYING...
...THIS COULD BE THE SAFEST PLACE IN THE WHOLE WORLD.

END SNACK BREAK

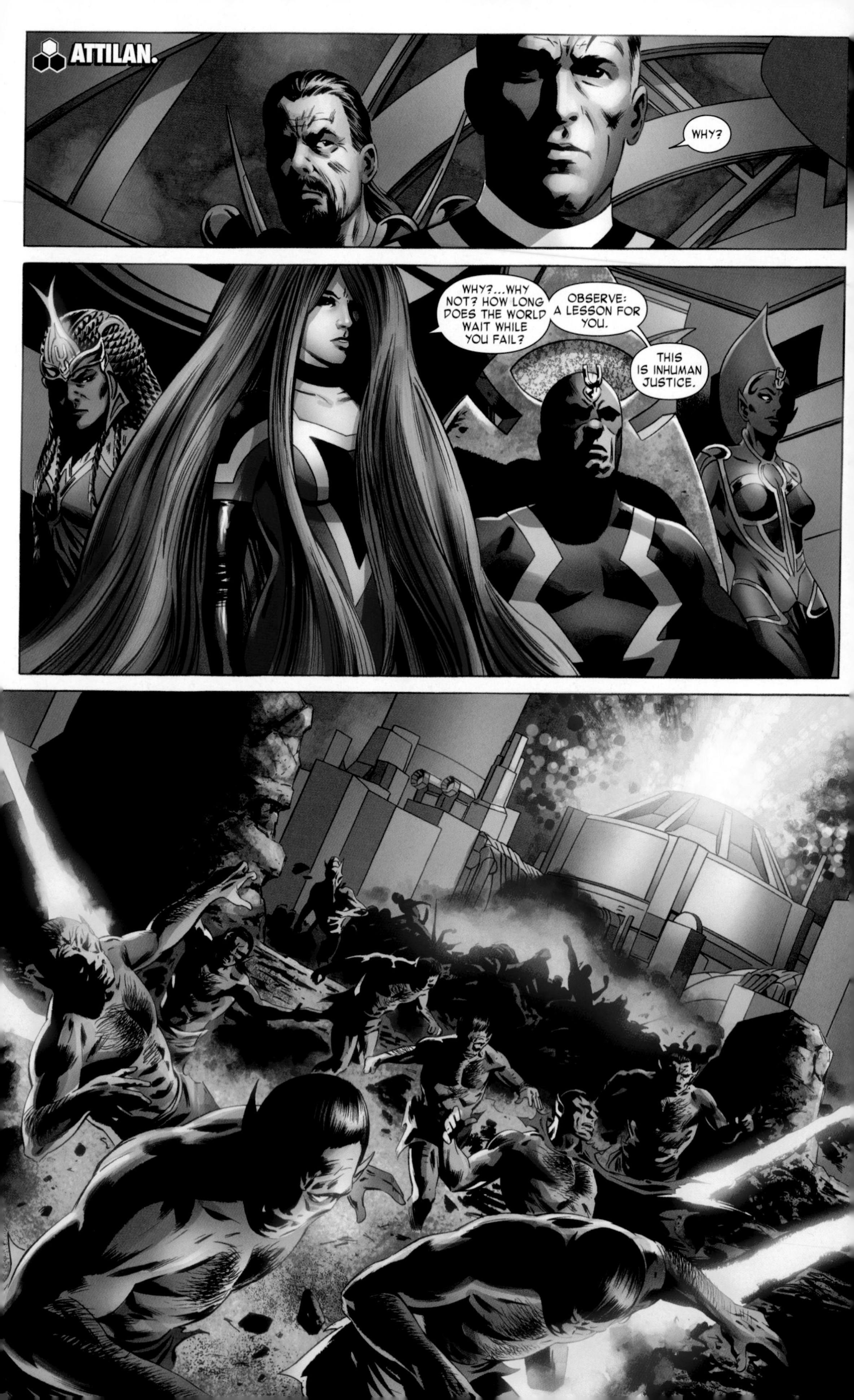
ATTILAN.
WHY?
WHY?...WHY NOT? HOW LONG DOES THE WORLD WAIT WHILE YOU FAIL?
OBSERVE: A LESSON FOR YOU.
THIS IS INHUMAN JUSTICE.

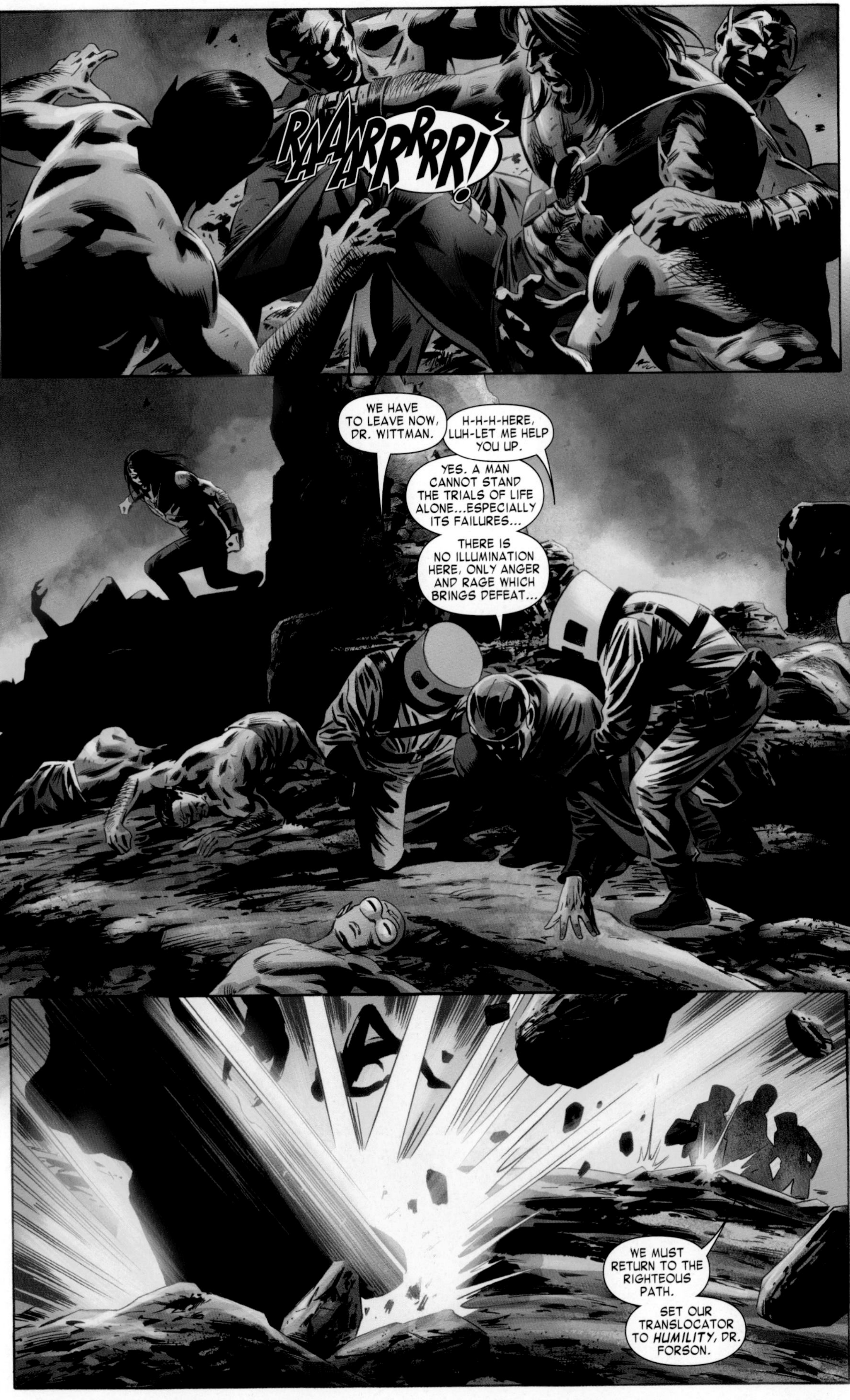
RAAARRRR!
WE HAVE TO LEAVE NOW, DR. WITTMAN.
H-H-H-HERE, LUH-LET ME HELP YOU UP.
YES. A MAN CANNOT STAND THE TRIALS OF LIFE ALONE...ESPECIALLY ITS FAILURES...
THERE IS NO ILLUMINATION HERE, ONLY ANGER AND RAGE WHICH BRINGS DEFEAT...
WE MUST RETURN TO THE RIGHTEOUS PATH.
SET OUR TRANSLOCATOR TO *HUMILITY*, DR. FORSON.

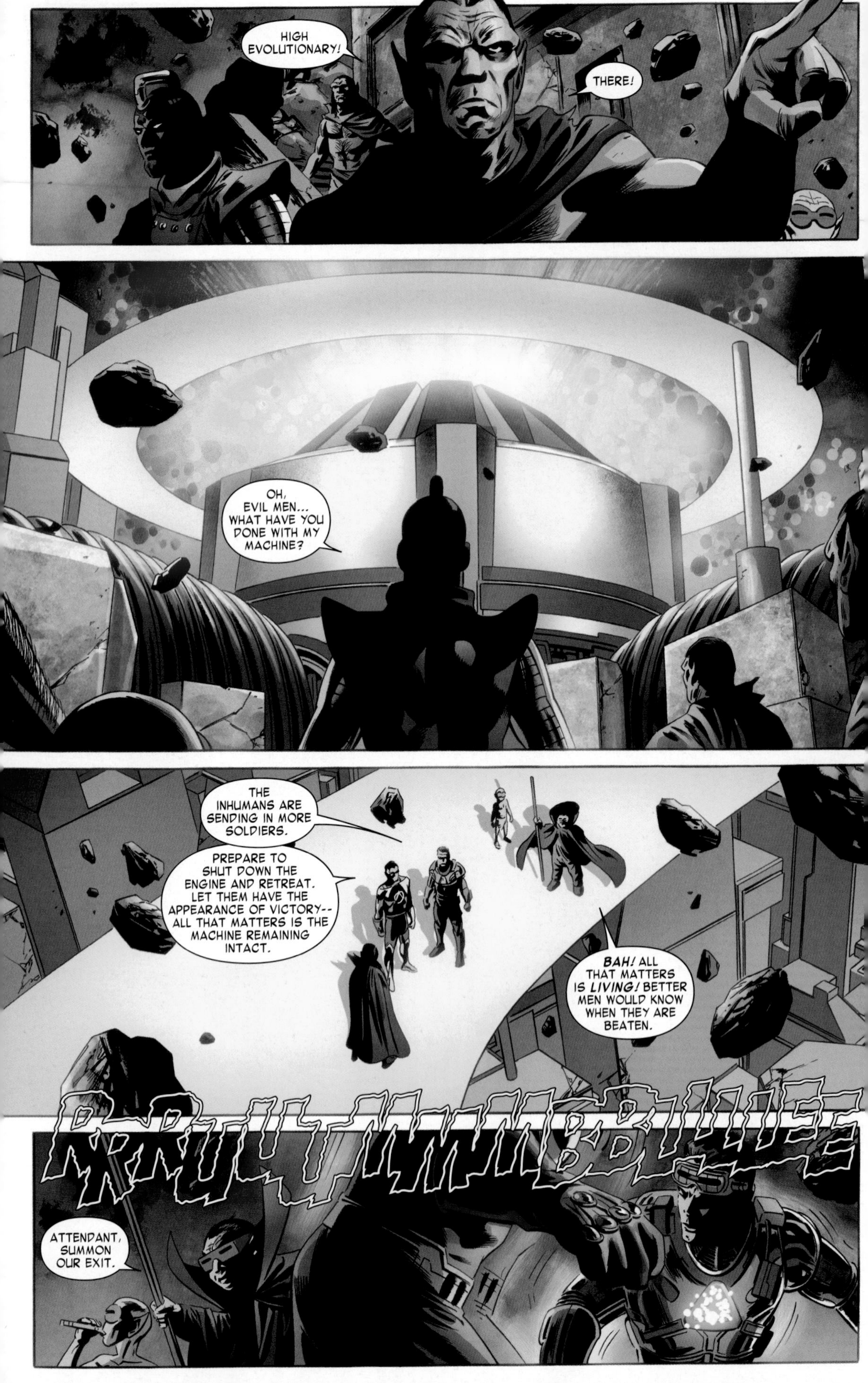
HIGH EVOLUTIONARY!
THERE!
OH, EVIL MEN... WHAT HAVE YOU DONE WITH MY MACHINE?
THE INHUMANS ARE SENDING IN MORE SOLDIERS.
PREPARE TO SHUT DOWN THE ENGINE AND RETREAT. LET THEM HAVE THE APPEARANCE OF VICTORY-- ALL THAT MATTERS IS THE MACHINE REMAINING INTACT.
BAH! ALL THAT MATTERS IS LIVING! BETTER MEN WOULD KNOW WHEN THEY ARE BEATEN.
ATTENDANT, SUMMON OUR EXIT.

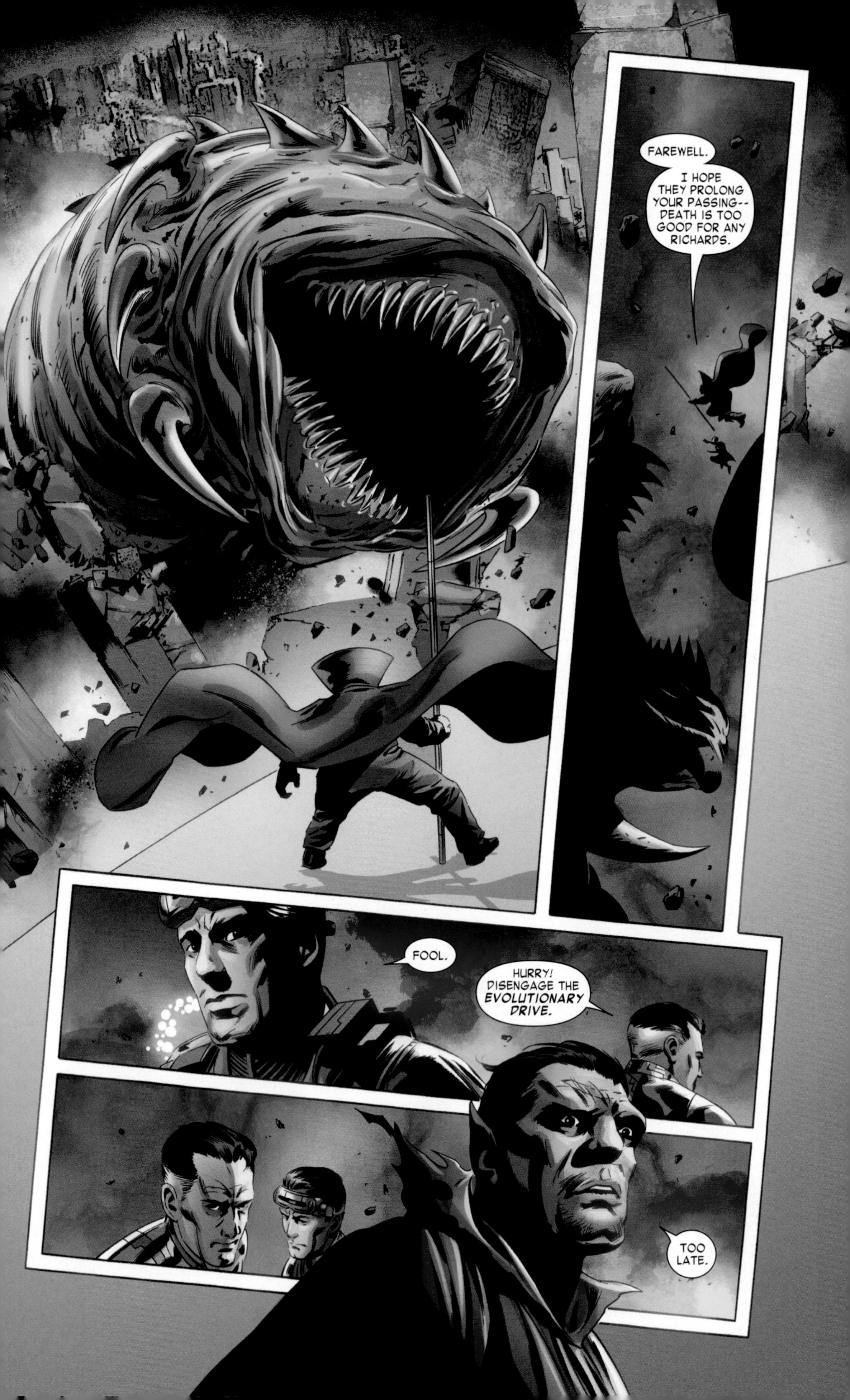
FAREWELL.
I HOPE THEY PROLONG YOUR PASSING-- DEATH IS TOO GOOD FOR ANY RICHARDS.
FOOL.
HURRY! DISENGAGE THE EVOLUTIONARY DRIVE.
TOO LATE.

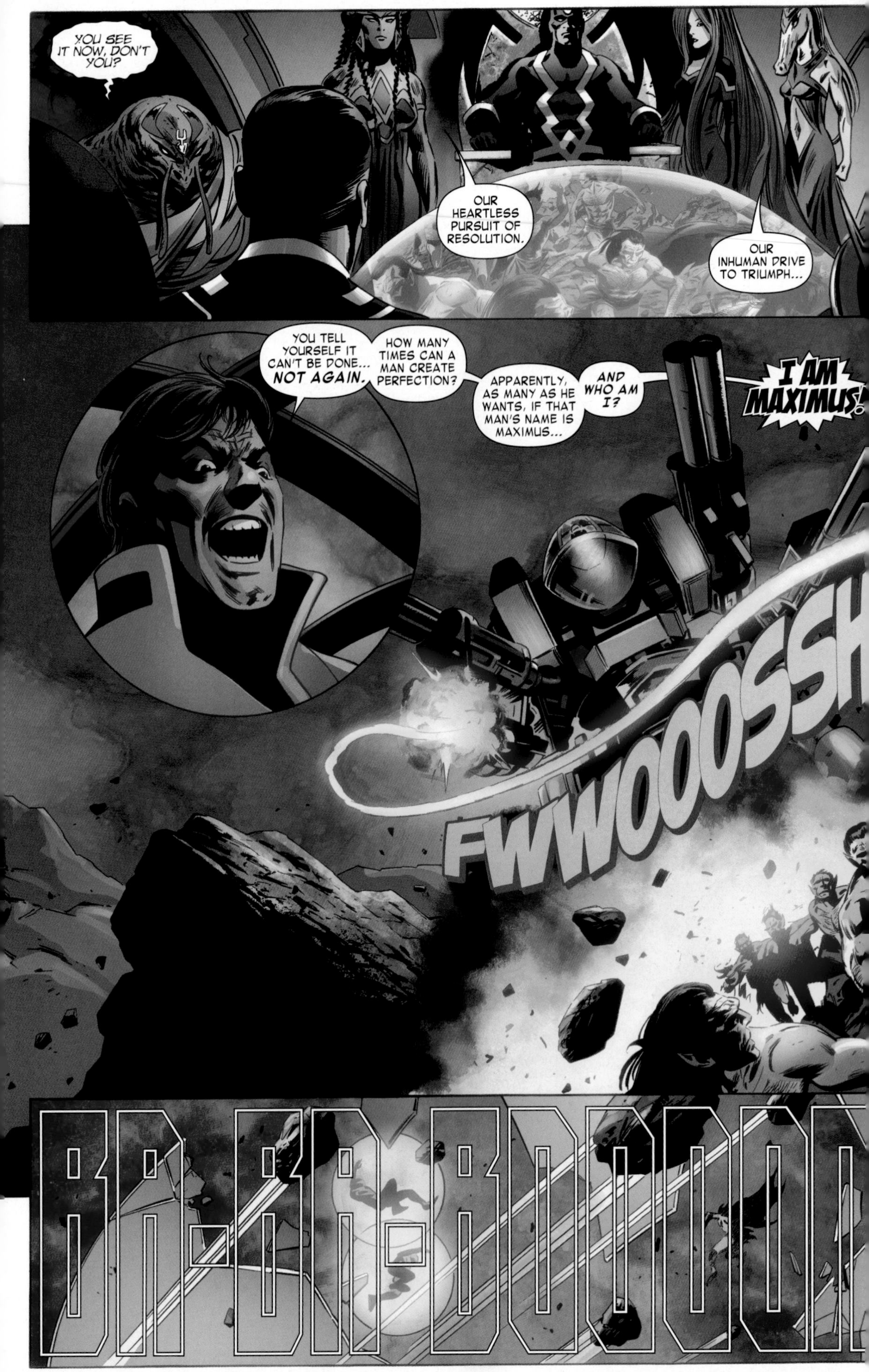
YOU SEE IT NOW, DON'T YOU?
OUR HEARTLESS PURSUIT OF RESOLUTION.
OUR INHUMAN DRIVE TO TRIUMPH...
YOU TELL YOURSELF IT CAN'T BE DONE... NOT AGAIN.
HOW MANY TIMES CAN A MAN CREATE PERFECTION?
APPARENTLY, AS MANY AS HE WANTS, IF THAT MAN'S NAME IS MAXIMUS...
AND WHO AM I?
I AM MAXIMUS!
FWWOOOSSH
BR-BR-BOOOOM

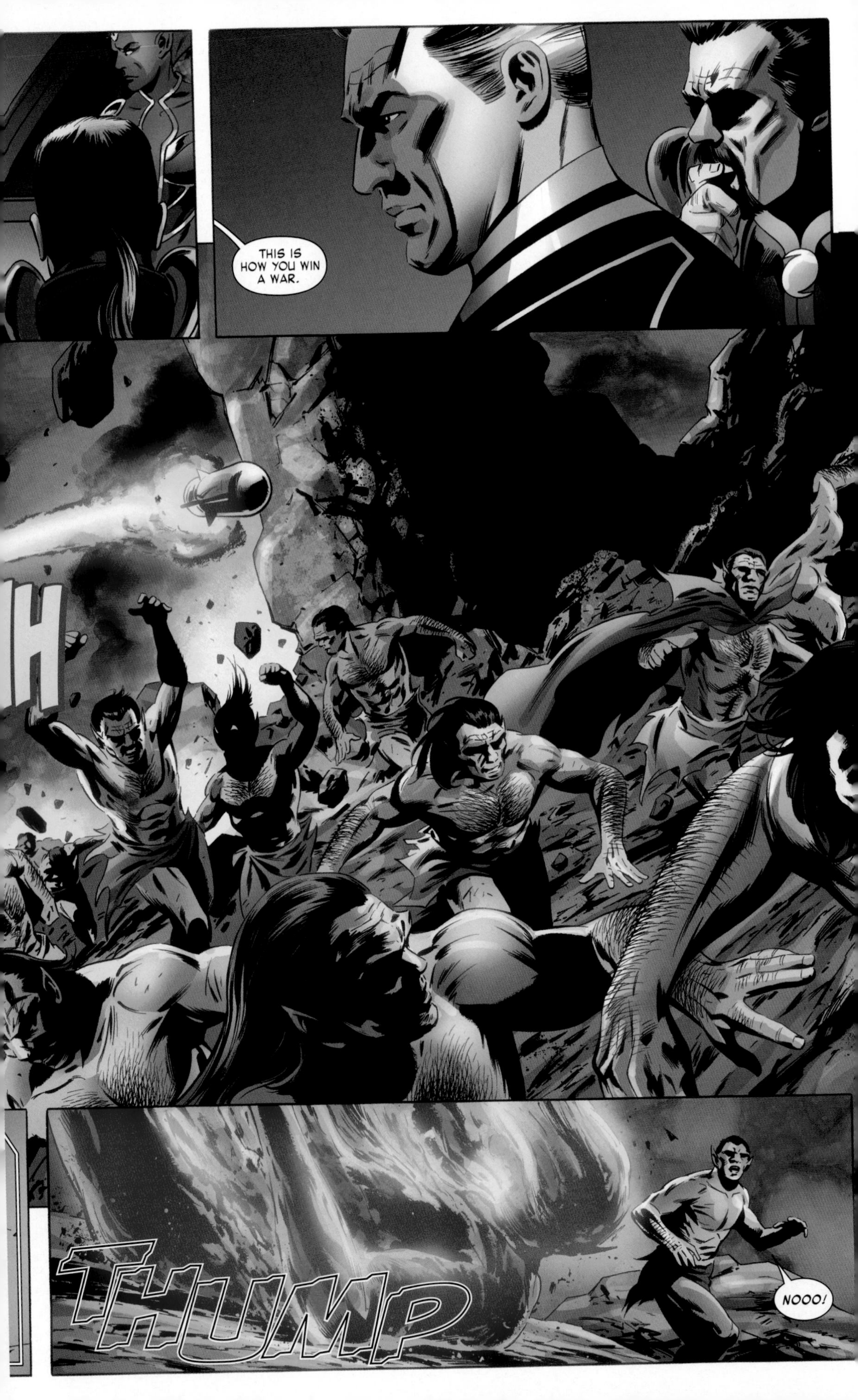
THIS IS HOW YOU WIN A WAR.
THUMP
NOOO!

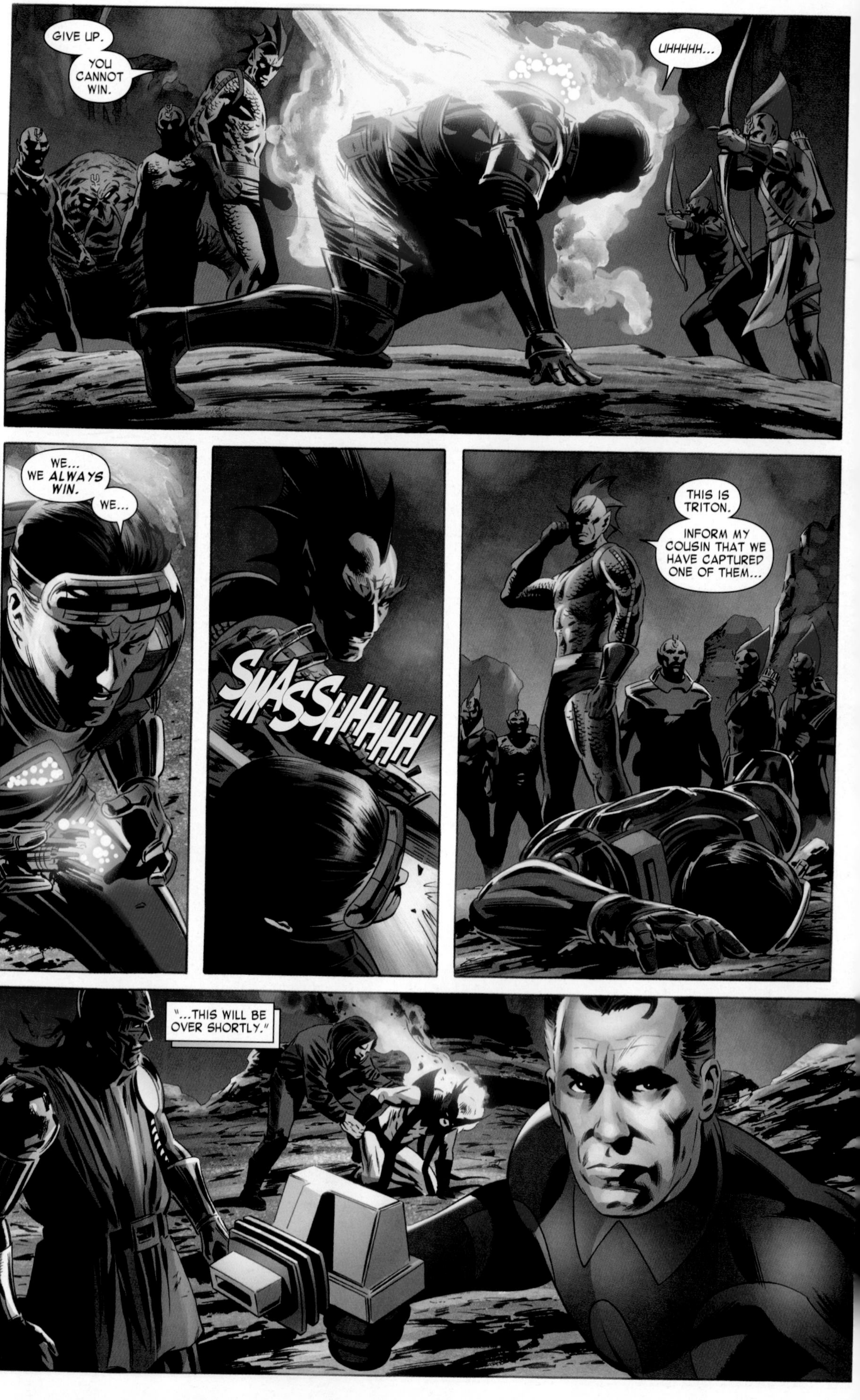
GIVE UP.
YOU CANNOT WIN.
UHHHHH...
WE... WE ALWAYS WIN.
WE...
SWASSHHHHH
THIS IS TRITON.
INFORM MY COUSIN THAT WE HAVE CAPTURED ONE OF THEM...
"...THIS WILL BE OVER SHORTLY."

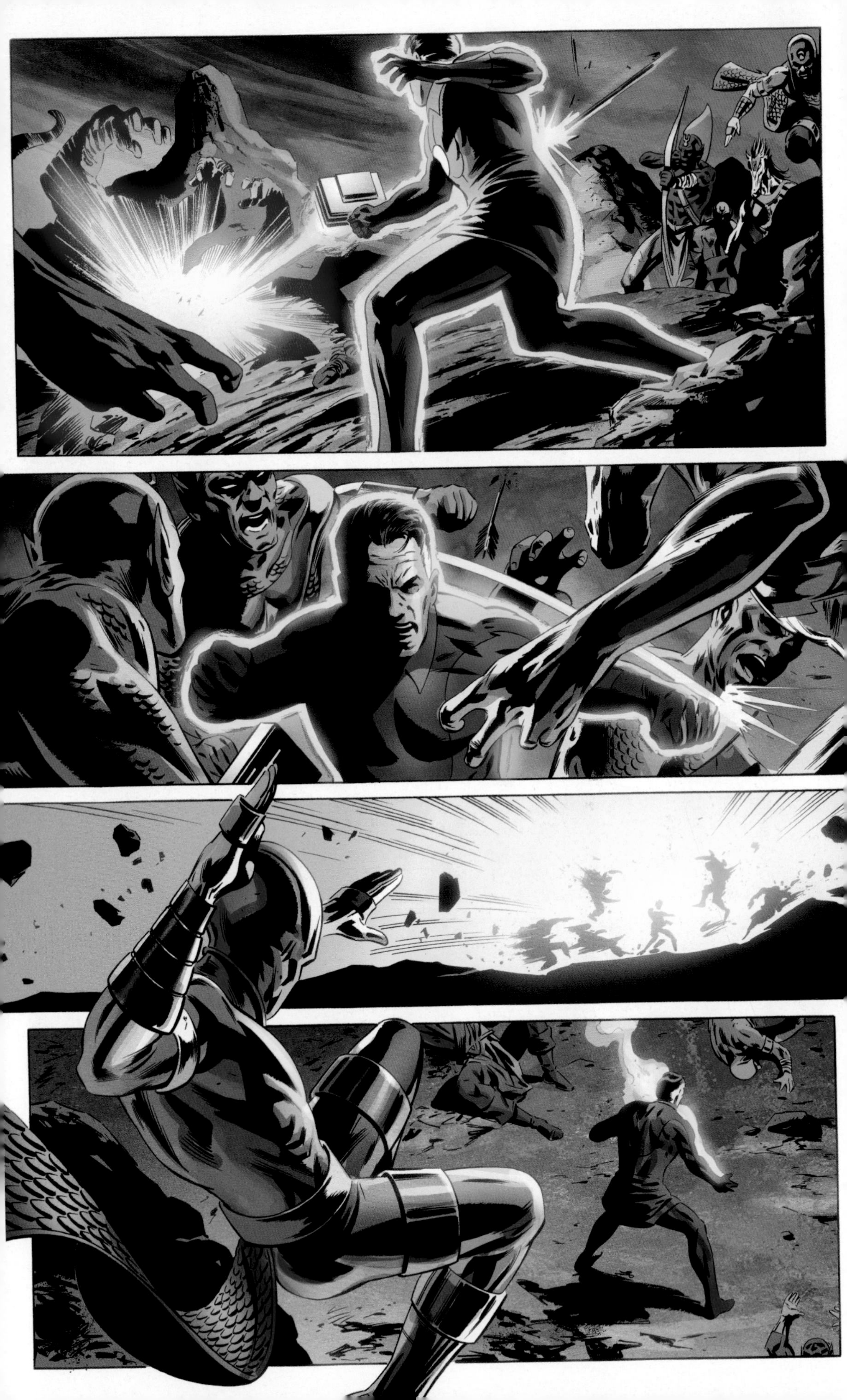

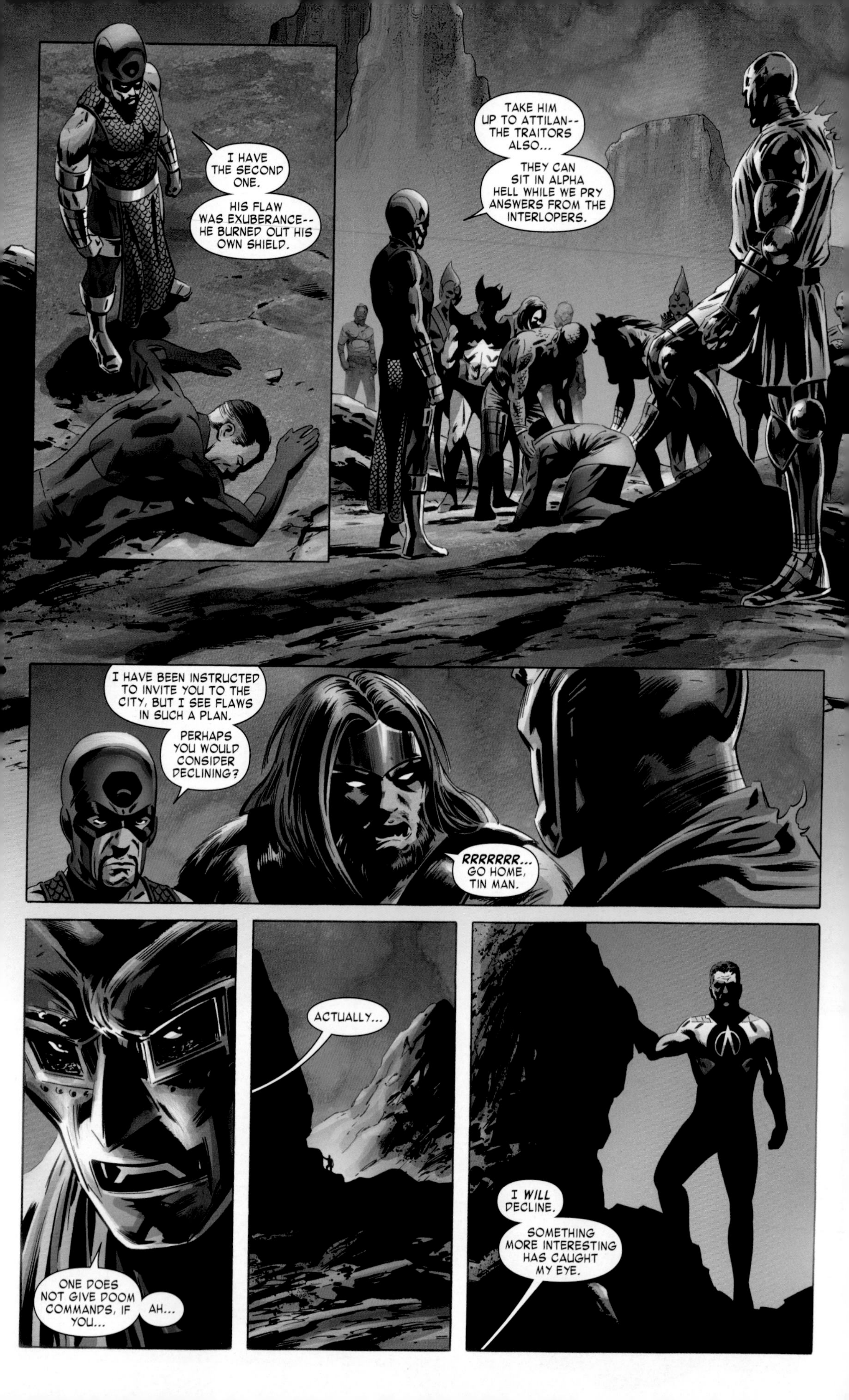
I HAVE THE SECOND ONE.
HIS FLAW WAS EXUBERANCE-- HE BURNED OUT HIS OWN SHIELD.
TAKE HIM UP TO ATTILAN-- THE TRAITORS ALSO...
THEY CAN SIT IN ALPHA HELL WHILE WE PRY ANSWERS FROM THE INTERLOPERS.
I HAVE BEEN INSTRUCTED TO INVITE YOU TO THE CITY, BUT I SEE FLAWS IN SUCH A PLAN.
PERHAPS YOU WOULD CONSIDER DECLINING?
RRRRRRR... GO HOME, TIN MAN.
ONE DOES NOT GIVE DOOM COMMANDS, IF YOU...
AH...
ACTUALLY...
I WILL DECLINE.
SOMETHING MORE INTERESTING HAS CAUGHT MY EYE.

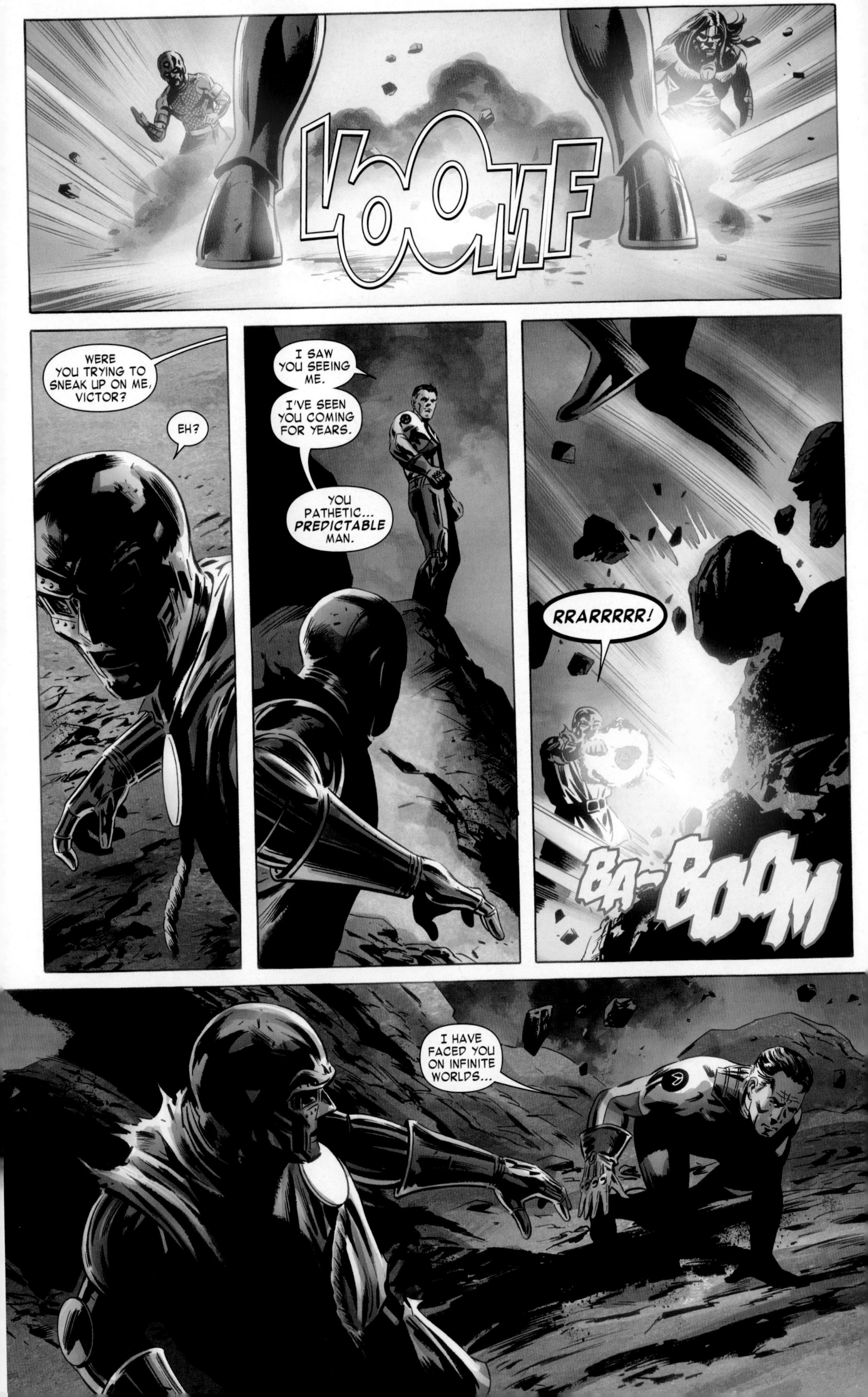
WOOMF
WERE YOU TRYING TO SNEAK UP ON ME, VICTOR?
EH?
I SAW YOU SEEING ME.
I'VE SEEN YOU COMING FOR YEARS.
YOU PATHETIC... *PREDICTABLE* MAN.
RRARRRRR!
BA-BOOM
I HAVE FACED YOU ON INFINITE WORLDS...

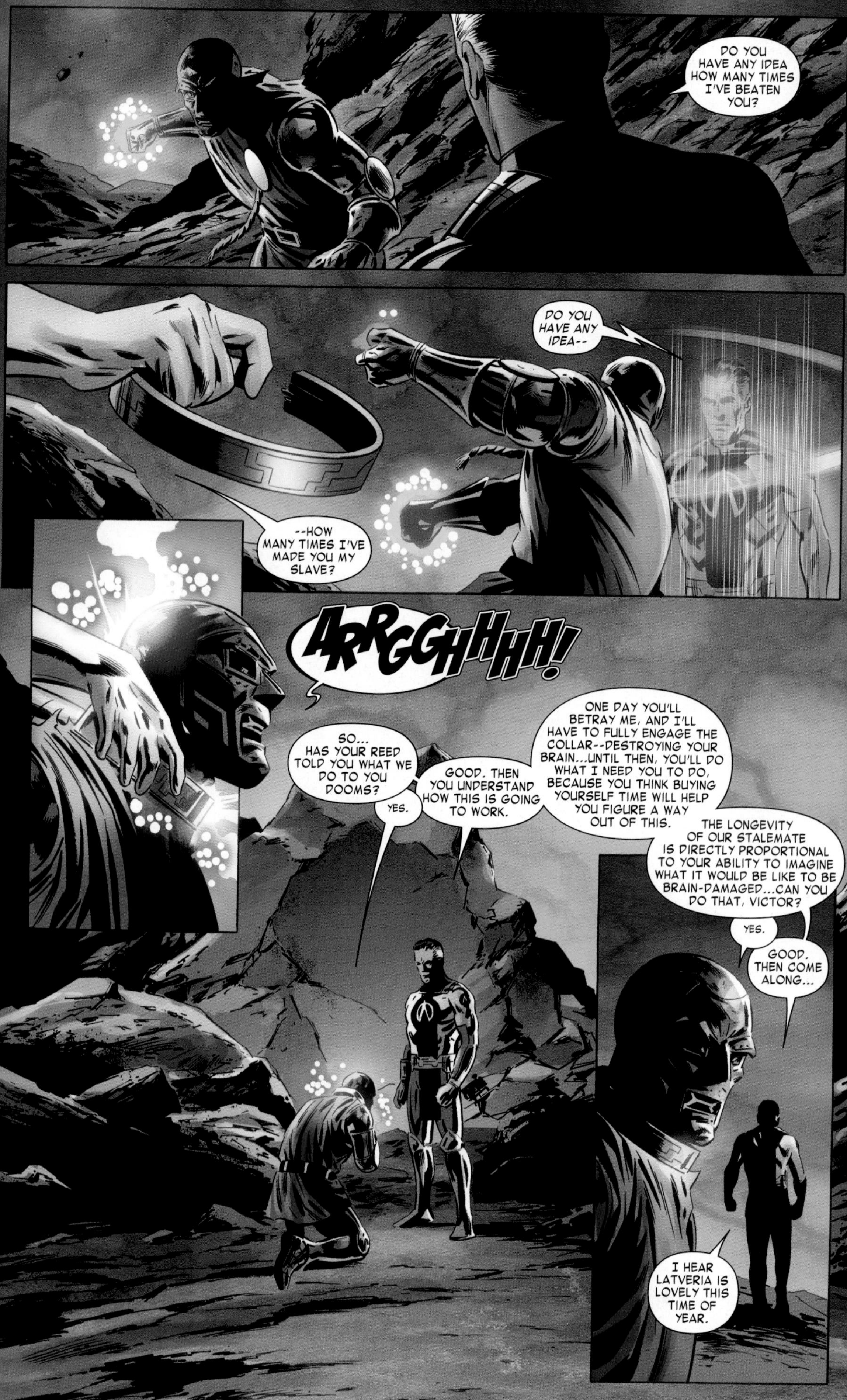
DO YOU HAVE ANY IDEA HOW MANY TIMES I'VE BEATEN YOU?
DO YOU HAVE ANY IDEA--
--HOW MANY TIMES I'VE MADE YOU MY SLAVE?
ARRGGHHHHH!
SO... HAS YOUR REED TOLD YOU WHAT WE DO TO YOU DOOMS?
YES.
GOOD. THEN YOU UNDERSTAND HOW THIS IS GOING TO WORK.
ONE DAY YOU'LL BETRAY ME, AND I'LL HAVE TO FULLY ENGAGE THE COLLAR--DESTROYING YOUR BRAIN...UNTIL THEN, YOU'LL DO WHAT I NEED YOU TO DO, BECAUSE YOU THINK BUYING YOURSELF TIME WILL HELP YOU FIGURE A WAY OUT OF THIS.
THE LONGEVITY OF OUR STALEMATE IS DIRECTLY PROPORTIONAL TO YOUR ABILITY TO IMAGINE WHAT IT WOULD BE LIKE TO BE BRAIN-DAMAGED...CAN YOU DO THAT, VICTOR?
YES.
GOOD. THEN COME ALONG...
I HEAR LATVERIA IS LOVELY THIS TIME OF YEAR.

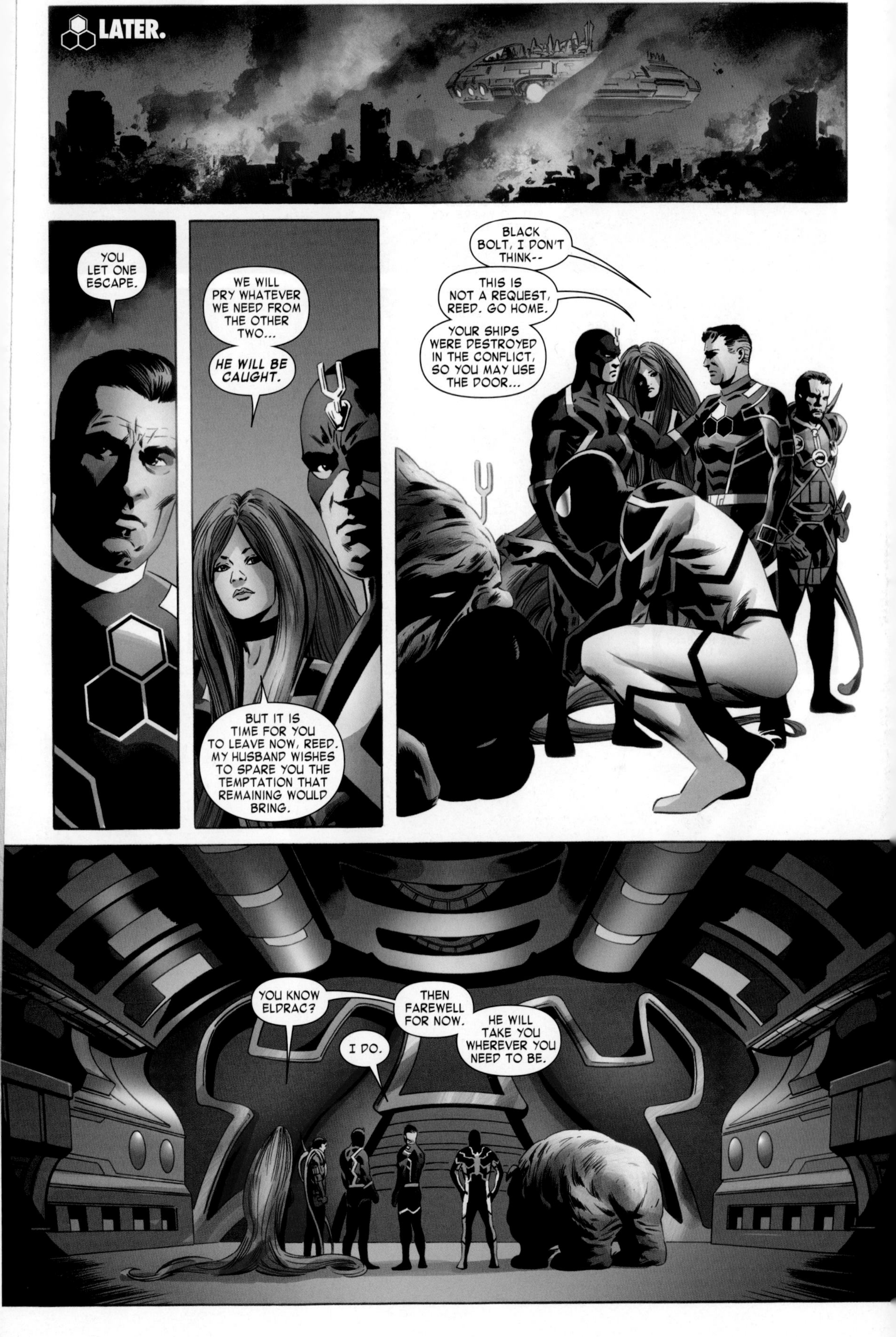
LATER.
YOU LET ONE ESCAPE.
WE WILL PRY WHATEVER WE NEED FROM THE OTHER TWO...
HE WILL BE CAUGHT.
BUT IT IS TIME FOR YOU TO LEAVE NOW, REED. MY HUSBAND WISHES TO SPARE YOU THE TEMPTATION THAT REMAINING WOULD BRING.
BLACK BOLT, I DON'T THINK--
THIS IS NOT A REQUEST, REED. GO HOME.
YOUR SHIPS WERE DESTROYED IN THE CONFLICT, SO YOU MAY USE THE DOOR...
YOU KNOW ELDRAC?
I DO.
THEN FAREWELL FOR NOW.
HE WILL TAKE YOU WHEREVER YOU NEED TO BE.

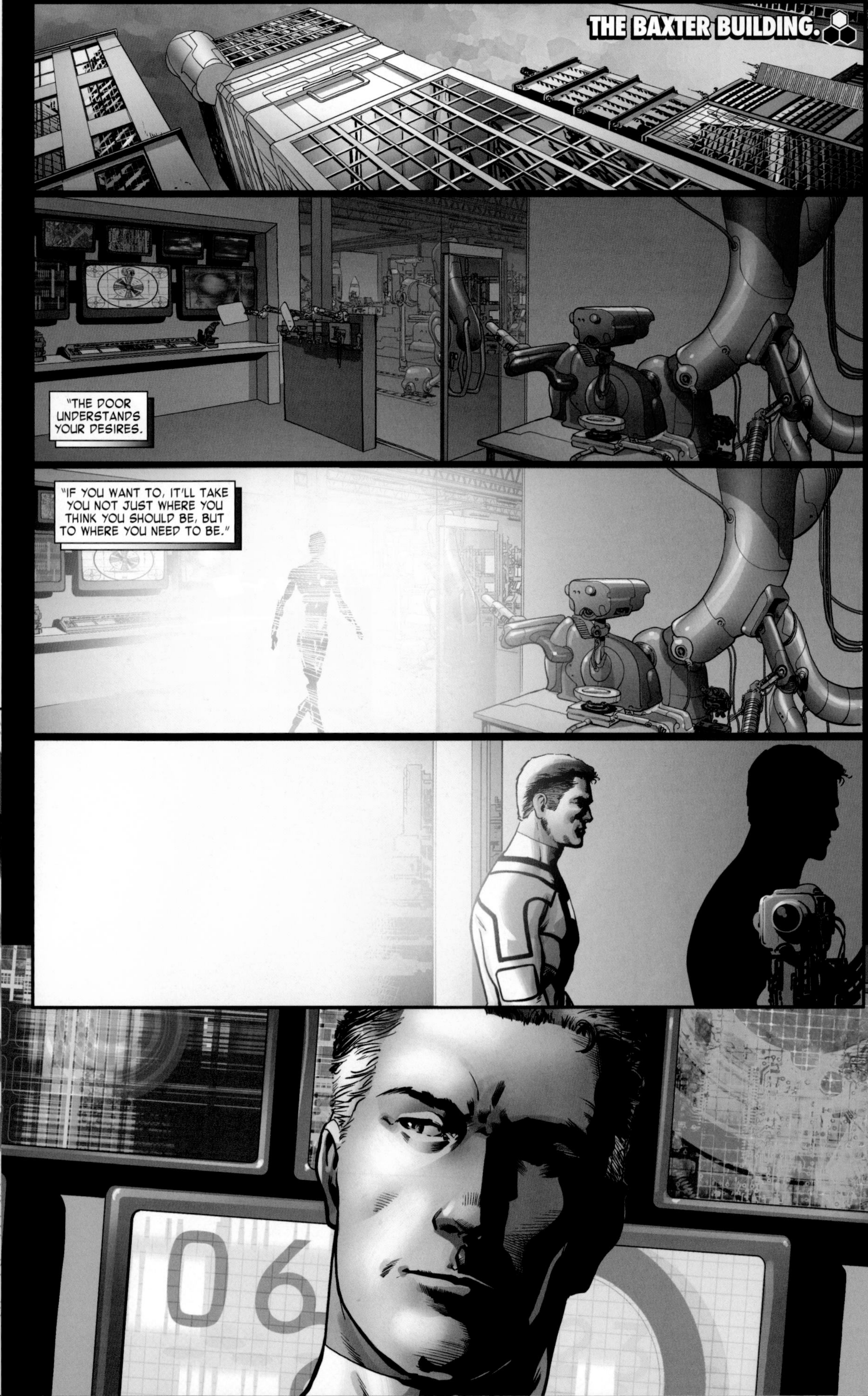
THE BAXTER BUILDING.
"THE DOOR UNDERSTANDS YOUR DESIRES.
"IF YOU WANT TO, IT'LL TAKE YOU NOT JUST WHERE YOU THINK YOU SHOULD BE, BUT TO WHERE YOU NEED TO BE."

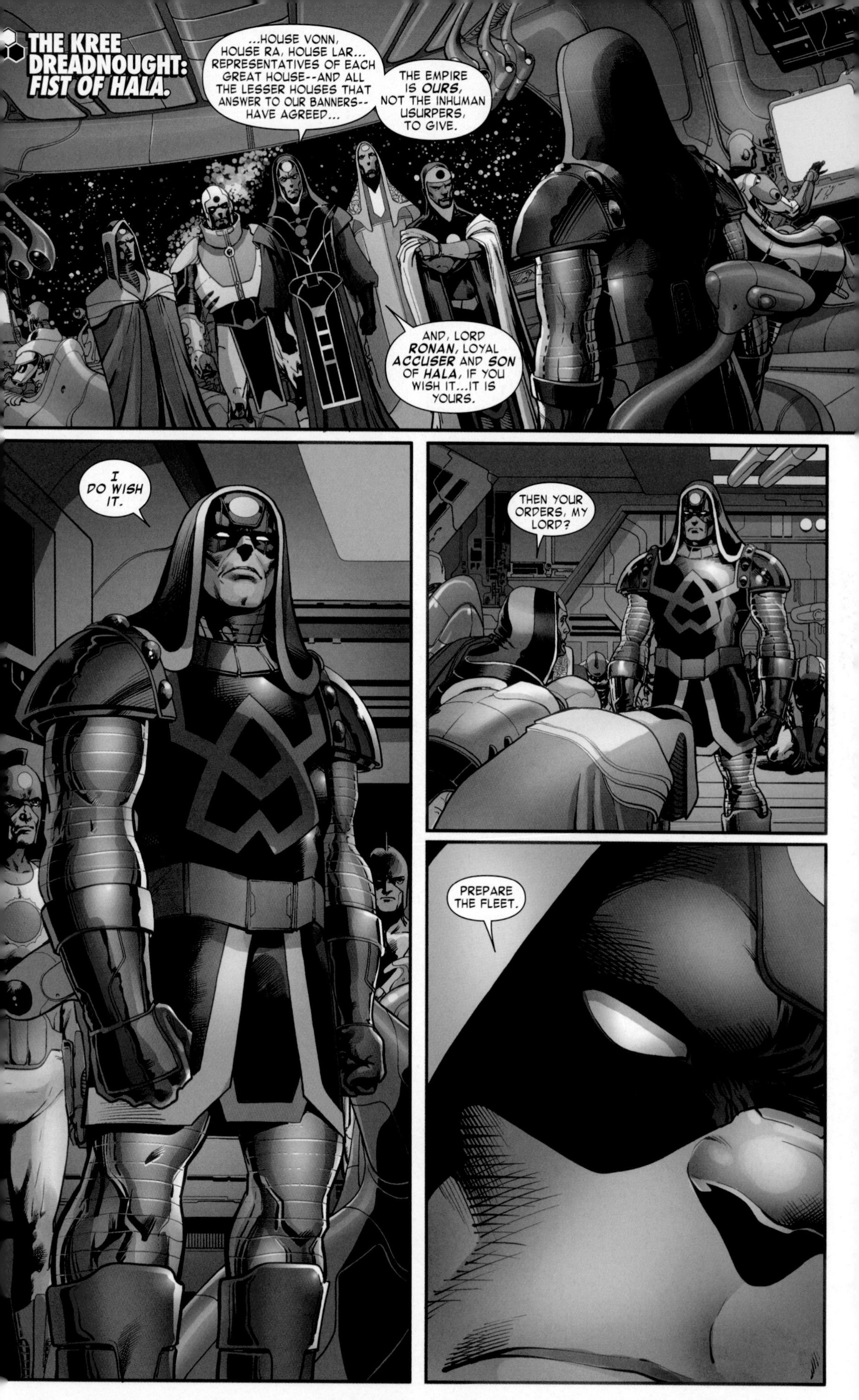
THE KREE DREADNOUGHT: FIST OF HALA.
...HOUSE VONN, HOUSE RA, HOUSE LAR... REPRESENTATIVES OF EACH GREAT HOUSE--AND ALL THE LESSER HOUSES THAT ANSWER TO OUR BANNERS--HAVE AGREED...
THE EMPIRE IS OURS, NOT THE INHUMAN USURPERS, TO GIVE.
AND, LORD RONAN, LOYAL ACCUSER AND SON OF HALA, IF YOU WISH IT...IT IS YOURS.
I DO WISH IT.
THEN YOUR ORDERS, MY LORD?
PREPARE THE FLEET.

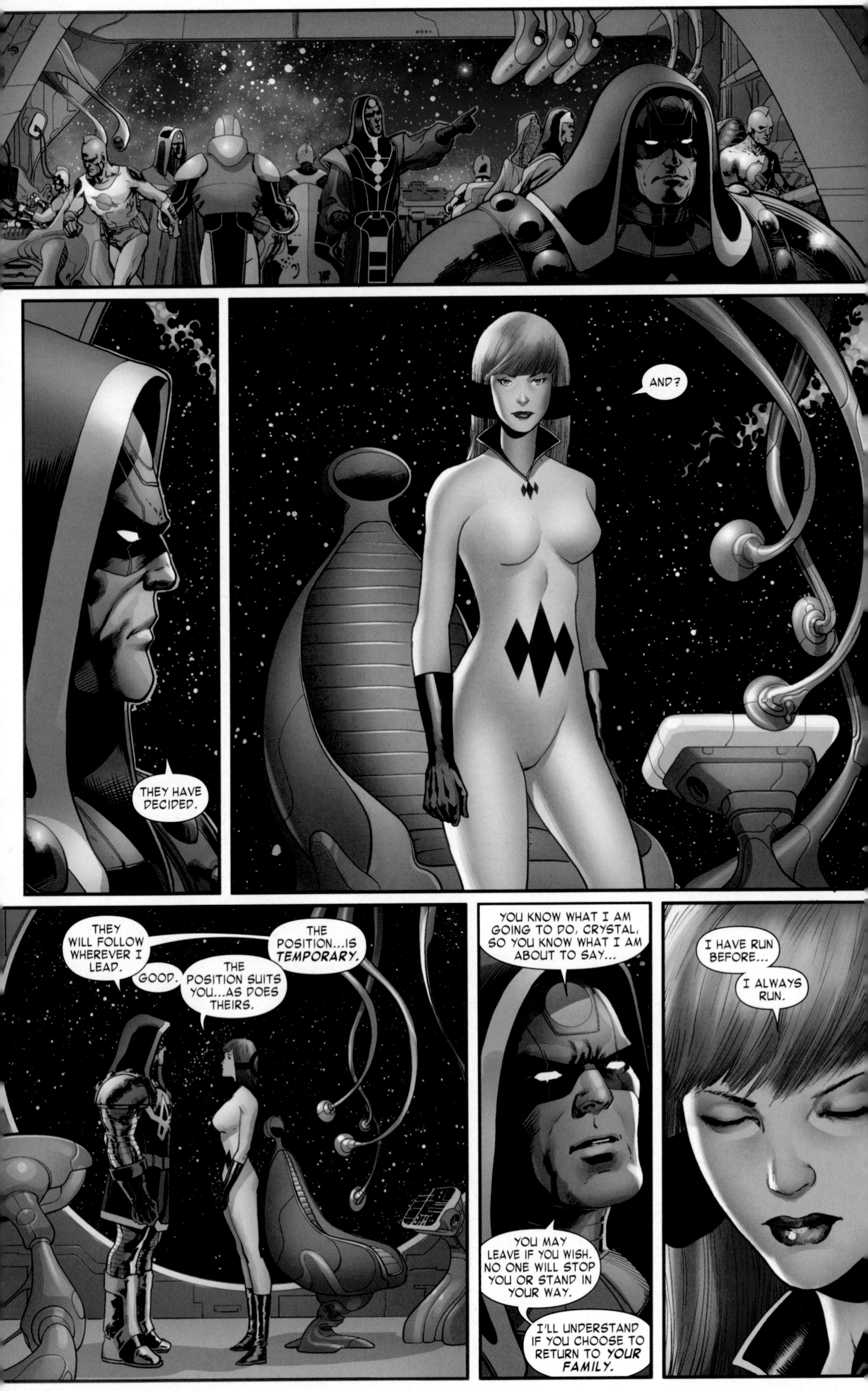
THEY HAVE DECIDED.
AND?
THEY WILL FOLLOW WHEREVER I LEAD.
GOOD.
THE POSITION SUITS YOU...AS DOES THEIRS.
THE POSITION...IS *TEMPORARY.*
YOU KNOW WHAT I AM GOING TO DO, CRYSTAL, SO YOU KNOW WHAT I AM ABOUT TO SAY...
YOU MAY LEAVE IF YOU WISH. NO ONE WILL STOP YOU OR STAND IN YOUR WAY.
I'LL UNDERSTAND IF YOU CHOOSE TO RETURN TO *YOUR FAMILY.*
I HAVE RUN BEFORE...
I ALWAYS RUN.

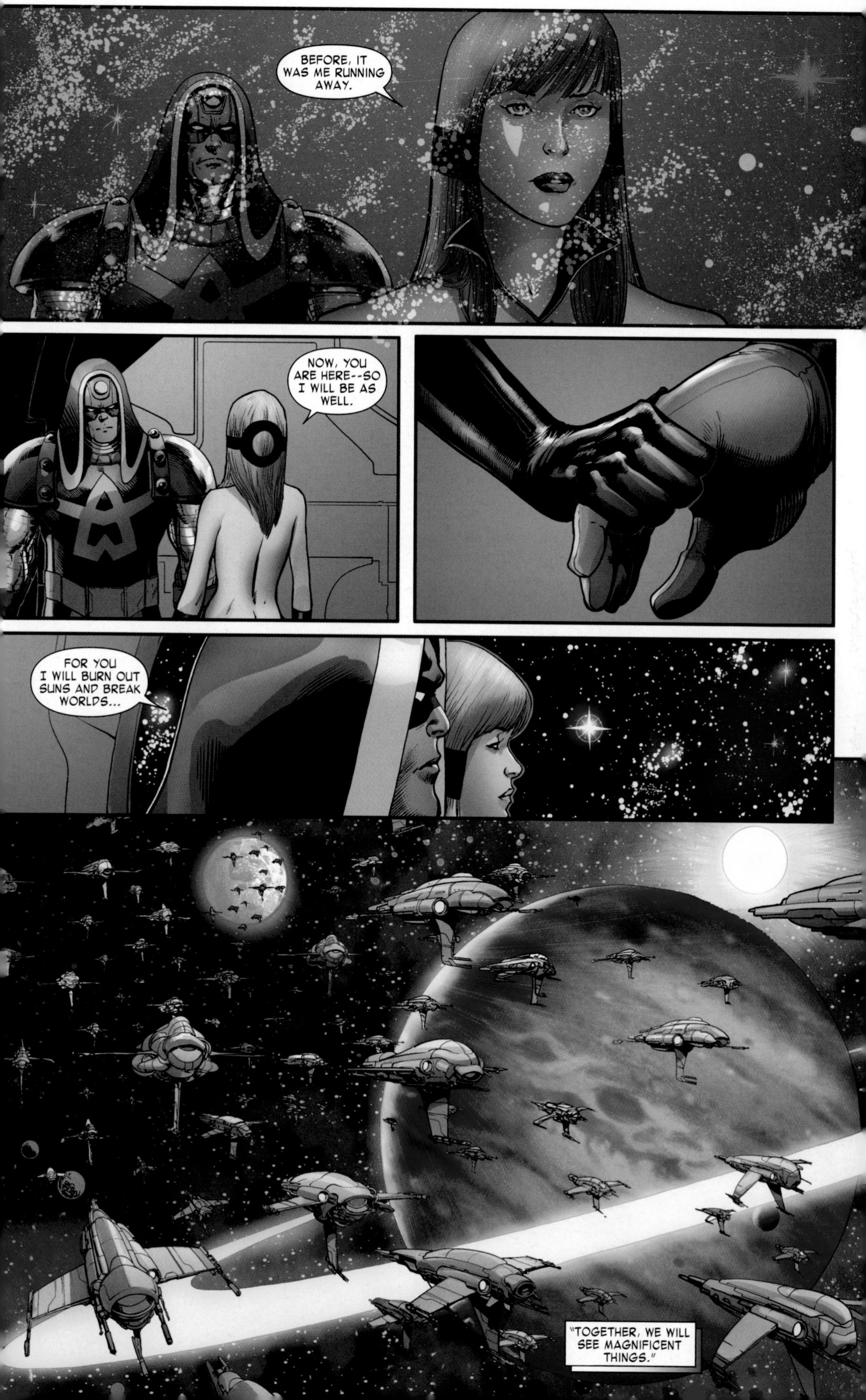
BEFORE, IT WAS ME RUNNING AWAY.
NOW, YOU ARE HERE--SO I WILL BE AS WELL.
FOR YOU I WILL BURN OUT SUNS AND BREAK WORLDS...
"TOGETHER, WE WILL SEE MAGNIFICENT THINGS."

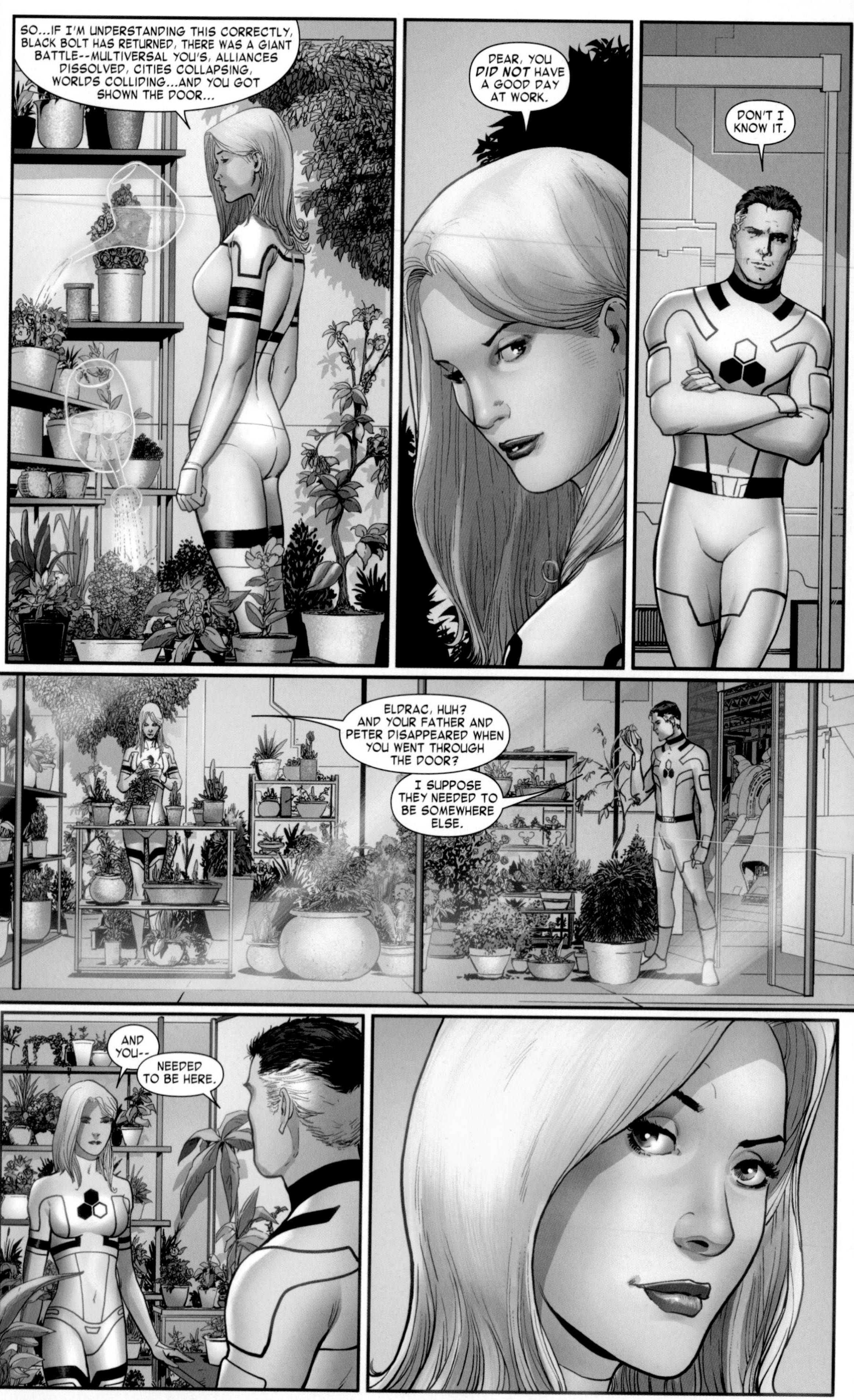
SO...IF I'M UNDERSTANDING THIS CORRECTLY, BLACK BOLT HAS RETURNED, THERE WAS A GIANT BATTLE--MULTIVERSAL YOU'S, ALLIANCES DISSOLVED, CITIES COLLAPSING, WORLDS COLLIDING...AND YOU GOT SHOWN THE DOOR...
DEAR, YOU *DID NOT* HAVE A GOOD DAY AT WORK.
DON'T I KNOW IT.
ELDRAC, HUH? AND YOUR FATHER AND PETER DISAPPEARED WHEN YOU WENT THROUGH THE DOOR?
I SUPPOSE THEY NEEDED TO BE SOMEWHERE ELSE.
AND YOU--
NEEDED TO BE HERE.

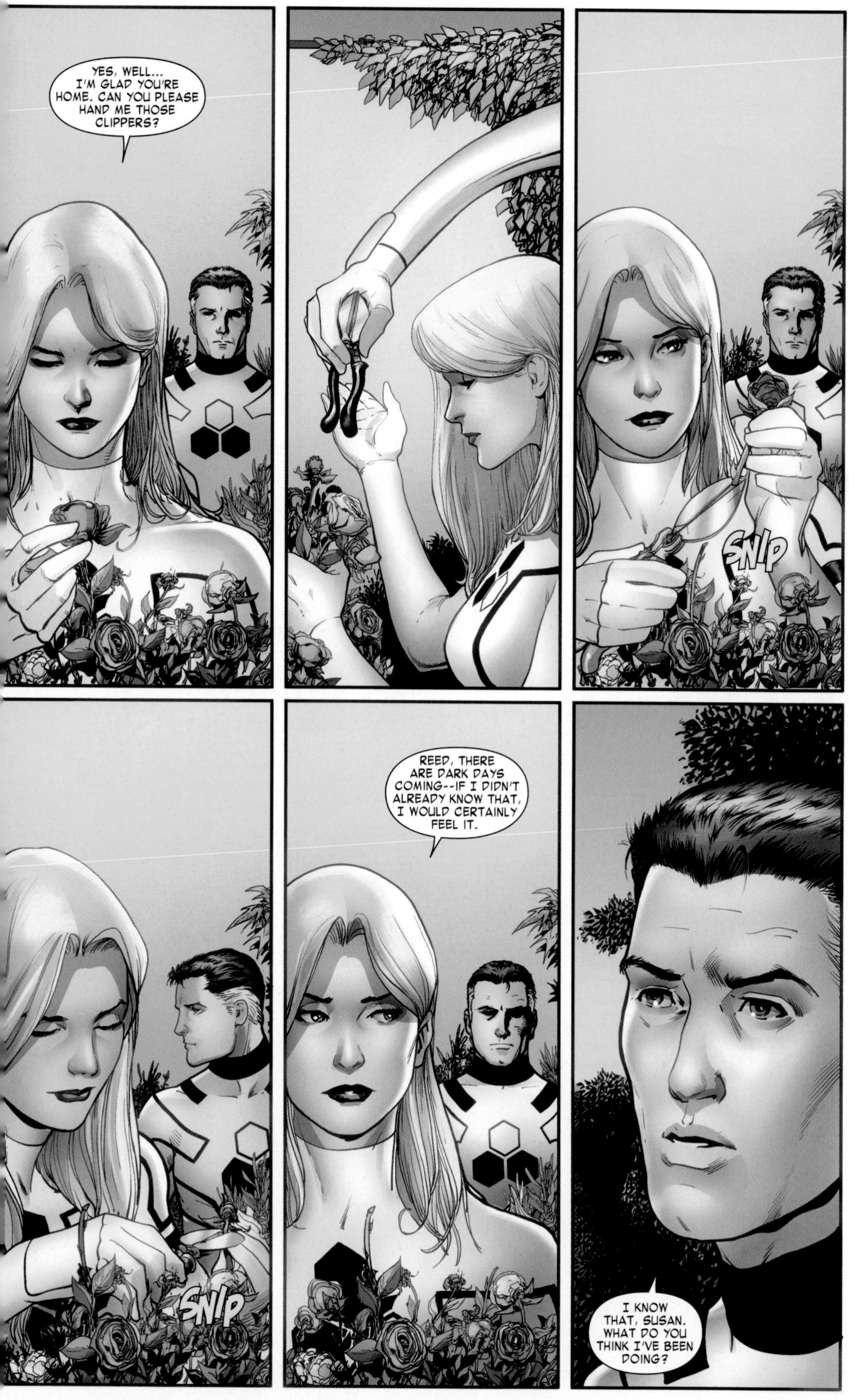
YES, WELL... I'M GLAD YOU'RE HOME. CAN YOU PLEASE HAND ME THOSE CLIPPERS?
SNIP
SNIP
REED, THERE ARE DARK DAYS COMING--IF I DIDN'T ALREADY KNOW THAT, I WOULD CERTAINLY FEEL IT.
I KNOW THAT, SUSAN. WHAT DO YOU THINK I'VE BEEN DOING?

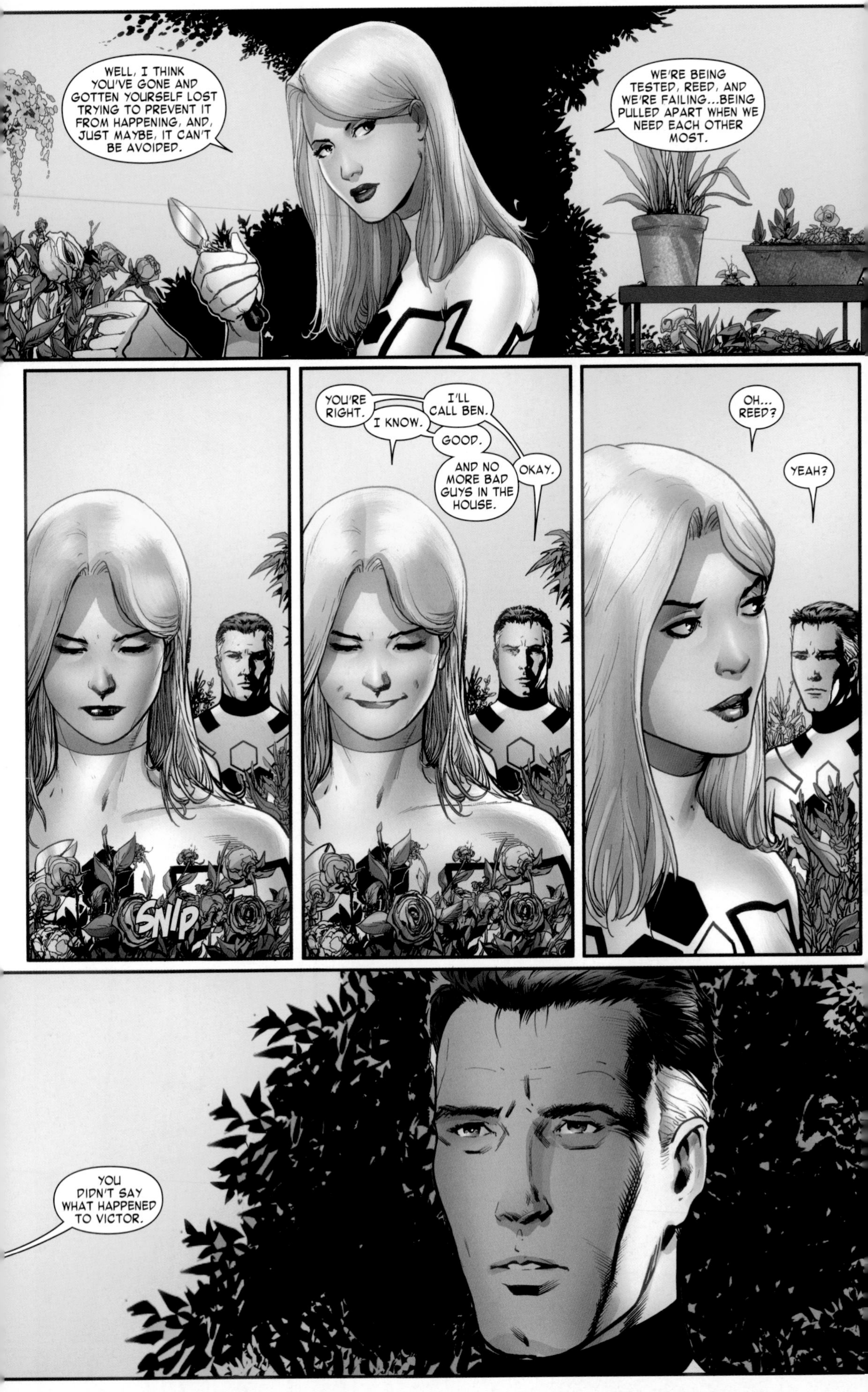
WELL, I THINK YOU'VE GONE AND GOTTEN YOURSELF LOST TRYING TO PREVENT IT FROM HAPPENING, AND, JUST MAYBE, IT CAN'T BE AVOIDED.
WE'RE BEING TESTED, REED, AND WE'RE FAILING...BEING PULLED APART WHEN WE NEED EACH OTHER MOST.
SNIP
YOU'RE RIGHT.
I KNOW.
I'LL CALL BEN.
GOOD.
AND NO MORE BAD GUYS IN THE HOUSE.
OKAY.
OH... REED?
YEAH?
YOU DIDN'T SAY WHAT HAPPENED TO VICTOR.

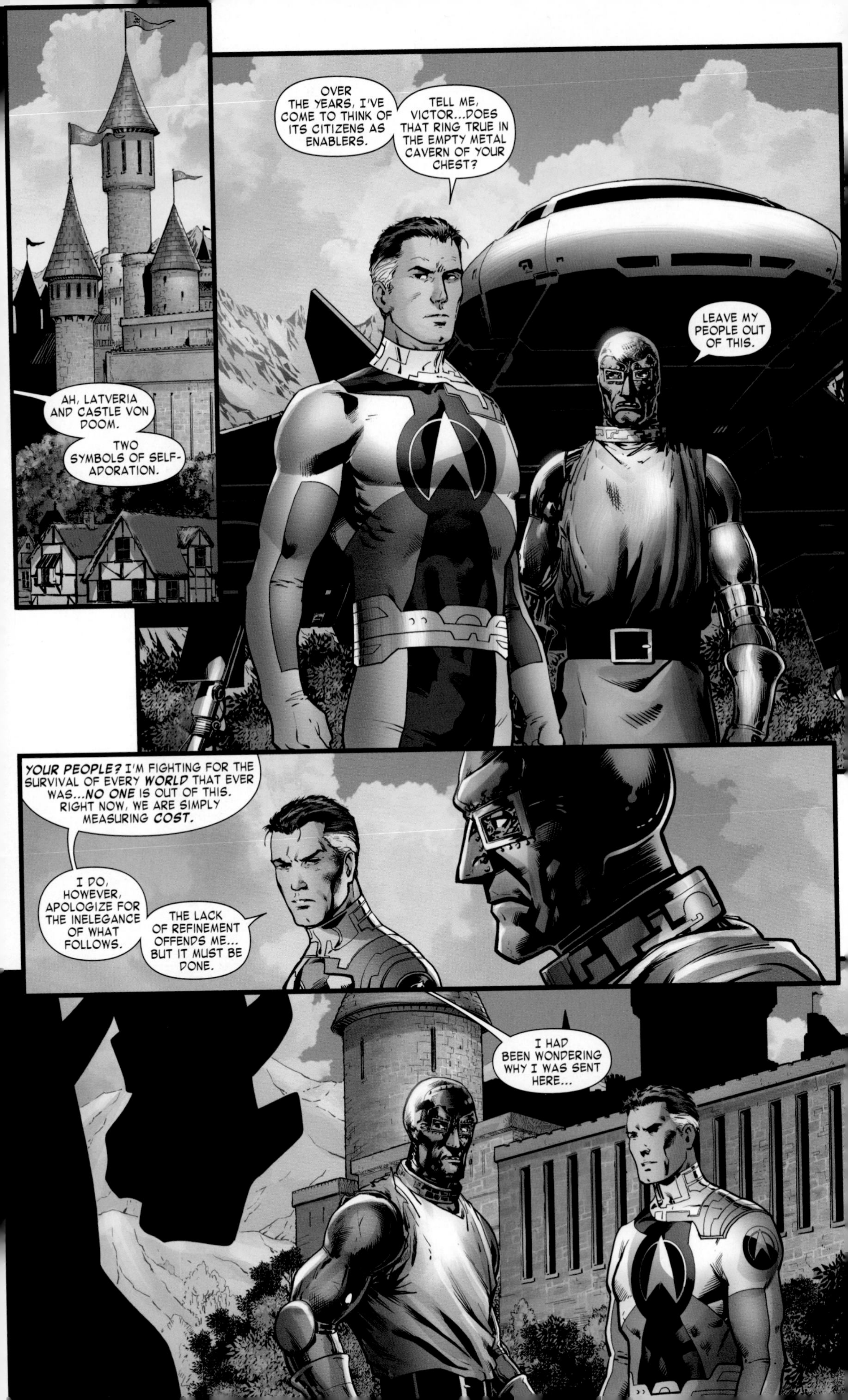
AH, LATVERIA AND CASTLE VON DOOM.
TWO SYMBOLS OF SELF-ADORATION.
OVER THE YEARS, I'VE COME TO THINK OF ITS CITIZENS AS ENABLERS.
TELL ME, VICTOR...DOES THAT RING TRUE IN THE EMPTY METAL CAVERN OF YOUR CHEST?
LEAVE MY PEOPLE OUT OF THIS.
YOUR PEOPLE? I'M FIGHTING FOR THE SURVIVAL OF EVERY WORLD THAT EVER WAS...NO ONE IS OUT OF THIS. RIGHT NOW, WE ARE SIMPLY MEASURING COST.
I DO, HOWEVER, APOLOGIZE FOR THE INELEGANCE OF WHAT FOLLOWS.
THE LACK OF REFINEMENT OFFENDS ME... BUT IT MUST BE DONE.
I HAD BEEN WONDERING WHY I WAS SENT HERE...

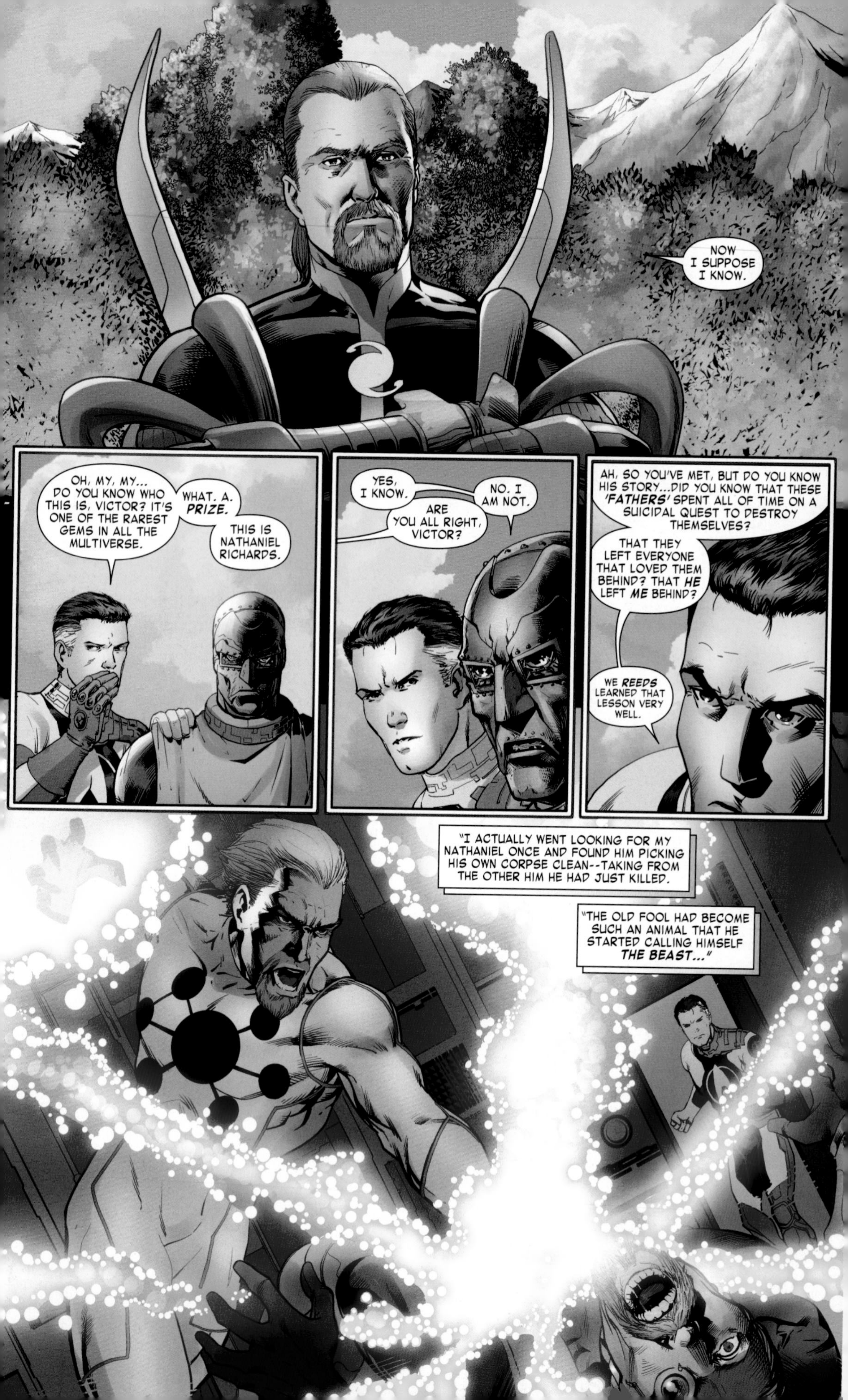
NOW I SUPPOSE I KNOW.
OH, MY, MY... DO YOU KNOW WHO THIS IS, VICTOR? IT'S ONE OF THE RAREST GEMS IN ALL THE MULTIVERSE.
WHAT. A. PRIZE.
THIS IS NATHANIEL RICHARDS.
YES, I KNOW.
ARE YOU ALL RIGHT, VICTOR?
NO. I AM NOT.
AH, SO YOU'VE MET, BUT DO YOU KNOW HIS STORY...DID YOU KNOW THAT THESE 'FATHERS' SPENT ALL OF TIME ON A SUICIDAL QUEST TO DESTROY THEMSELVES?
THAT THEY LEFT EVERYONE THAT LOVED THEM BEHIND? THAT HE LEFT ME BEHIND?
WE REEDS LEARNED THAT LESSON VERY WELL.
"I ACTUALLY WENT LOOKING FOR MY NATHANIEL ONCE AND FOUND HIM PICKING HIS OWN CORPSE CLEAN--TAKING FROM THE OTHER HIM HE HAD JUST KILLED.
"THE OLD FOOL HAD BECOME SUCH AN ANIMAL THAT HE STARTED CALLING HIMSELF THE BEAST..."

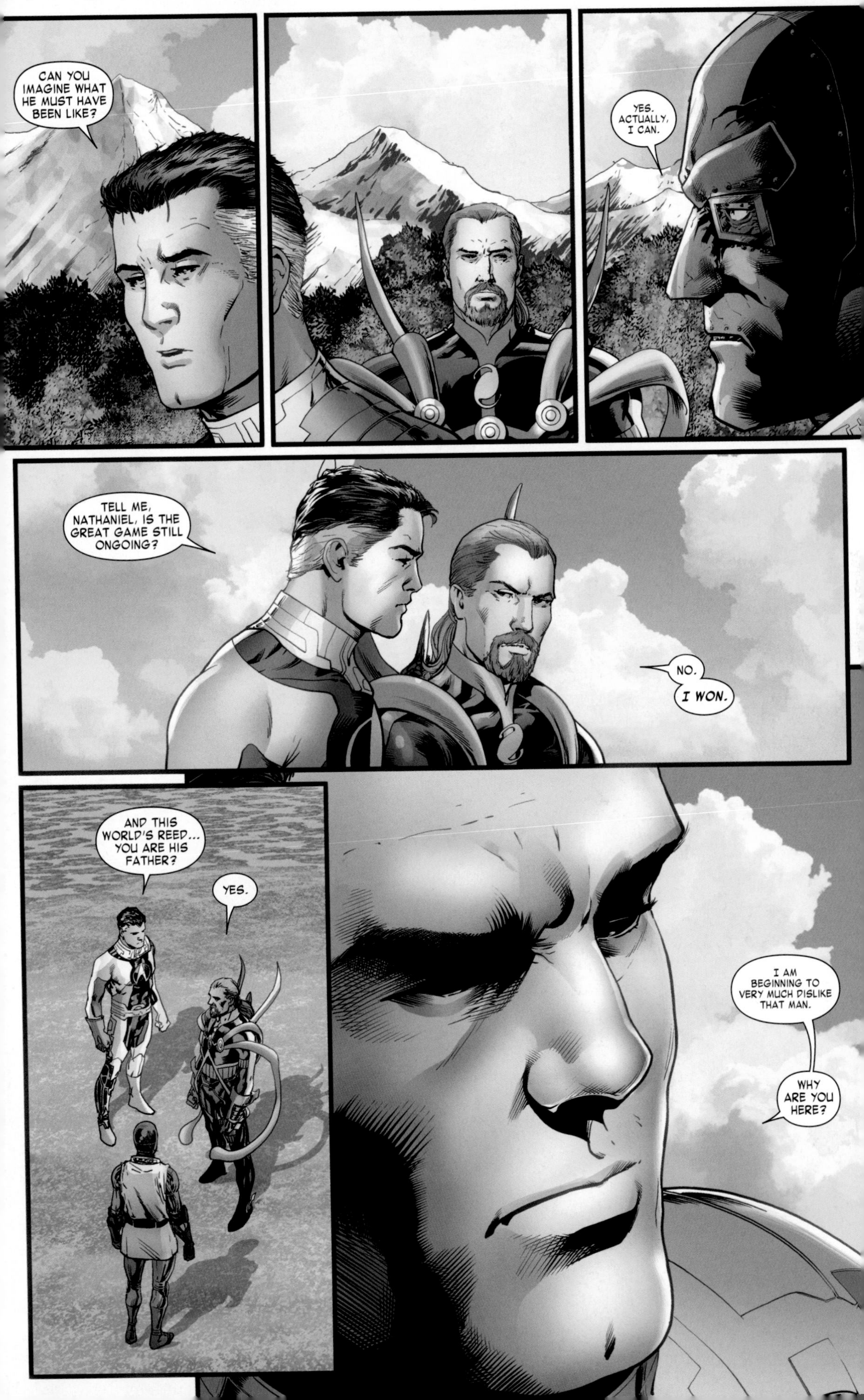
CAN YOU IMAGINE WHAT HE MUST HAVE BEEN LIKE?
YES. ACTUALLY, I CAN.
TELL ME, NATHANIEL, IS THE GREAT GAME STILL ONGOING?
NO.
I WON.
AND THIS WORLD'S REED... YOU ARE HIS FATHER?
YES.
I AM BEGINNING TO VERY MUCH DISLIKE THAT MAN.
WHY ARE YOU HERE?

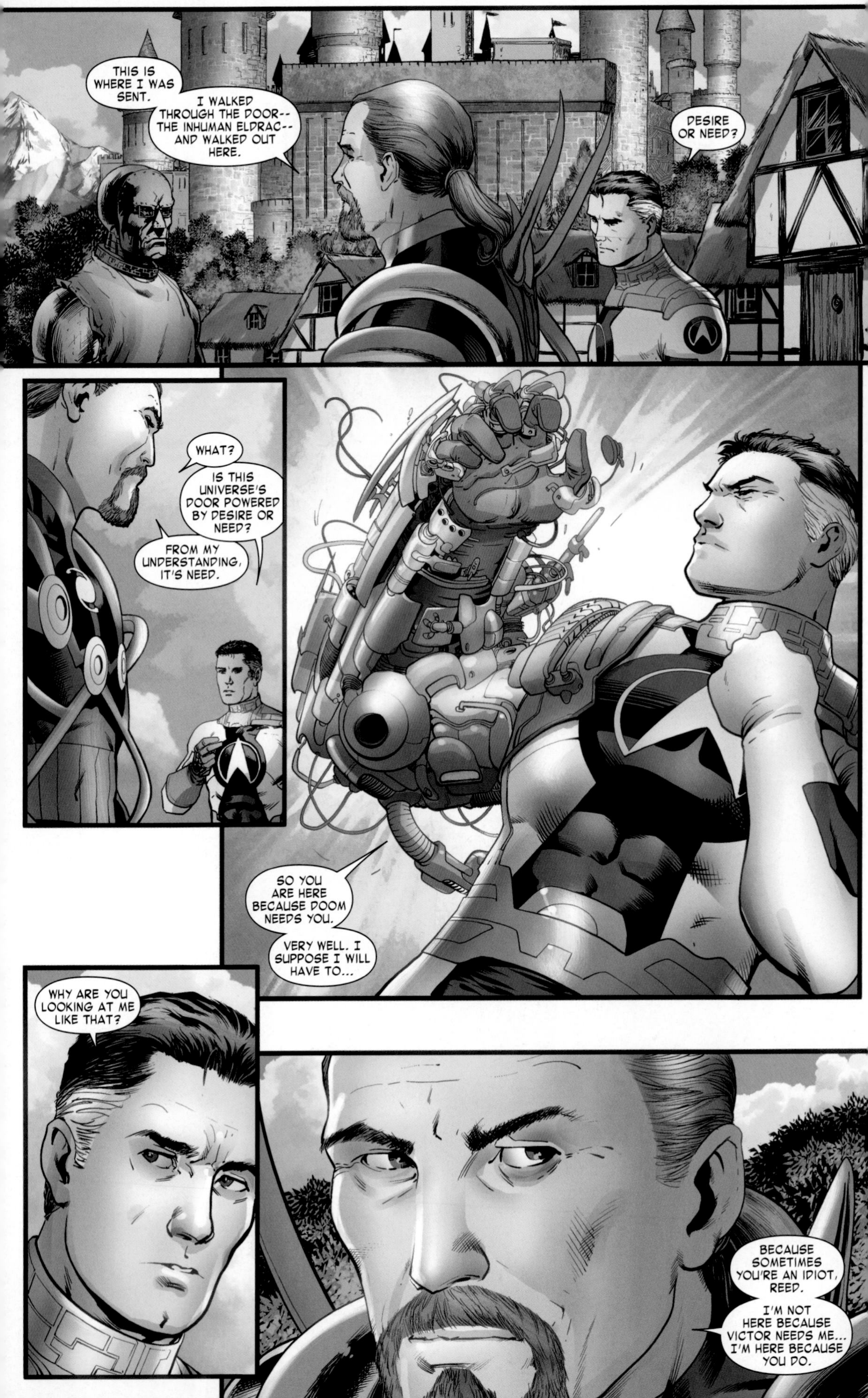
THIS IS WHERE I WAS SENT.
I WALKED THROUGH THE DOOR-- THE INHUMAN ELDRAC-- AND WALKED OUT HERE.
DESIRE OR NEED?
WHAT?
IS THIS UNIVERSE'S DOOR POWERED BY DESIRE OR NEED?
FROM MY UNDERSTANDING, IT'S NEED.
SO YOU ARE HERE BECAUSE DOOM NEEDS YOU.
VERY WELL. I SUPPOSE I WILL HAVE TO...
WHY ARE YOU LOOKING AT ME LIKE THAT?
BECAUSE SOMETIMES YOU'RE AN IDIOT, REED.
I'M NOT HERE BECAUSE VICTOR NEEDS ME... I'M HERE BECAUSE YOU DO.

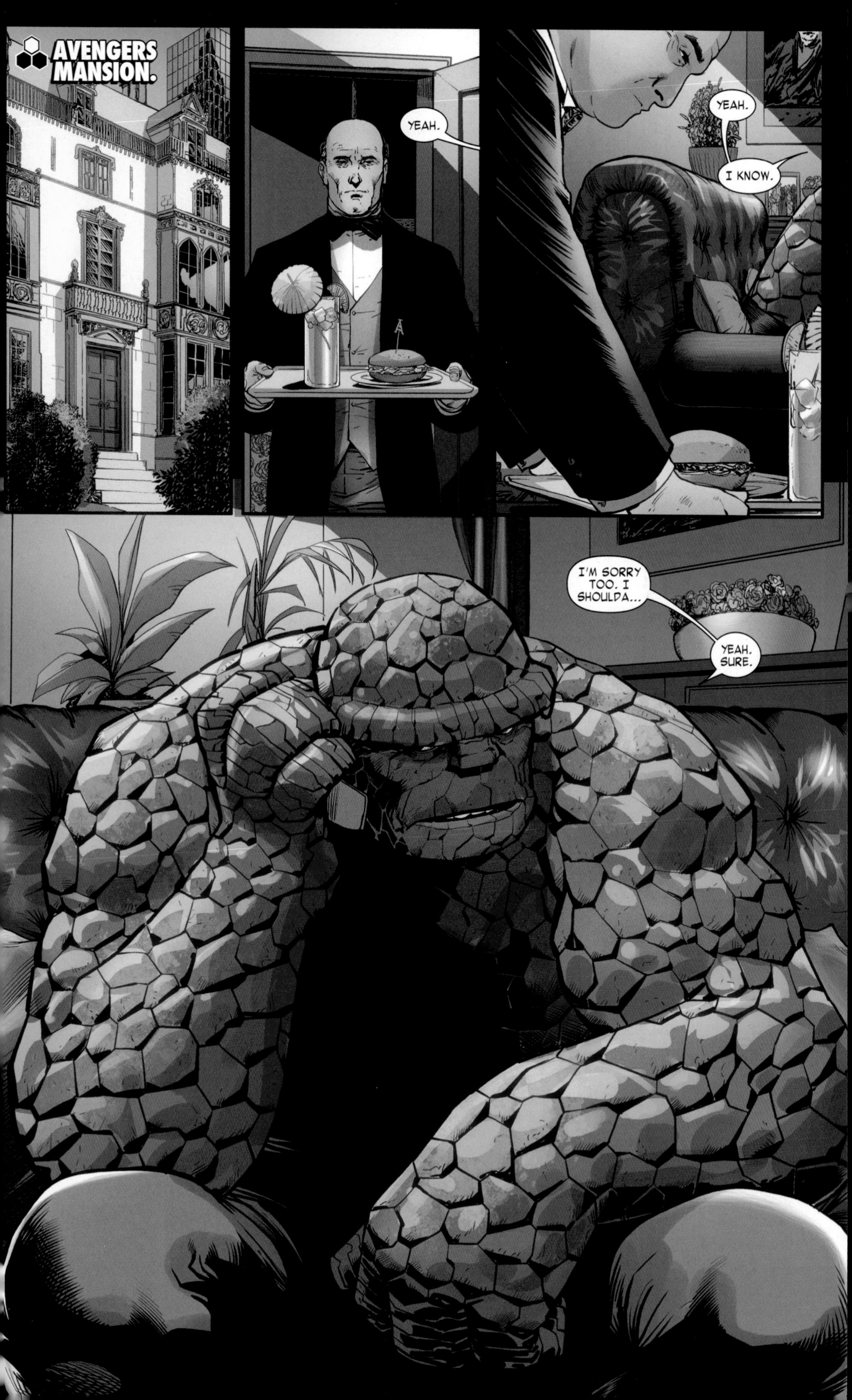
AVENGERS MANSION.
YEAH.
YEAH.
I KNOW.
I'M SORRY TOO. I SHOULDA...
YEAH. SURE.

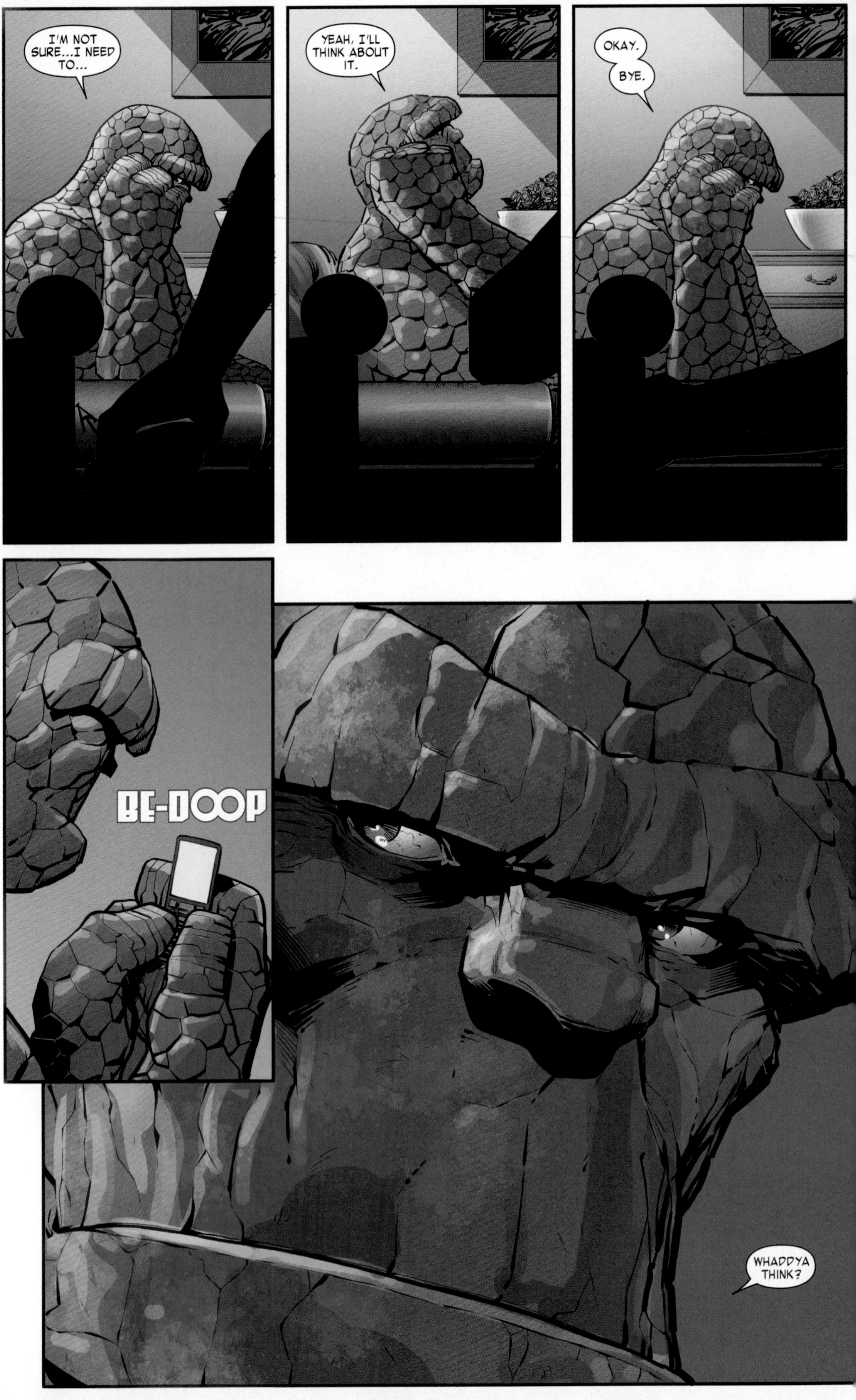
I'M NOT SURE...I NEED TO...
YEAH, I'LL THINK ABOUT IT.
OKAY.
BYE.
BE-DOOP
WHADDYA THINK?

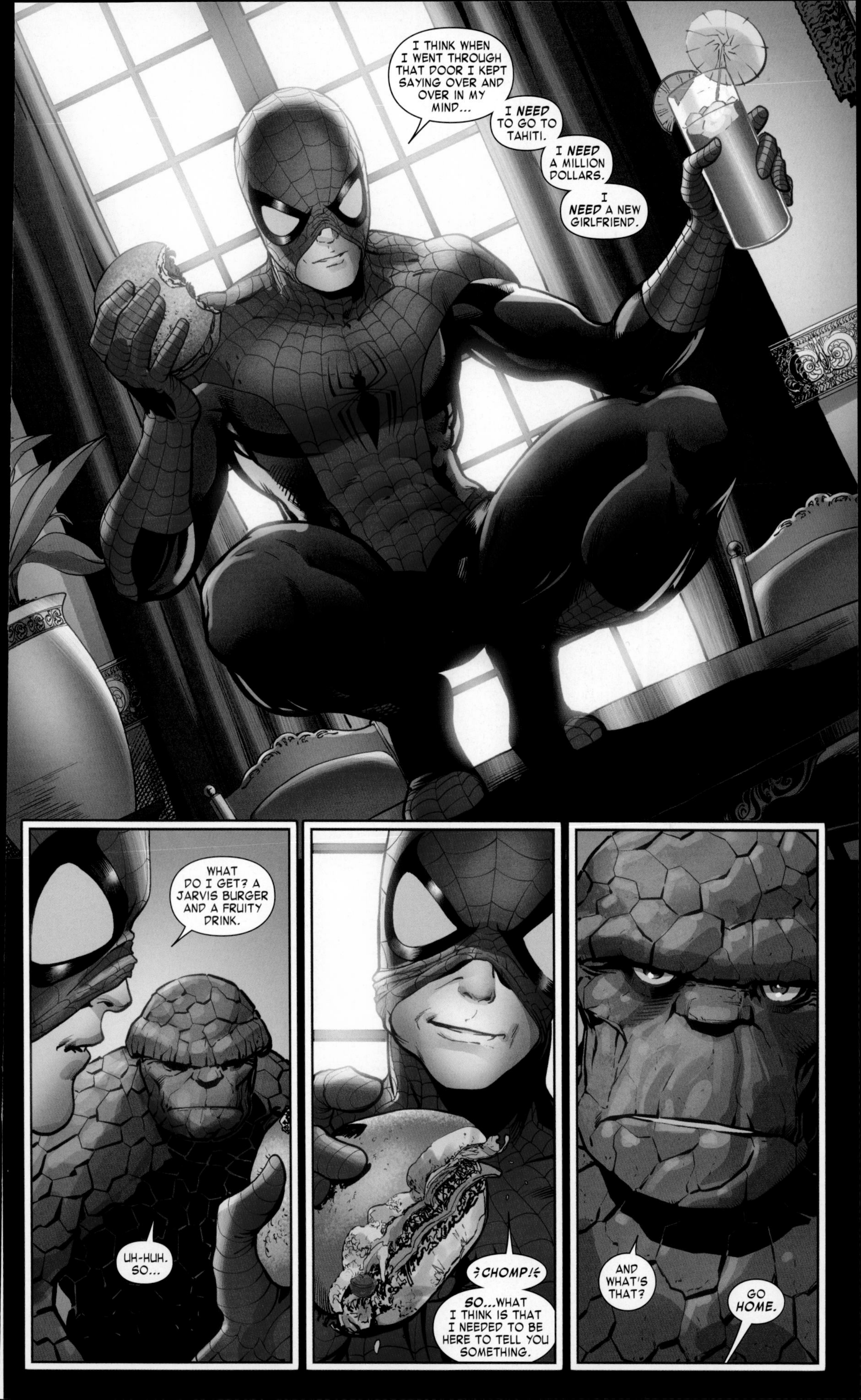

I THINK WHEN I WENT THROUGH THAT DOOR I KEPT SAYING OVER AND OVER IN MY MIND...
I NEED TO GO TO TAHITI.
I NEED A MILLION DOLLARS.
I NEED A NEW GIRLFRIEND.
WHAT DO I GET? A JARVIS BURGER AND A FRUITY DRINK.
UH-HUH. SO...
CHOMP!
SO...WHAT I THINK IS THAT I NEEDED TO BE HERE TO TELL YOU SOMETHING.
AND WHAT'S THAT?
GO HOME.

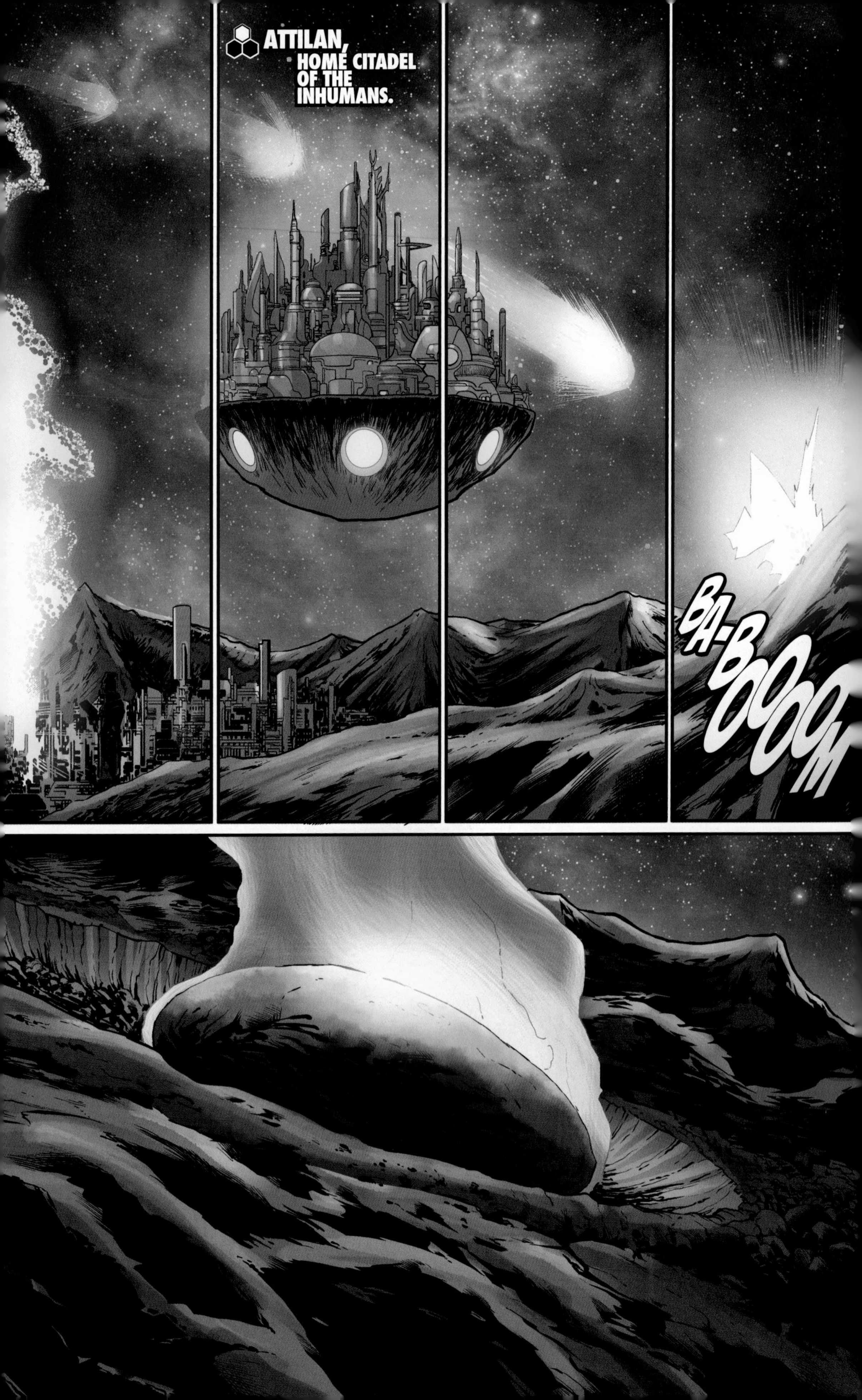
ATTILAN, HOME CITADEL OF THE INHUMANS.
BA-BOOOM

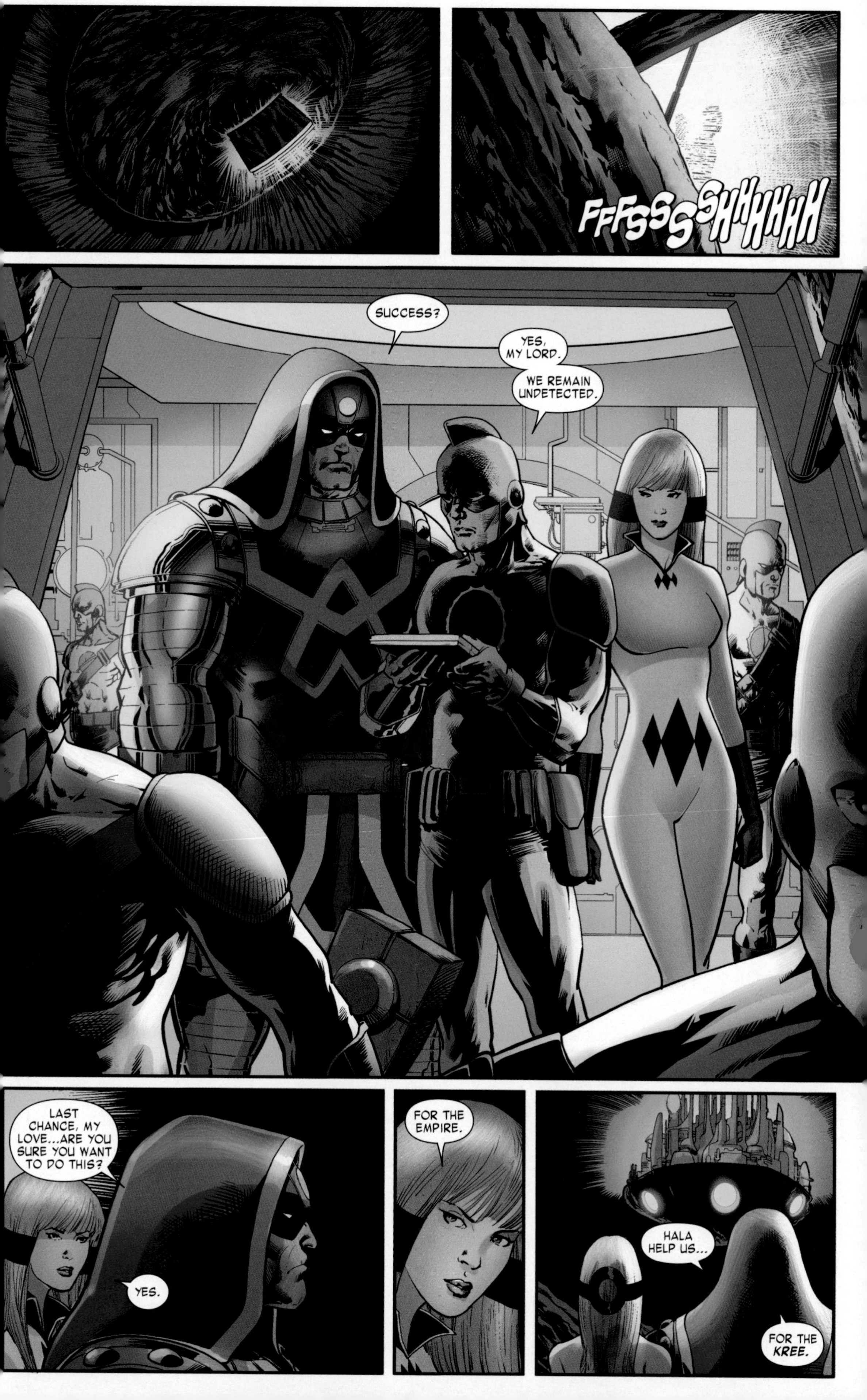
FFFSSSSHHHHHH
SUCCESS?
YES, MY LORD.
WE REMAIN UNDETECTED.
LAST CHANCE, MY LOVE...ARE YOU SURE YOU WANT TO DO THIS?
YES.
FOR THE EMPIRE.
HALA HELP US...
FOR THE *KREE.*

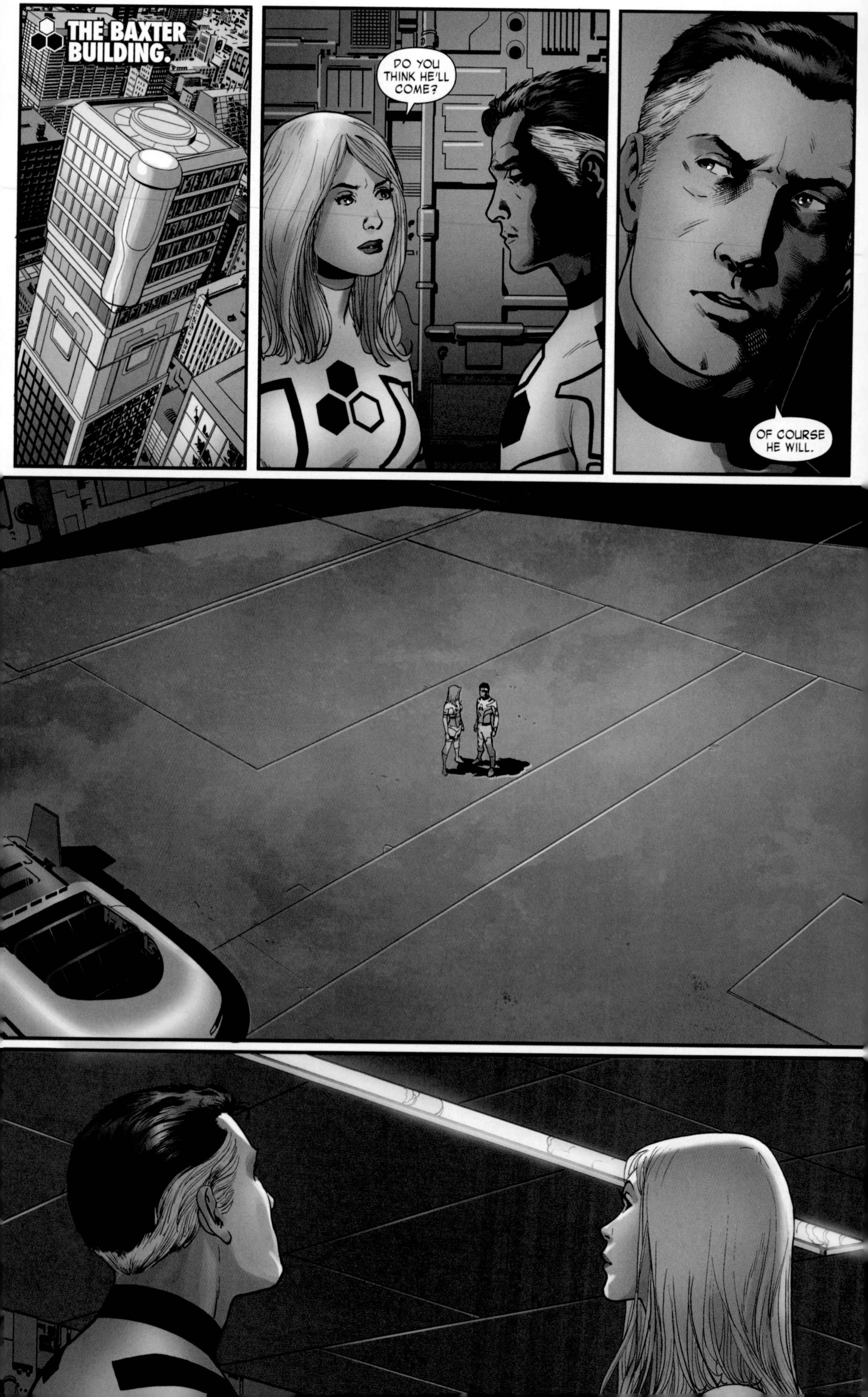
THE BAXTER BUILDING.
DO YOU THINK HE'LL COME?
OF COURSE HE WILL.

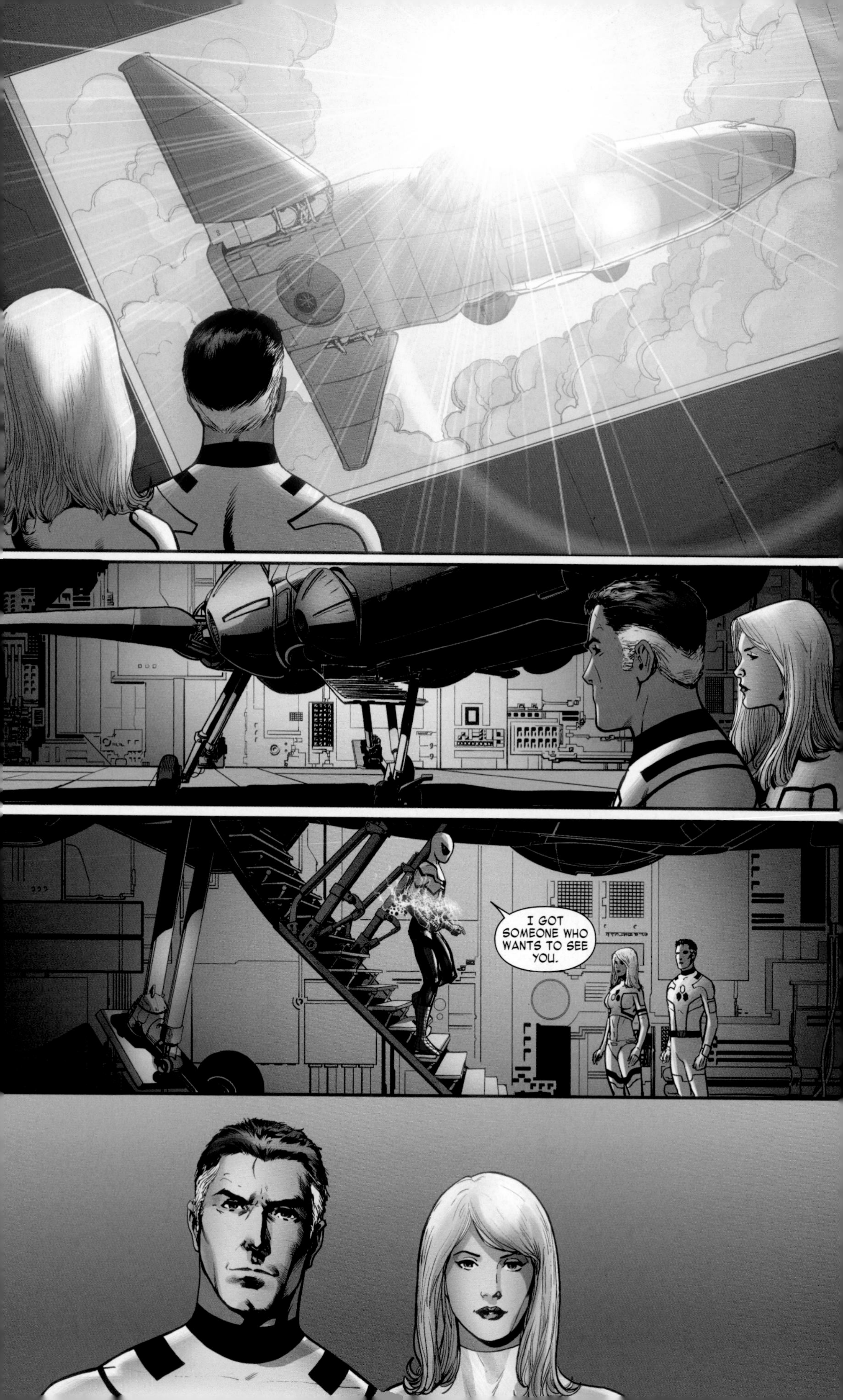
I GOT SOMEONE WHO WANTS TO SEE YOU.

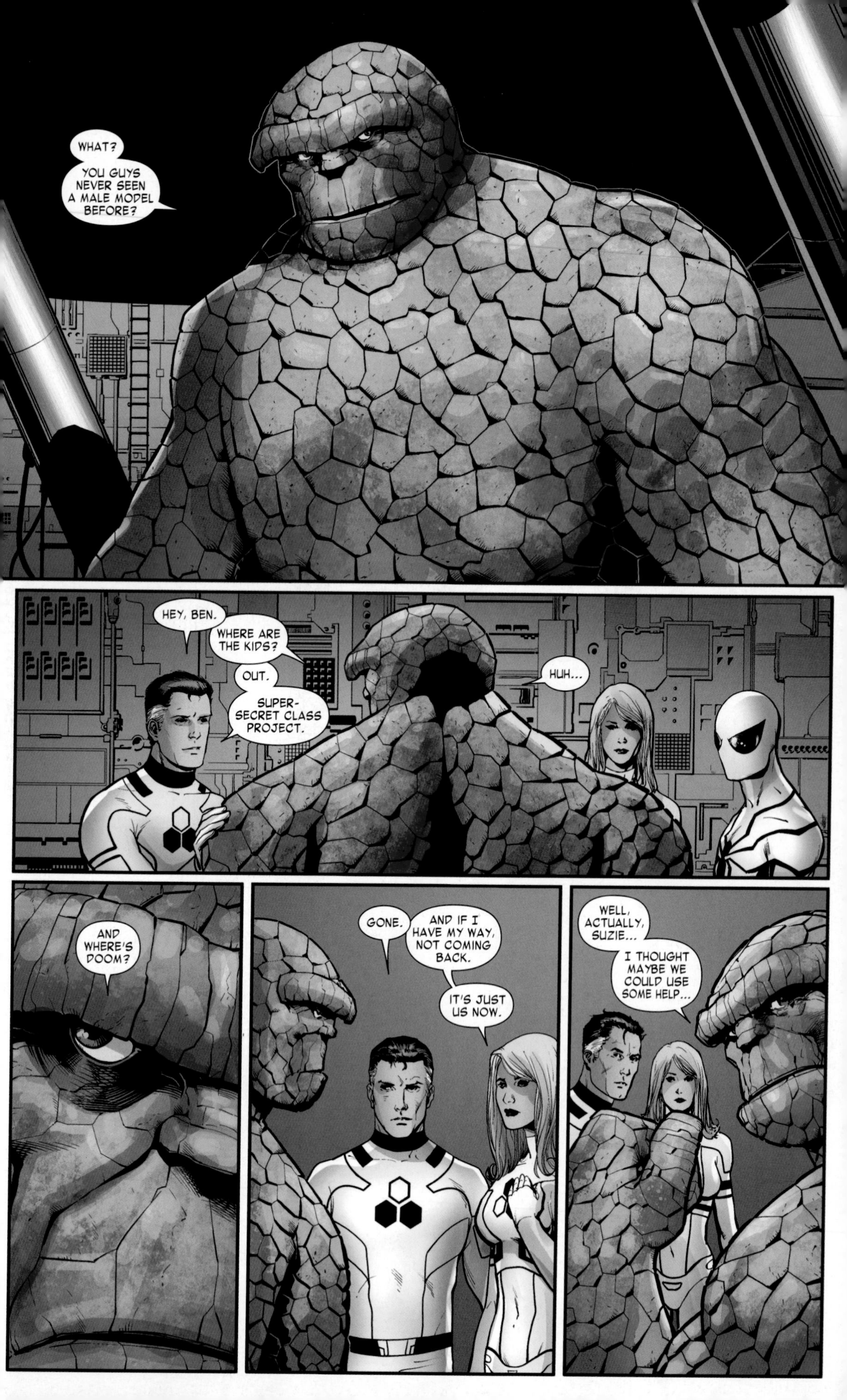
WHAT?
YOU GUYS NEVER SEEN A MALE MODEL BEFORE?
HEY, BEN.
WHERE ARE THE KIDS?
OUT.
SUPER-SECRET CLASS PROJECT.
HUH...
AND WHERE'S DOOM?
GONE.
AND IF I HAVE MY WAY, NOT COMING BACK.
IT'S JUST US NOW.
WELL, ACTUALLY, SUZIE...
I THOUGHT MAYBE WE COULD USE SOME HELP...

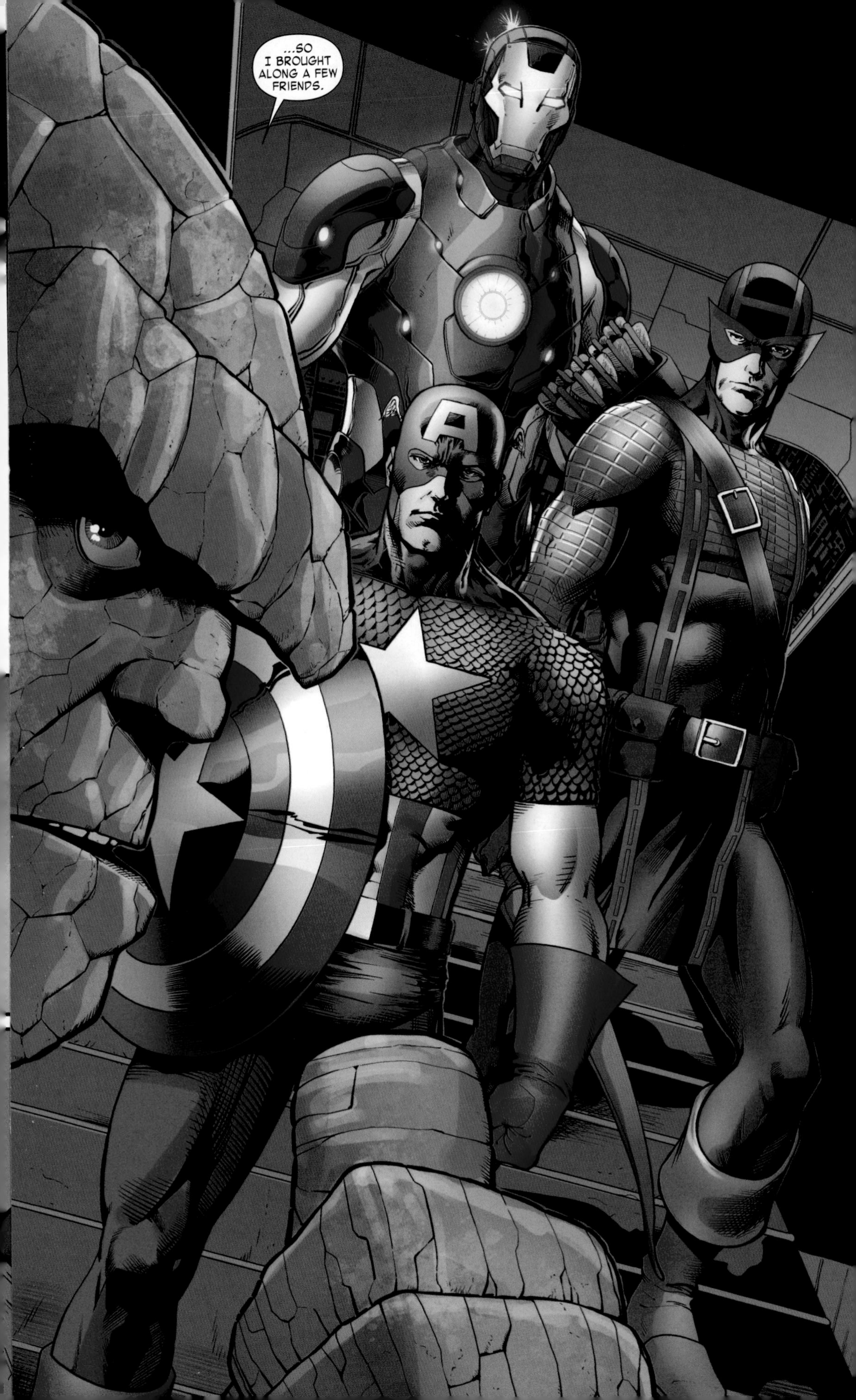
...SO I BROUGHT ALONG A FEW FRIENDS.

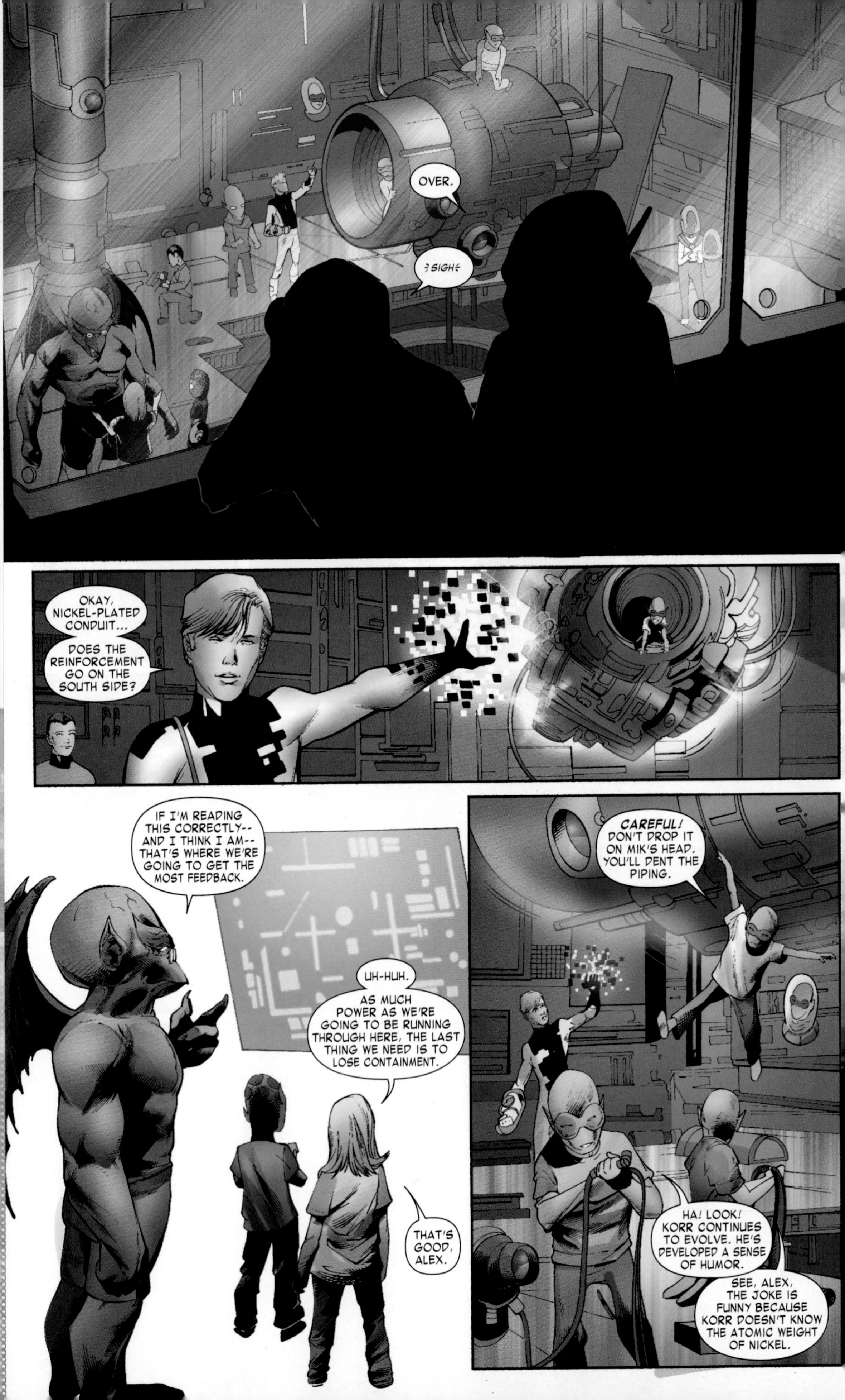
OVER.
=SIGH=
OKAY, NICKEL-PLATED CONDUIT...
DOES THE REINFORCEMENT GO ON THE SOUTH SIDE?
IF I'M READING THIS CORRECTLY-- AND I THINK I AM-- THAT'S WHERE WE'RE GOING TO GET THE MOST FEEDBACK.
UH-HUH.
AS MUCH POWER AS WE'RE GOING TO BE RUNNING THROUGH HERE, THE LAST THING WE NEED IS TO LOSE CONTAINMENT.
THAT'S GOOD, ALEX.
CAREFUL! DON'T DROP IT ON MIK'S HEAD. YOU'LL DENT THE PIPING.
HA! LOOK! KORR CONTINUES TO EVOLVE. HE'S DEVELOPED A SENSE OF HUMOR.
SEE, ALEX, THE JOKE IS FUNNY BECAUSE KORR DOESN'T KNOW THE ATOMIC WEIGHT OF NICKEL.

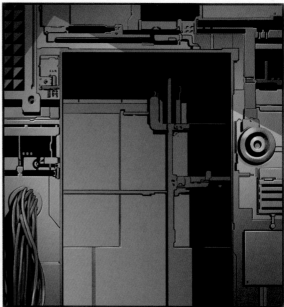

DO TOO!
IT'S 58.6934.

AHEM.

I'M GONNA NEED TO SEE SOME IDENTIFICATION.

I'M SORRY?

IDENTIFICATION. I NEED TO SEE SOME.

MAKE SURE YOU'RE NOT ONE OF THOSE JERK REEDS.

WATCH YOUR LANGUAGE, YOUNG MAN.

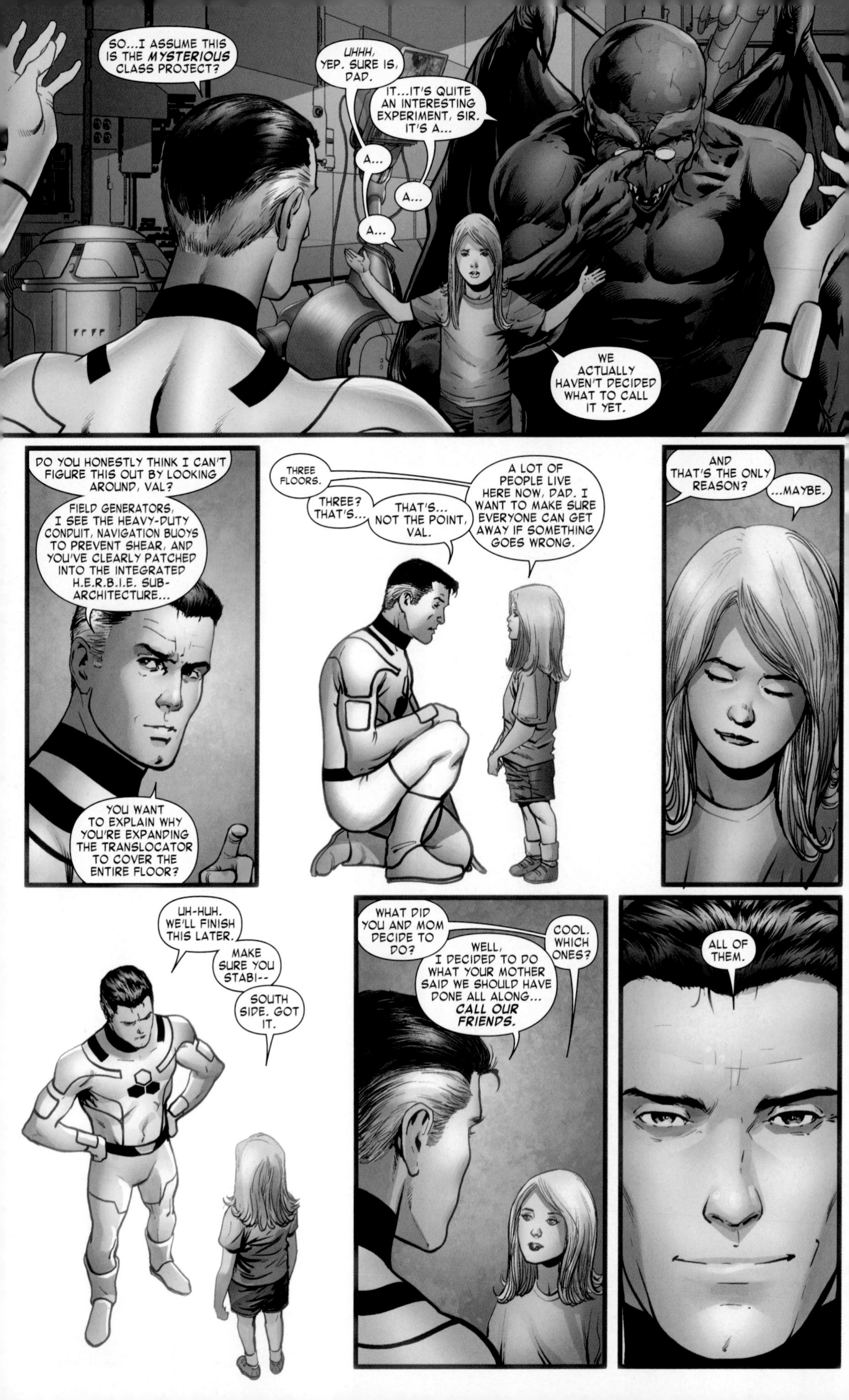
SO...I ASSUME THIS IS THE MYSTERIOUS CLASS PROJECT?
UHHH, YEP. SURE IS, DAD.
IT...IT'S QUITE AN INTERESTING EXPERIMENT, SIR. IT'S A...
A...
A...
A...
WE ACTUALLY HAVEN'T DECIDED WHAT TO CALL IT YET.
DO YOU HONESTLY THINK I CAN'T FIGURE THIS OUT BY LOOKING AROUND, VAL?
FIELD GENERATORS, I SEE THE HEAVY-DUTY CONDUIT, NAVIGATION BUOYS TO PREVENT SHEAR, AND YOU'VE CLEARLY PATCHED INTO THE INTEGRATED H.E.R.B.I.E. SUB-ARCHITECTURE...
YOU WANT TO EXPLAIN WHY YOU'RE EXPANDING THE TRANSLOCATOR TO COVER THE ENTIRE FLOOR?
THREE FLOORS.
THREE? THAT'S...
THAT'S... NOT THE POINT, VAL.
A LOT OF PEOPLE LIVE HERE NOW, DAD. I WANT TO MAKE SURE EVERYONE CAN GET AWAY IF SOMETHING GOES WRONG.
AND THAT'S THE ONLY REASON?
...MAYBE.
UH-HUH. WE'LL FINISH THIS LATER.
MAKE SURE YOU STABI--
SOUTH SIDE. GOT IT.
WHAT DID YOU AND MOM DECIDE TO DO?
WELL, I DECIDED TO DO WHAT YOUR MOTHER SAID WE SHOULD HAVE DONE ALL ALONG... CALL OUR FRIENDS.
COOL. WHICH ONES?
ALL OF THEM.

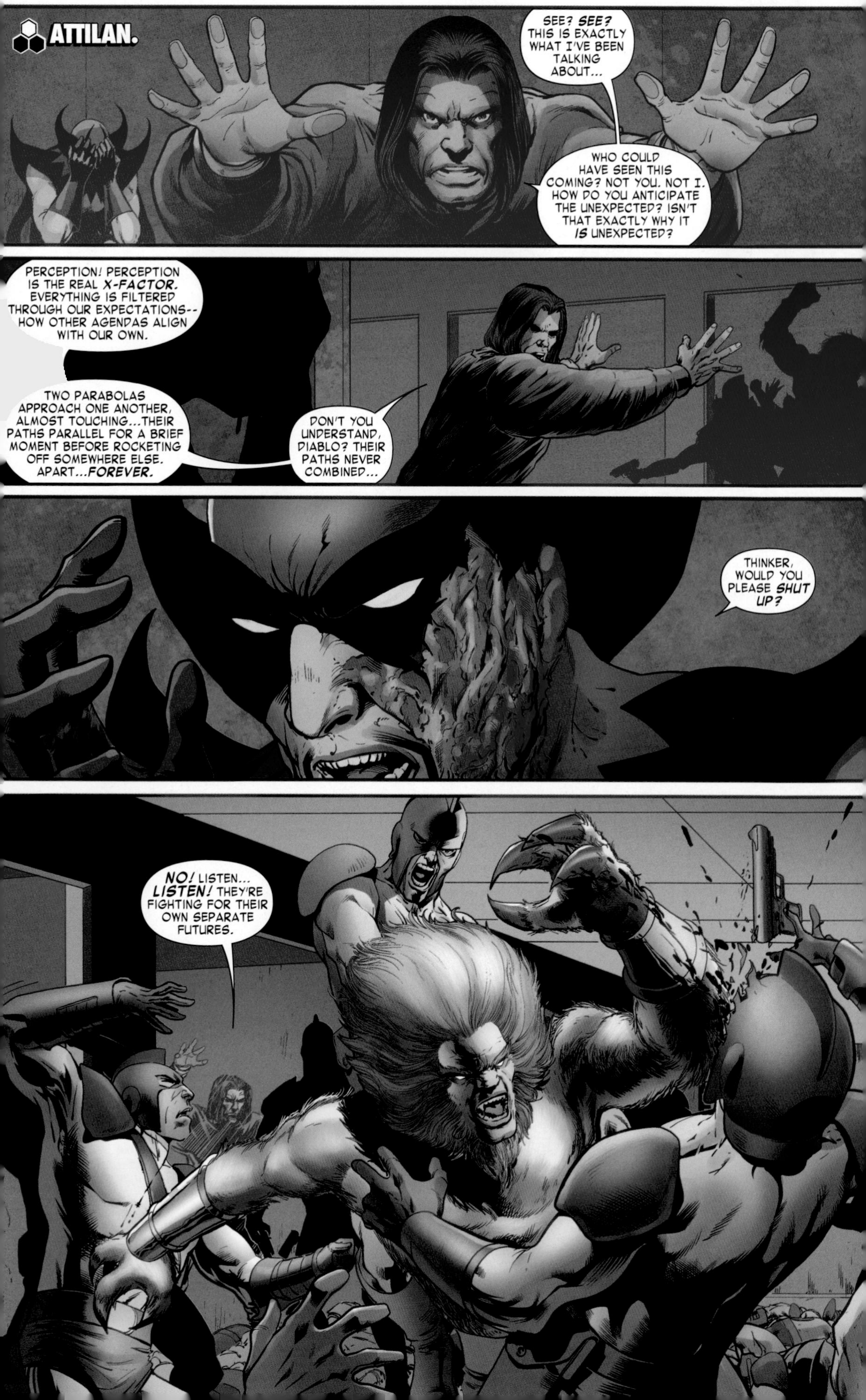
ATTILAN.
SEE? SEE? THIS IS EXACTLY WHAT I'VE BEEN TALKING ABOUT...
WHO COULD HAVE SEEN THIS COMING? NOT YOU. NOT I. HOW DO YOU ANTICIPATE THE UNEXPECTED? ISN'T THAT EXACTLY WHY IT IS UNEXPECTED?
PERCEPTION! PERCEPTION IS THE REAL X-FACTOR. EVERYTHING IS FILTERED THROUGH OUR EXPECTATIONS-- HOW OTHER AGENDAS ALIGN WITH OUR OWN.
TWO PARABOLAS APPROACH ONE ANOTHER, ALMOST TOUCHING...THEIR PATHS PARALLEL FOR A BRIEF MOMENT BEFORE ROCKETING OFF SOMEWHERE ELSE. APART...FOREVER.
DON'T YOU UNDERSTAND, DIABLO? THEIR PATHS NEVER COMBINED...
THINKER, WOULD YOU PLEASE SHUT UP?
NO! LISTEN... LISTEN! THEY'RE FIGHTING FOR THEIR OWN SEPARATE FUTURES.

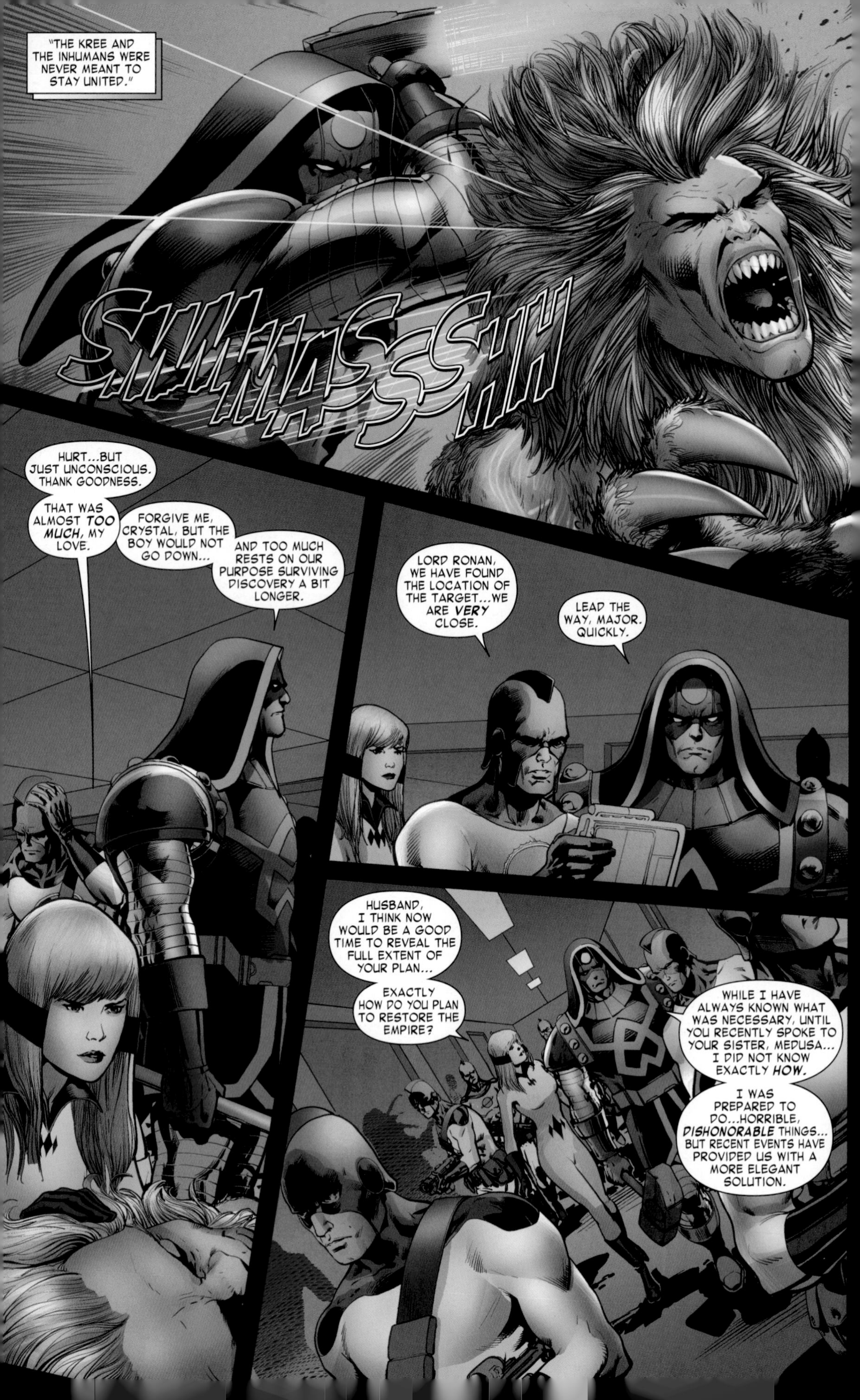
"THE KREE AND THE INHUMANS WERE NEVER MEANT TO STAY UNITED."
SHHHMASSSHH
HURT...BUT JUST UNCONSCIOUS. THANK GOODNESS.
THAT WAS ALMOST *TOO MUCH*, MY LOVE.
FORGIVE ME, CRYSTAL, BUT THE BOY WOULD NOT GO DOWN...
AND TOO MUCH RESTS ON OUR PURPOSE SURVIVING DISCOVERY A BIT LONGER.
LORD RONAN, WE HAVE FOUND THE LOCATION OF THE TARGET...WE ARE *VERY* CLOSE.
LEAD THE WAY, MAJOR. QUICKLY.
HUSBAND, I THINK NOW WOULD BE A GOOD TIME TO REVEAL THE FULL EXTENT OF YOUR PLAN...
EXACTLY HOW DO YOU PLAN TO RESTORE THE EMPIRE?
WHILE I HAVE ALWAYS KNOWN WHAT WAS NECESSARY, UNTIL YOU RECENTLY SPOKE TO YOUR SISTER, MEDUSA... I DID NOT KNOW EXACTLY *HOW*.
I WAS PREPARED TO DO...HORRIBLE, *DISHONORABLE* THINGS... BUT RECENT EVENTS HAVE PROVIDED US WITH A MORE ELEGANT SOLUTION.

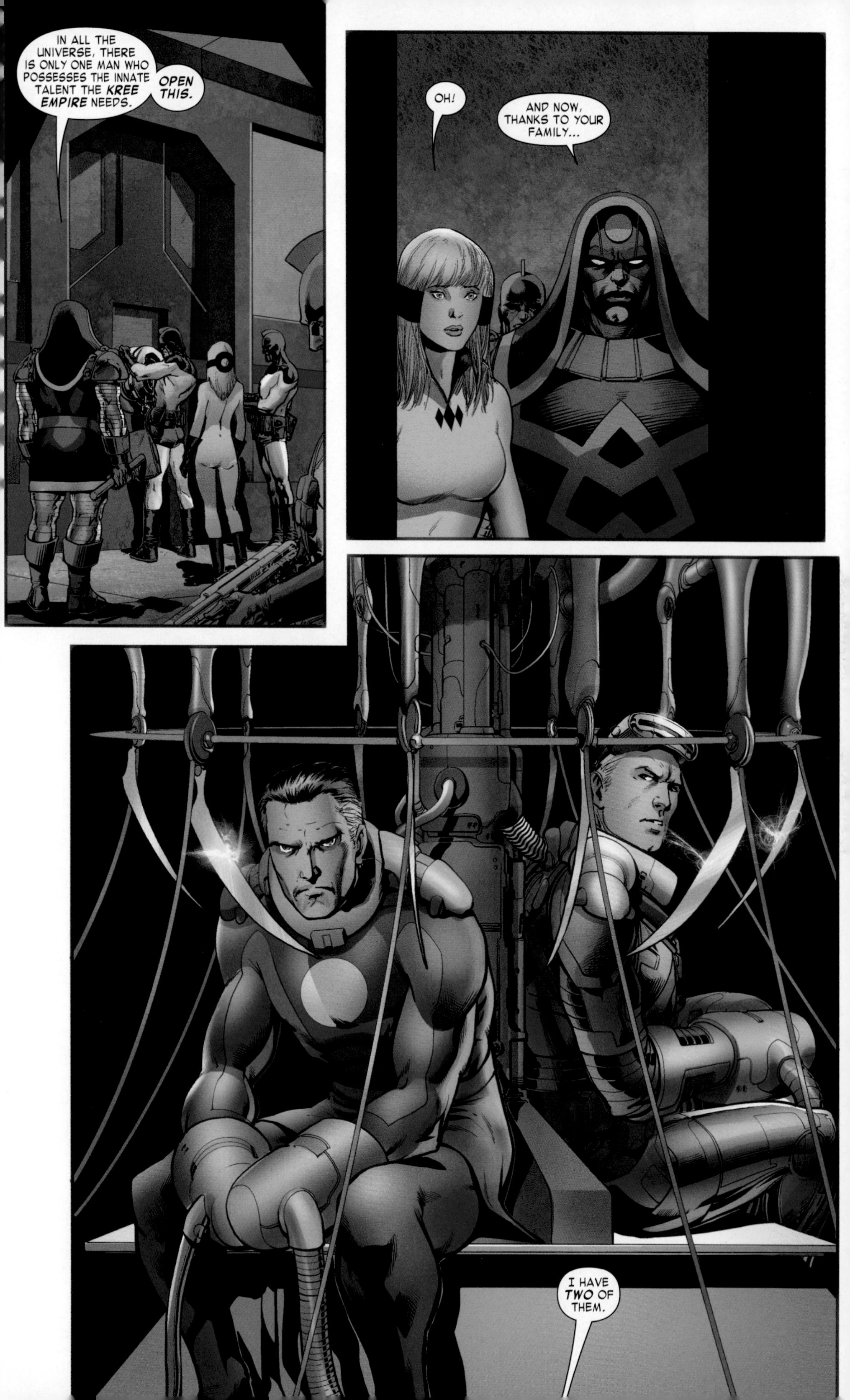

IN ALL THE UNIVERSE, THERE IS ONLY ONE MAN WHO POSSESSES THE INNATE TALENT THE KREE EMPIRE NEEDS.
OPEN THIS.
OH!
AND NOW, THANKS TO YOUR FAMILY...
I HAVE TWO OF THEM.

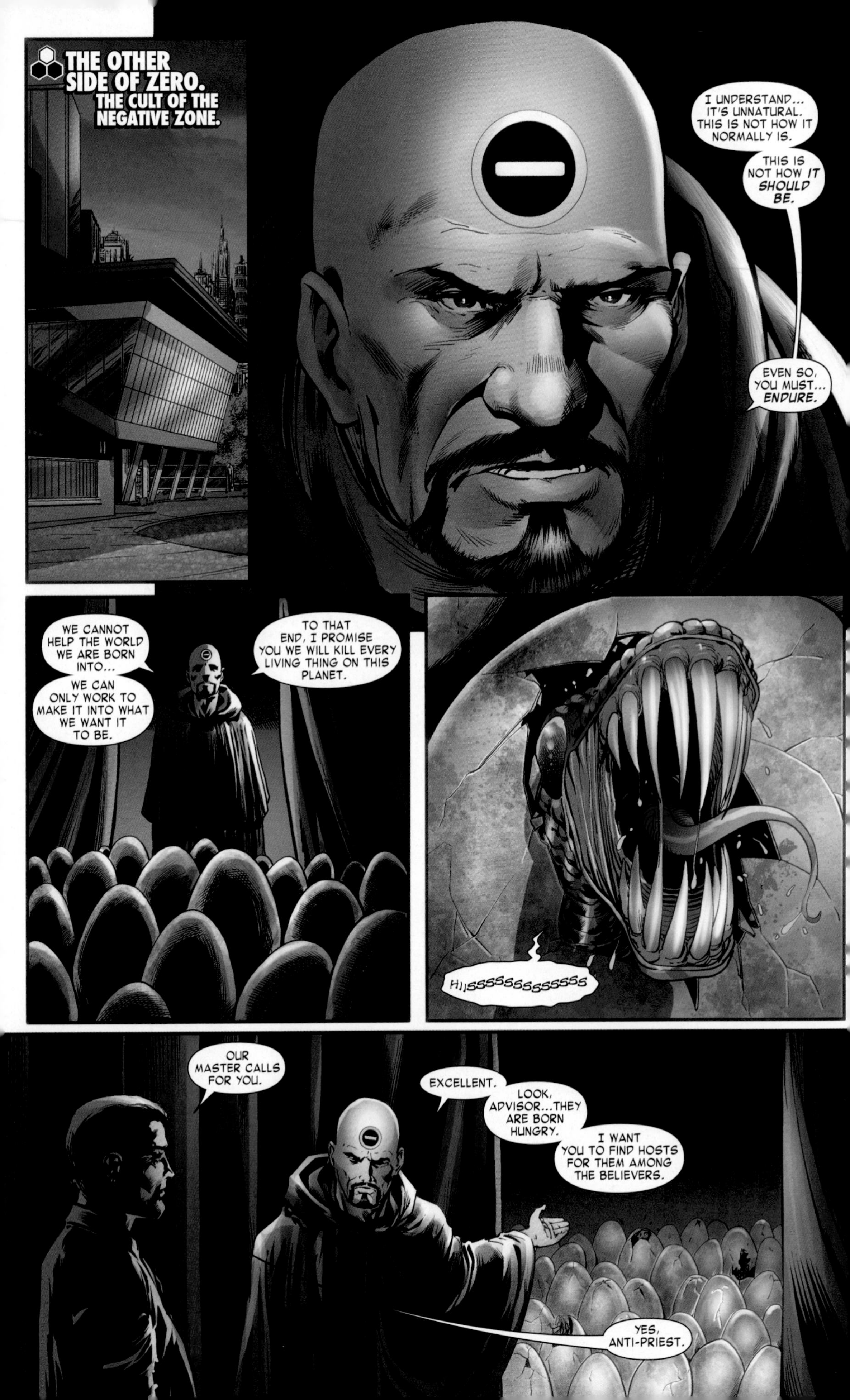
THE OTHER SIDE OF ZERO.
THE CULT OF THE NEGATIVE ZONE.
I UNDERSTAND... IT'S UNNATURAL. THIS IS NOT HOW IT NORMALLY IS.
THIS IS NOT HOW IT SHOULD BE.
EVEN SO, YOU MUST... ENDURE.
WE CANNOT HELP THE WORLD WE ARE BORN INTO...
WE CAN ONLY WORK TO MAKE IT INTO WHAT WE WANT IT TO BE.
TO THAT END, I PROMISE YOU WE WILL KILL EVERY LIVING THING ON THIS PLANET.
HIISSSSSSSSSSSSS
OUR MASTER CALLS FOR YOU.
EXCELLENT.
LOOK, ADVISOR...THEY ARE BORN HUNGRY.
I WANT YOU TO FIND HOSTS FOR THEM AMONG THE BELIEVERS.
YES, ANTI-PRIEST.

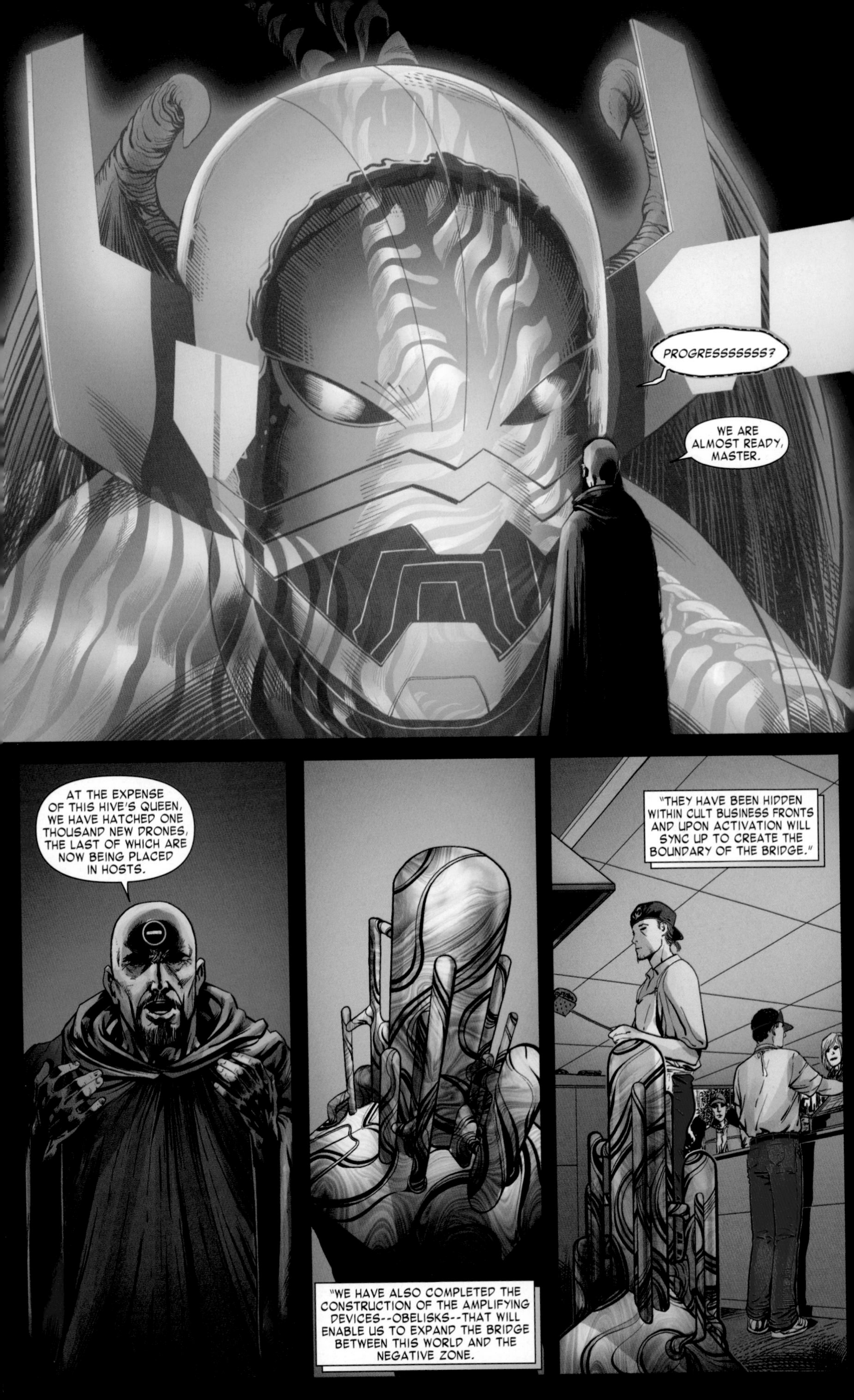
PROGRESSSSSSS?
WE ARE ALMOST READY, MASTER.
AT THE EXPENSE OF THIS HIVE'S QUEEN, WE HAVE HATCHED ONE THOUSAND NEW DRONES, THE LAST OF WHICH ARE NOW BEING PLACED IN HOSTS.
"WE HAVE ALSO COMPLETED THE CONSTRUCTION OF THE AMPLIFYING DEVICES--OBELISKS--THAT WILL ENABLE US TO EXPAND THE BRIDGE BETWEEN THIS WORLD AND THE NEGATIVE ZONE.
"THEY HAVE BEEN HIDDEN WITHIN CULT BUSINESS FRONTS AND UPON ACTIVATION WILL SYNC UP TO CREATE THE BOUNDARY OF THE BRIDGE."

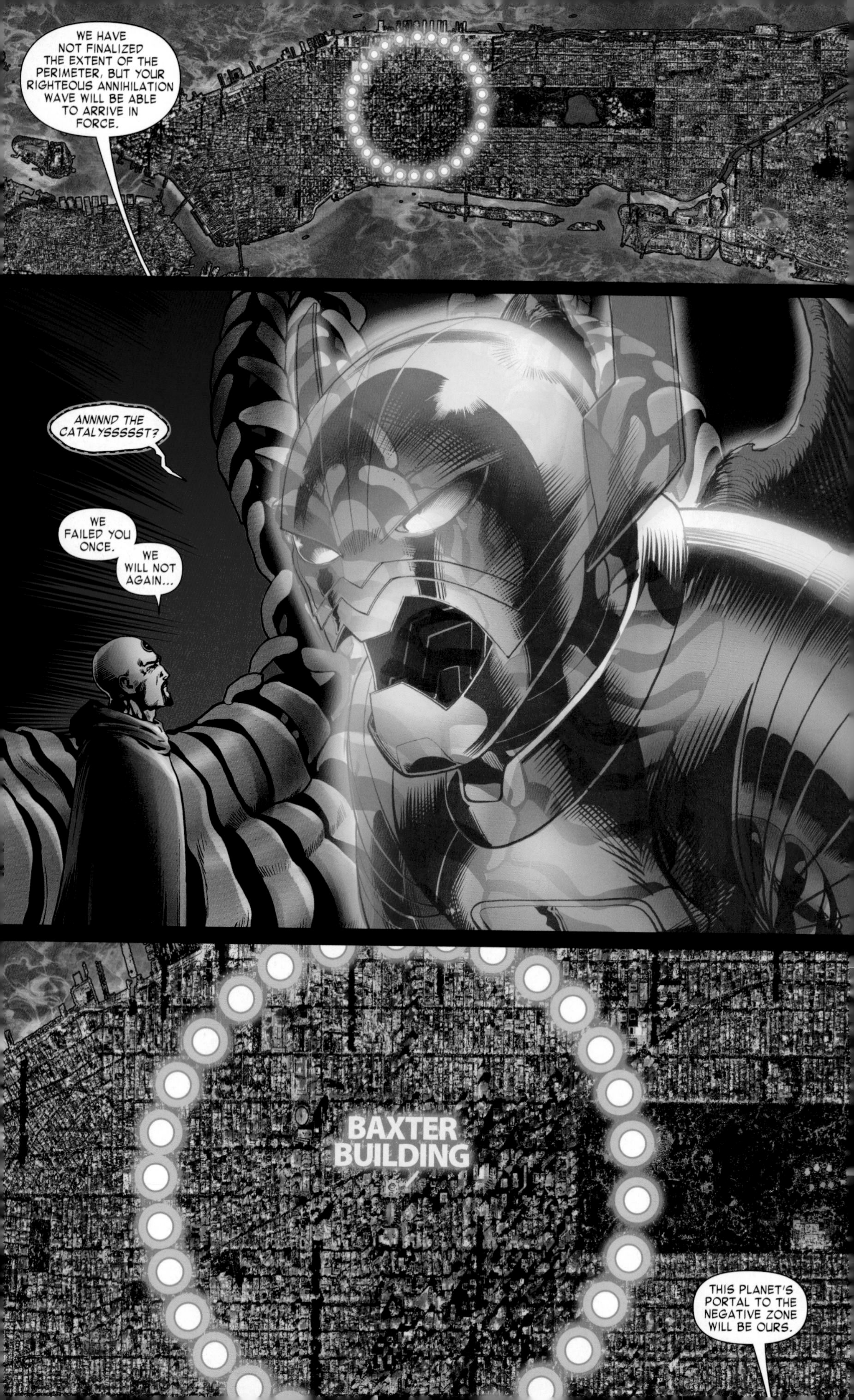
WE HAVE NOT FINALIZED THE EXTENT OF THE PERIMETER, BUT YOUR RIGHTEOUS ANNIHILATION WAVE WILL BE ABLE TO ARRIVE IN FORCE.
ANNNND THE CATALYSSSSST?
WE FAILED YOU ONCE.
WE WILL NOT AGAIN...
BAXTER BUILDING
THIS PLANET'S PORTAL TO THE NEGATIVE ZONE WILL BE OURS.

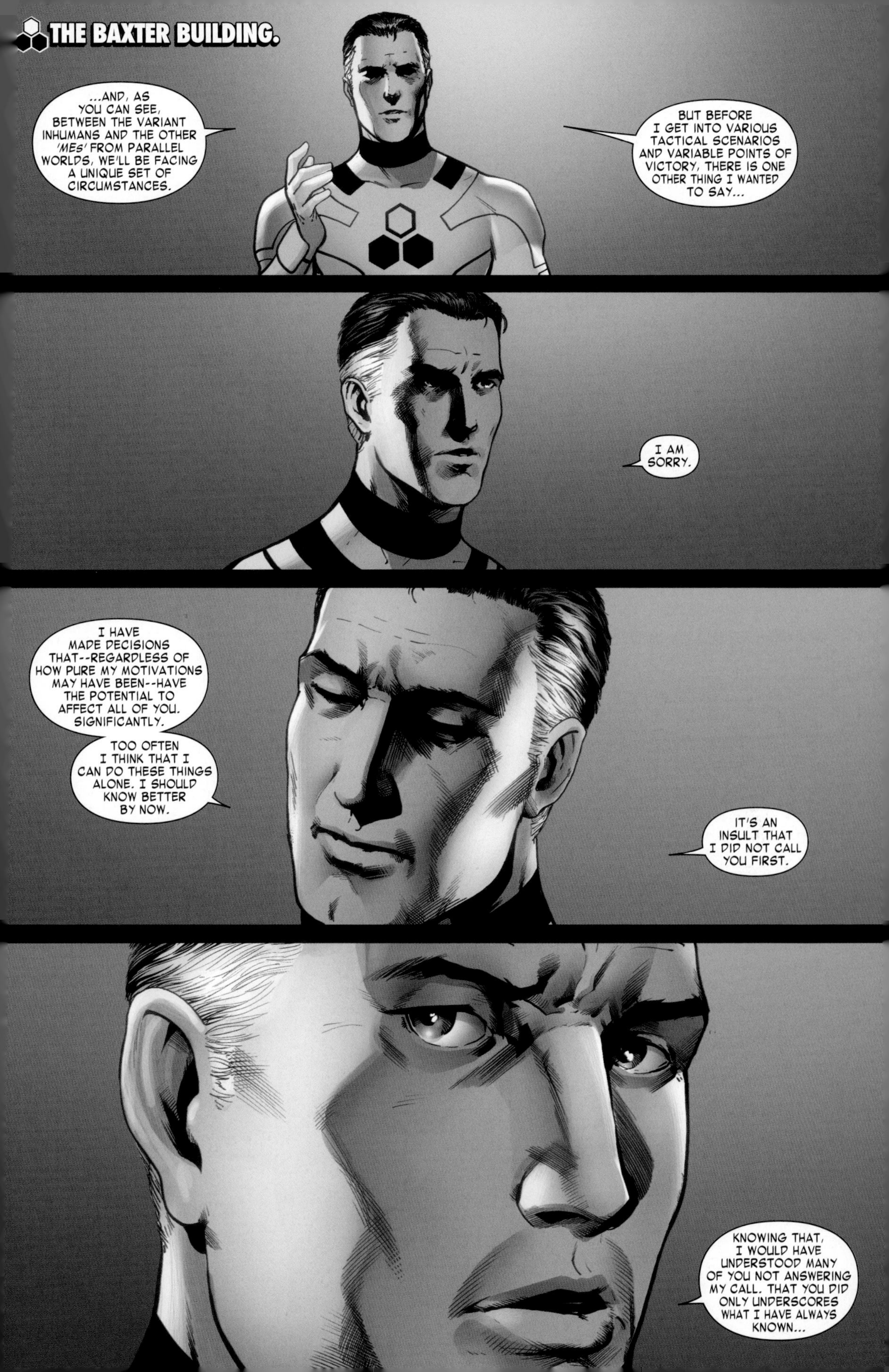
THE BAXTER BUILDING.
...AND, AS YOU CAN SEE, BETWEEN THE VARIANT INHUMANS AND THE OTHER 'MES' FROM PARALLEL WORLDS, WE'LL BE FACING A UNIQUE SET OF CIRCUMSTANCES.
BUT BEFORE I GET INTO VARIOUS TACTICAL SCENARIOS AND VARIABLE POINTS OF VICTORY, THERE IS ONE OTHER THING I WANTED TO SAY...
I AM SORRY.
I HAVE MADE DECISIONS THAT--REGARDLESS OF HOW PURE MY MOTIVATIONS MAY HAVE BEEN--HAVE THE POTENTIAL TO AFFECT ALL OF YOU. SIGNIFICANTLY.
TOO OFTEN I THINK THAT I CAN DO THESE THINGS ALONE. I SHOULD KNOW BETTER BY NOW.
IT'S AN INSULT THAT I DID NOT CALL YOU FIRST.
KNOWING THAT, I WOULD HAVE UNDERSTOOD MANY OF YOU NOT ANSWERING MY CALL. THAT YOU DID ONLY UNDERSCORES WHAT I HAVE ALWAYS KNOWN...

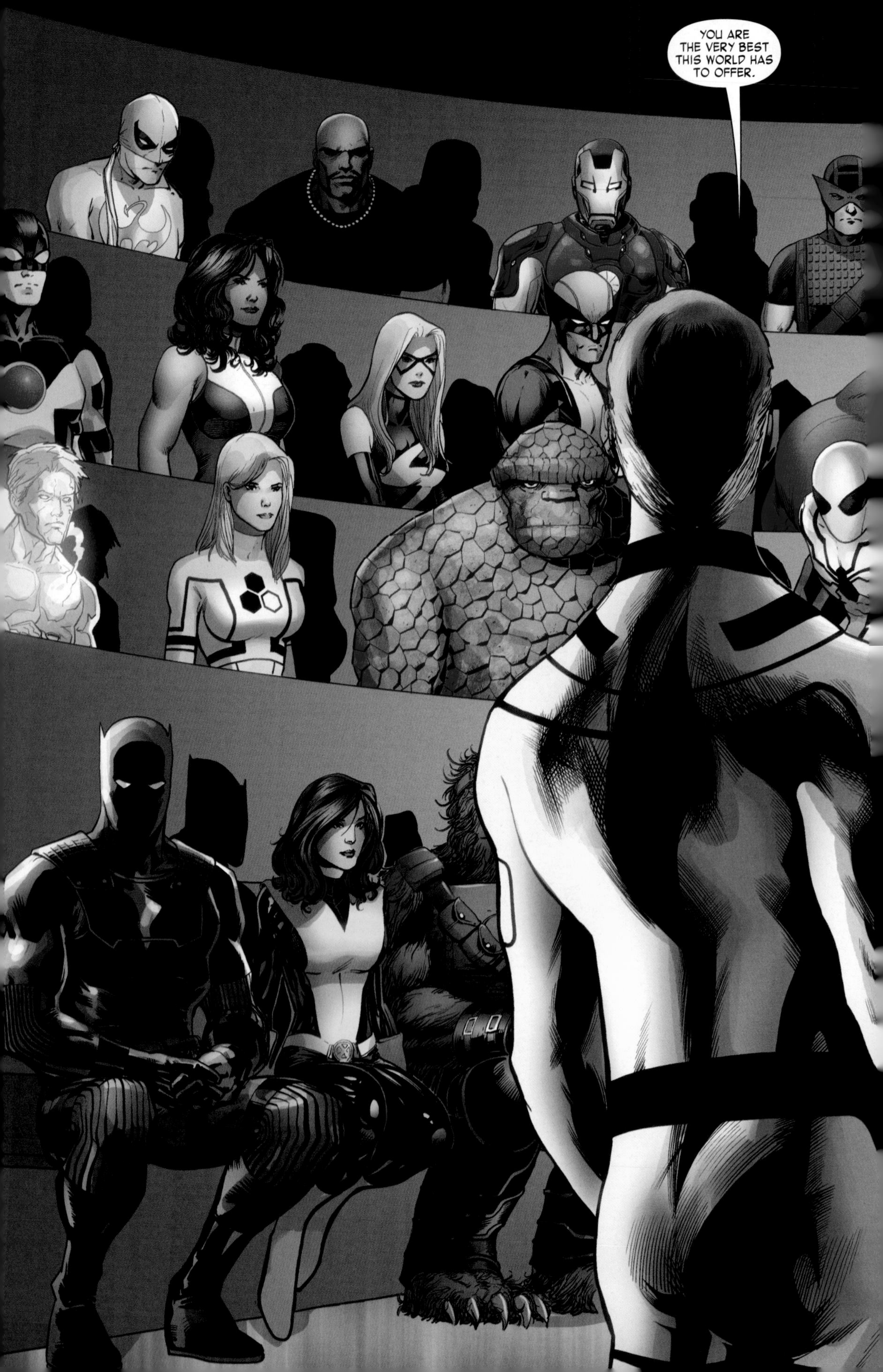
YOU ARE THE VERY BEST THIS WORLD HAS TO OFFER.

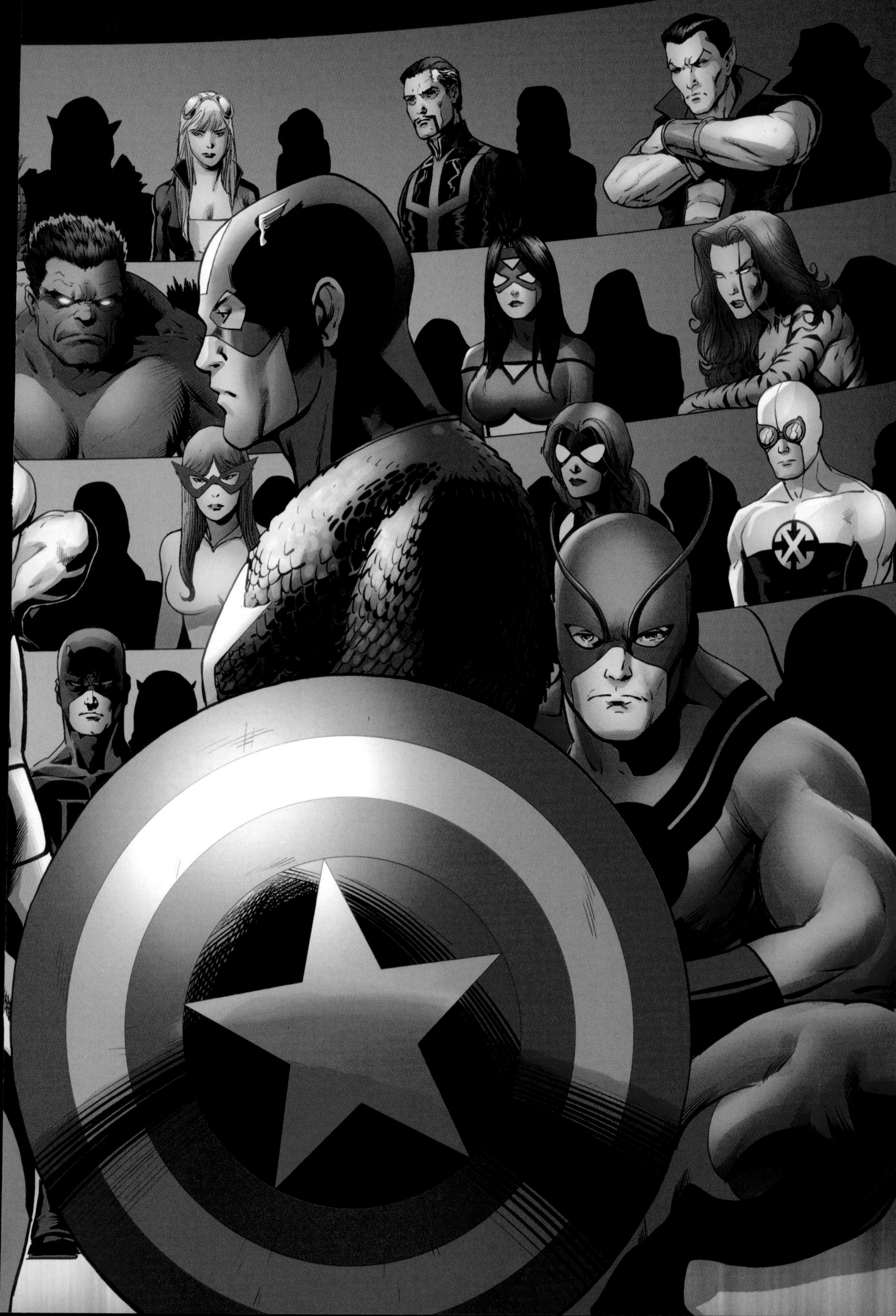

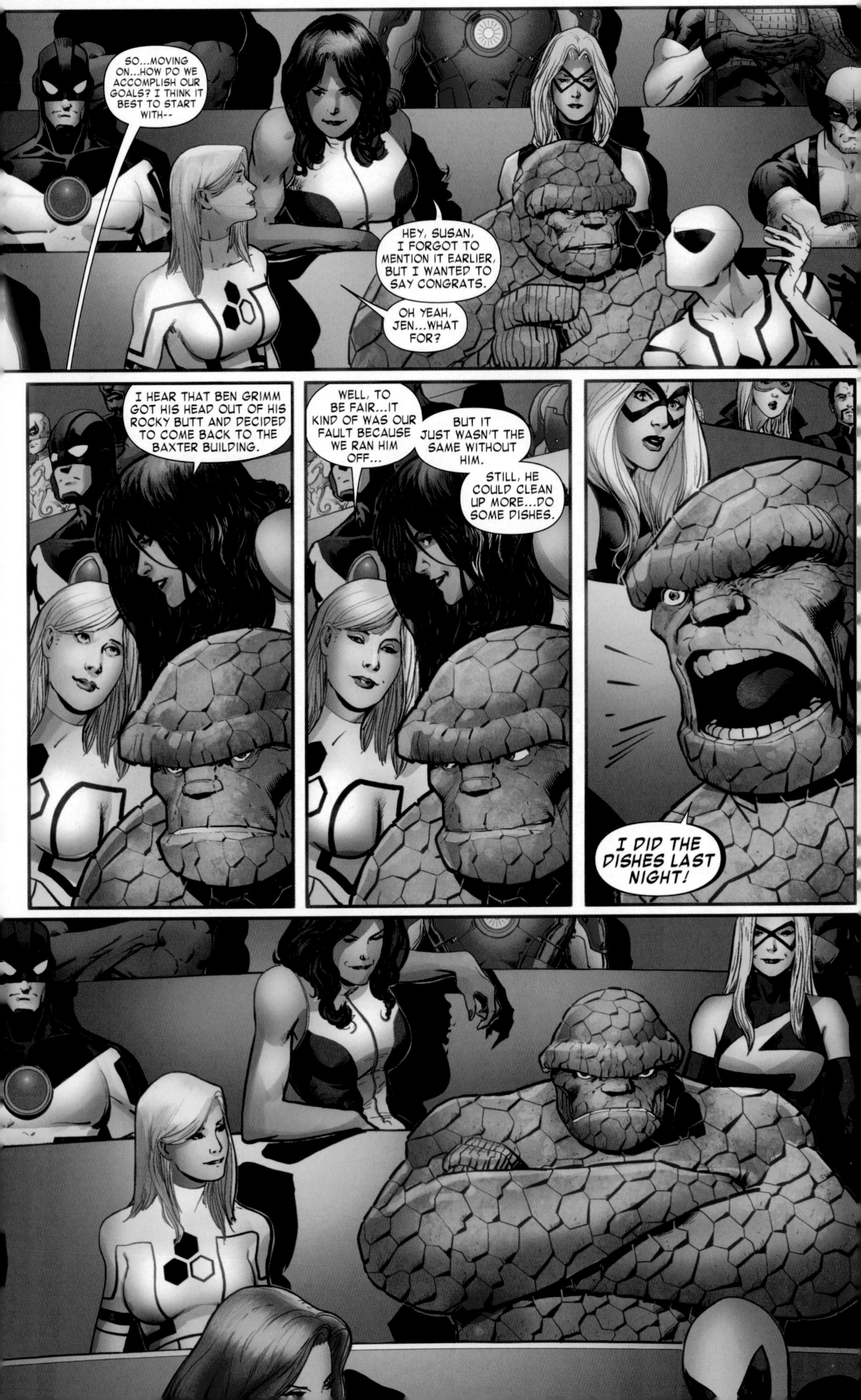
SO...MOVING ON...HOW DO WE ACCOMPLISH OUR GOALS? I THINK IT BEST TO START WITH--
HEY, SUSAN, I FORGOT TO MENTION IT EARLIER, BUT I WANTED TO SAY CONGRATS.
OH YEAH, JEN...WHAT FOR?
I HEAR THAT BEN GRIMM GOT HIS HEAD OUT OF HIS ROCKY BUTT AND DECIDED TO COME BACK TO THE BAXTER BUILDING.
WELL, TO BE FAIR...IT KIND OF WAS OUR FAULT BECAUSE WE RAN HIM OFF...
BUT IT JUST WASN'T THE SAME WITHOUT HIM.
STILL, HE COULD CLEAN UP MORE...DO SOME DISHES.
I DID THE DISHES LAST NIGHT!

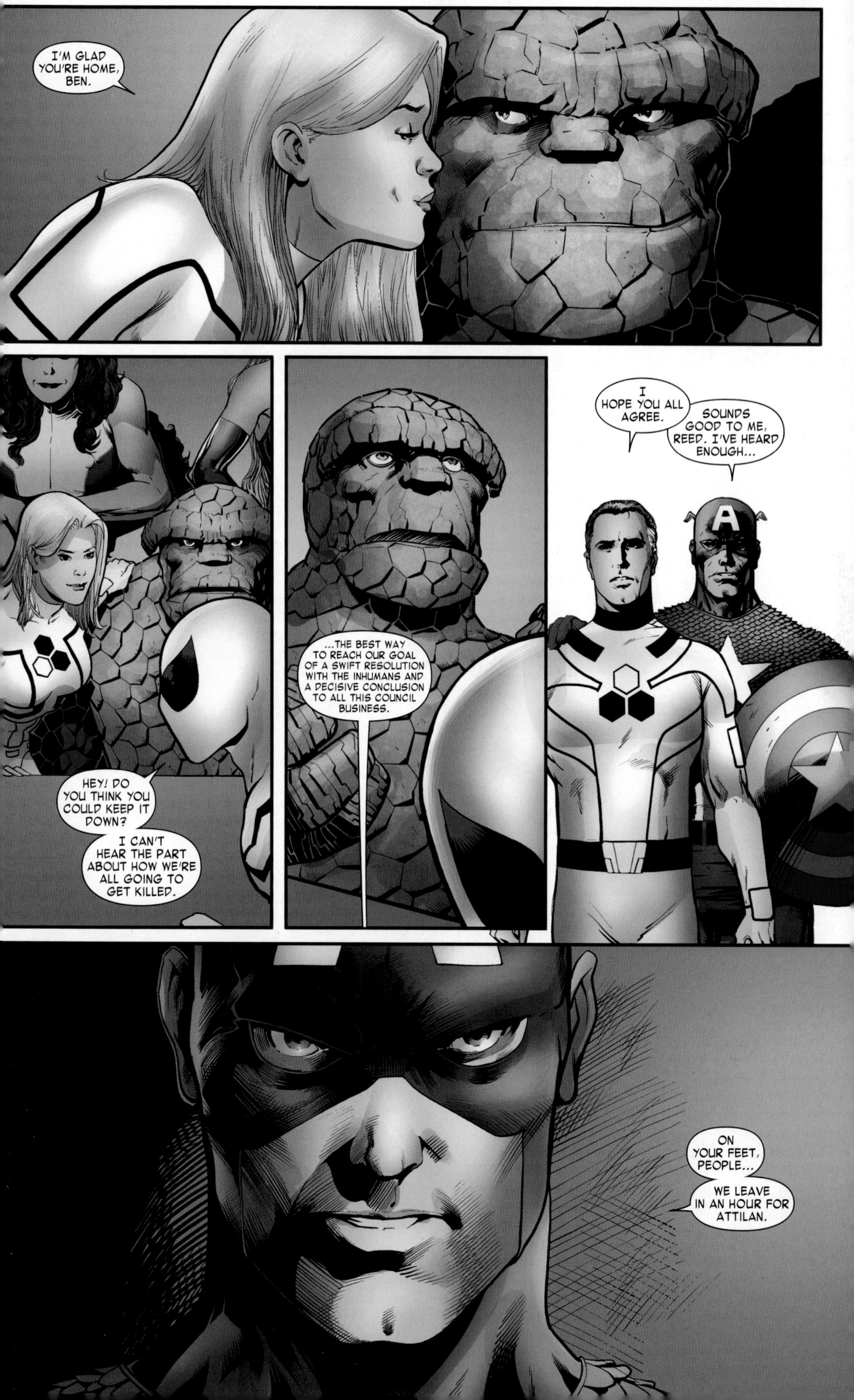
I'M GLAD YOU'RE HOME, BEN.
HEY! DO YOU THINK YOU COULD KEEP IT DOWN?
I CAN'T HEAR THE PART ABOUT HOW WE'RE ALL GOING TO GET KILLED.
...THE BEST WAY TO REACH OUR GOAL OF A SWIFT RESOLUTION WITH THE INHUMANS AND A DECISIVE CONCLUSION TO ALL THIS COUNCIL BUSINESS.
I HOPE YOU ALL AGREE.
SOUNDS GOOD TO ME, REED. I'VE HEARD ENOUGH...
ON YOUR FEET, PEOPLE...
WE LEAVE IN AN HOUR FOR ATTILAN.

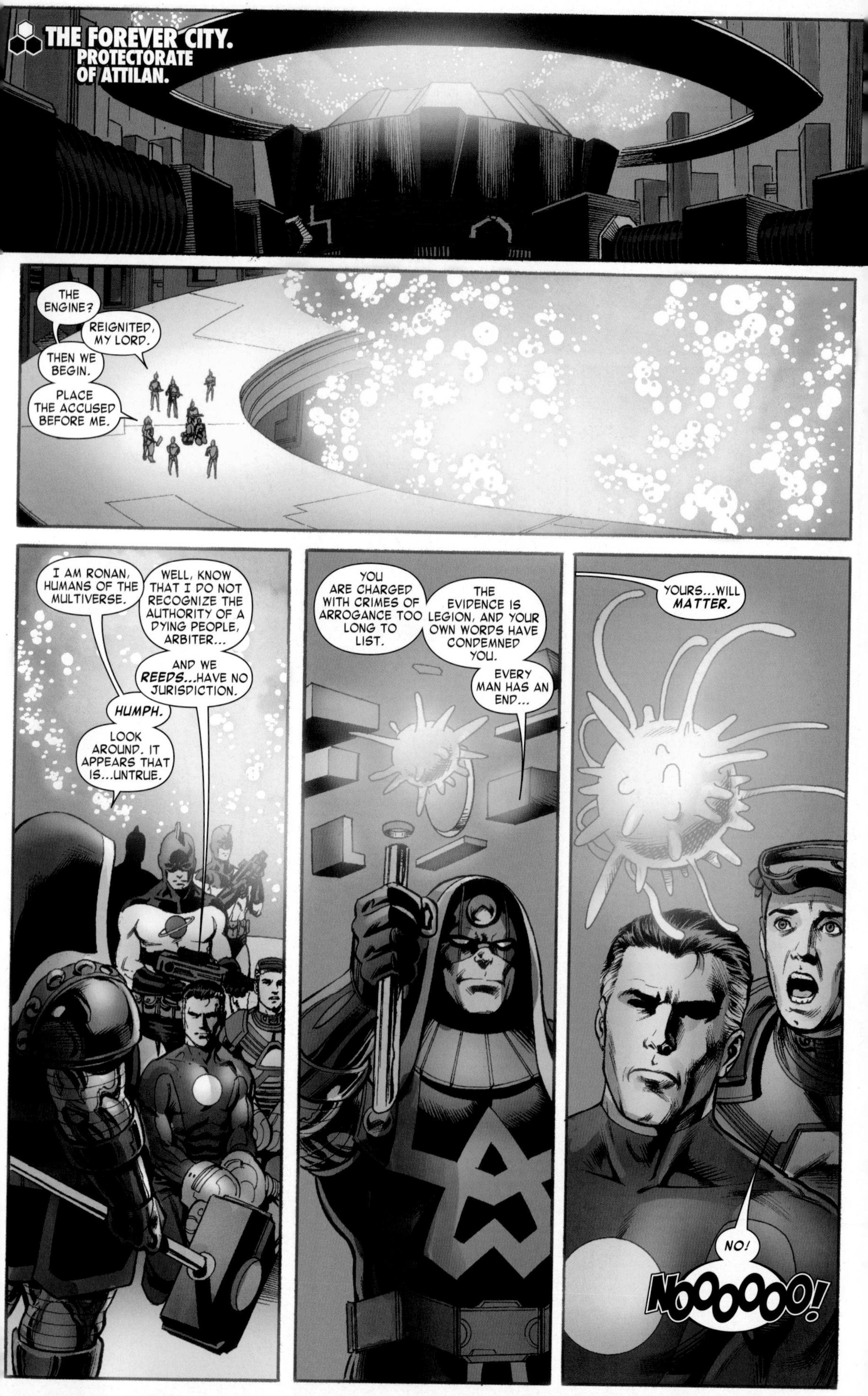
THE FOREVER CITY. PROTECTORATE OF ATTILAN.
THE ENGINE?
REIGNITED, MY LORD.
THEN WE BEGIN.
PLACE THE ACCUSED BEFORE ME.
I AM RONAN, HUMANS OF THE MULTIVERSE.
WELL, KNOW THAT I DO NOT RECOGNIZE THE AUTHORITY OF A DYING PEOPLE, ARBITER...
AND WE REEDS...HAVE NO JURISDICTION.
HUMPH.
LOOK AROUND. IT APPEARS THAT IS...UNTRUE.
YOU ARE CHARGED WITH CRIMES OF ARROGANCE TOO LONG TO LIST.
THE EVIDENCE IS LEGION, AND YOUR OWN WORDS HAVE CONDEMNED YOU.
EVERY MAN HAS AN END...
YOURS...WILL MATTER.
NO!
NOOOOOO!

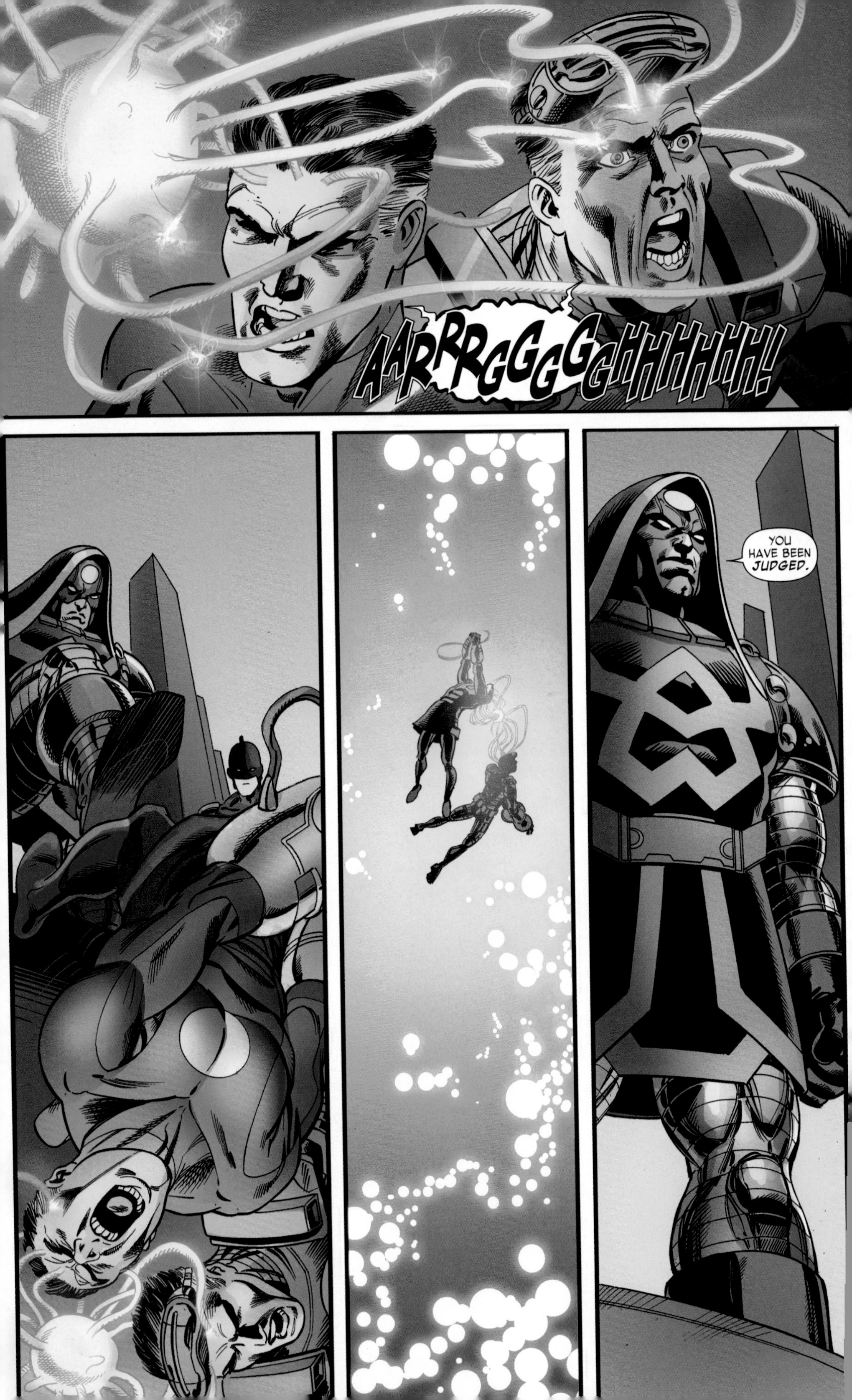
AARRRGGGGGHHHHHHH!
YOU HAVE BEEN JUDGED.

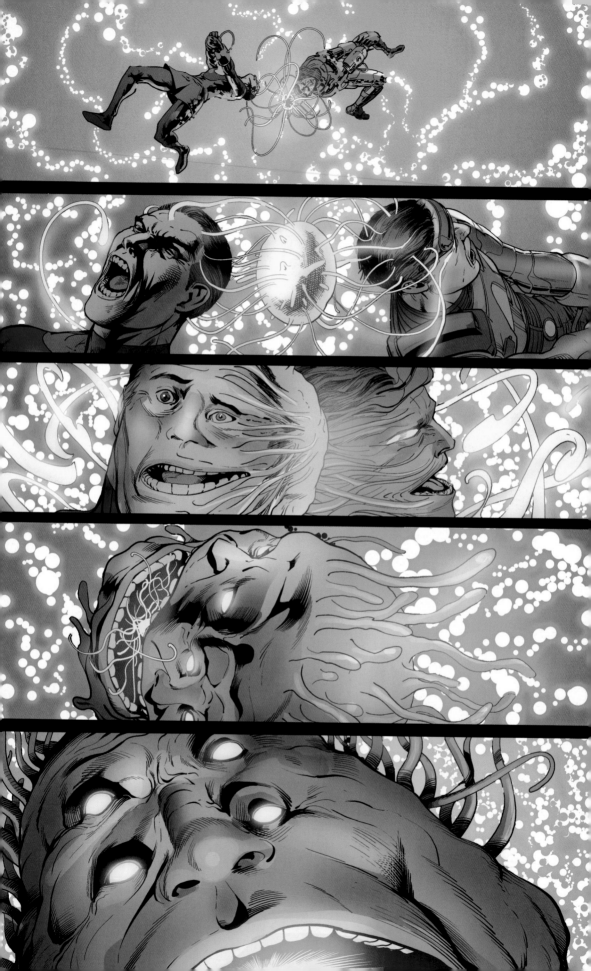

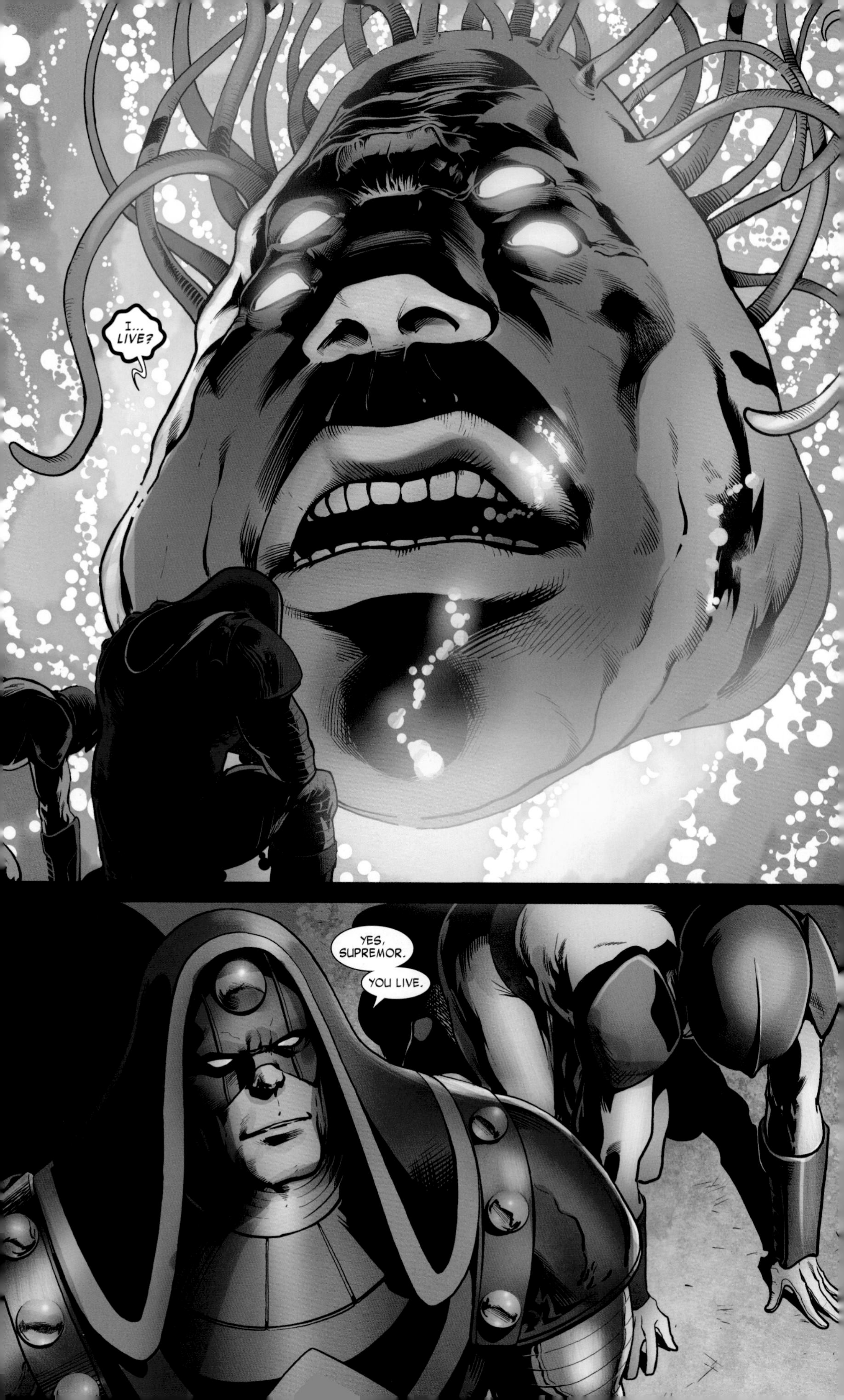
I... LIVE?
YES, SUPREMOR.
YOU LIVE.

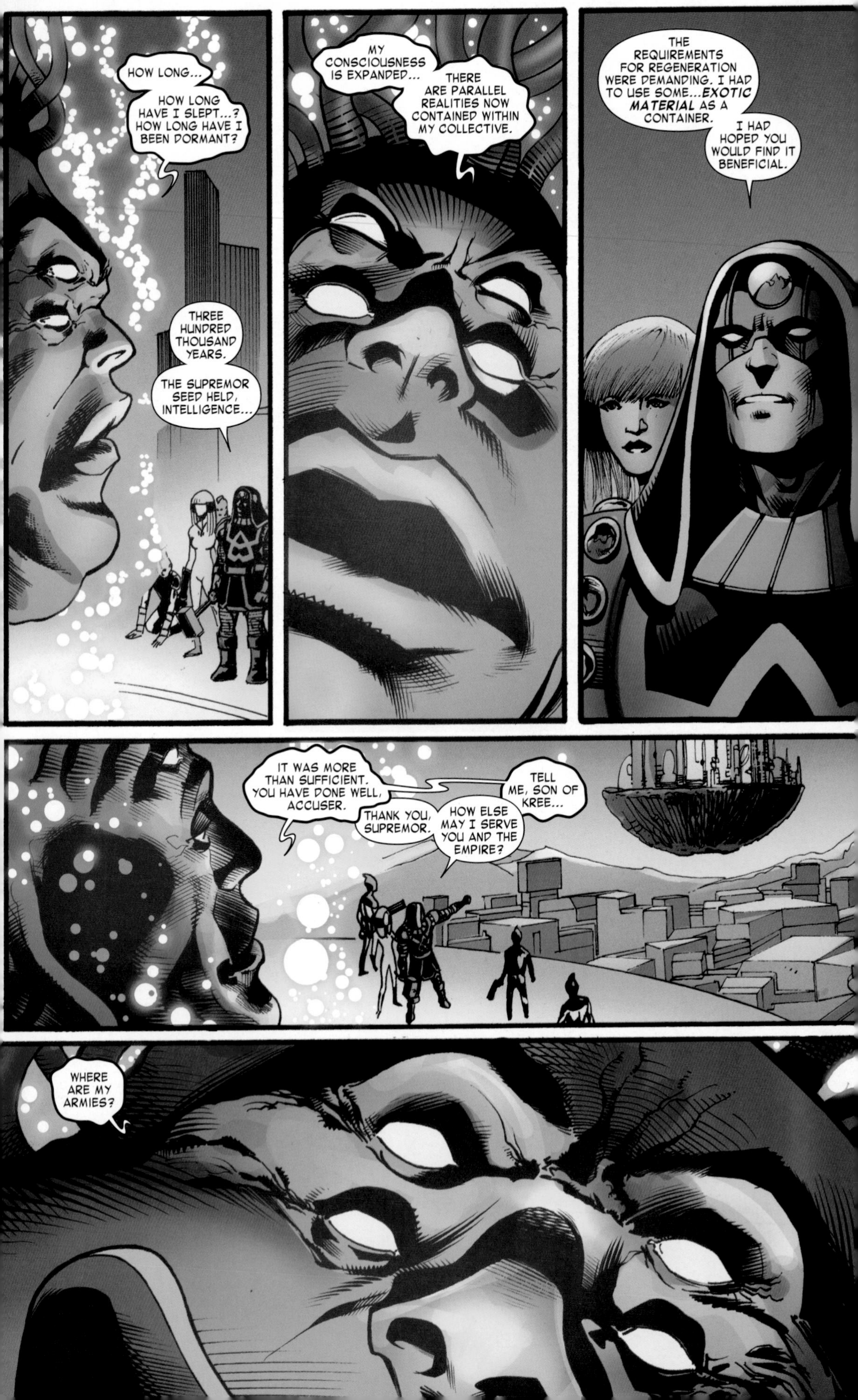
HOW LONG...
HOW LONG HAVE I SLEPT...? HOW LONG HAVE I BEEN DORMANT?
THREE HUNDRED THOUSAND YEARS.
THE SUPREMOR SEED HELD, INTELLIGENCE...
MY CONSCIOUSNESS IS EXPANDED...
THERE ARE PARALLEL REALITIES NOW CONTAINED WITHIN MY COLLECTIVE.
THE REQUIREMENTS FOR REGENERATION WERE DEMANDING. I HAD TO USE SOME...EXOTIC MATERIAL AS A CONTAINER.
I HAD HOPED YOU WOULD FIND IT BENEFICIAL.
IT WAS MORE THAN SUFFICIENT. YOU HAVE DONE WELL, ACCUSER.
THANK YOU, SUPREMOR.
HOW ELSE MAY I SERVE YOU AND THE EMPIRE?
TELL ME, SON OF KREE...
WHERE ARE MY ARMIES?

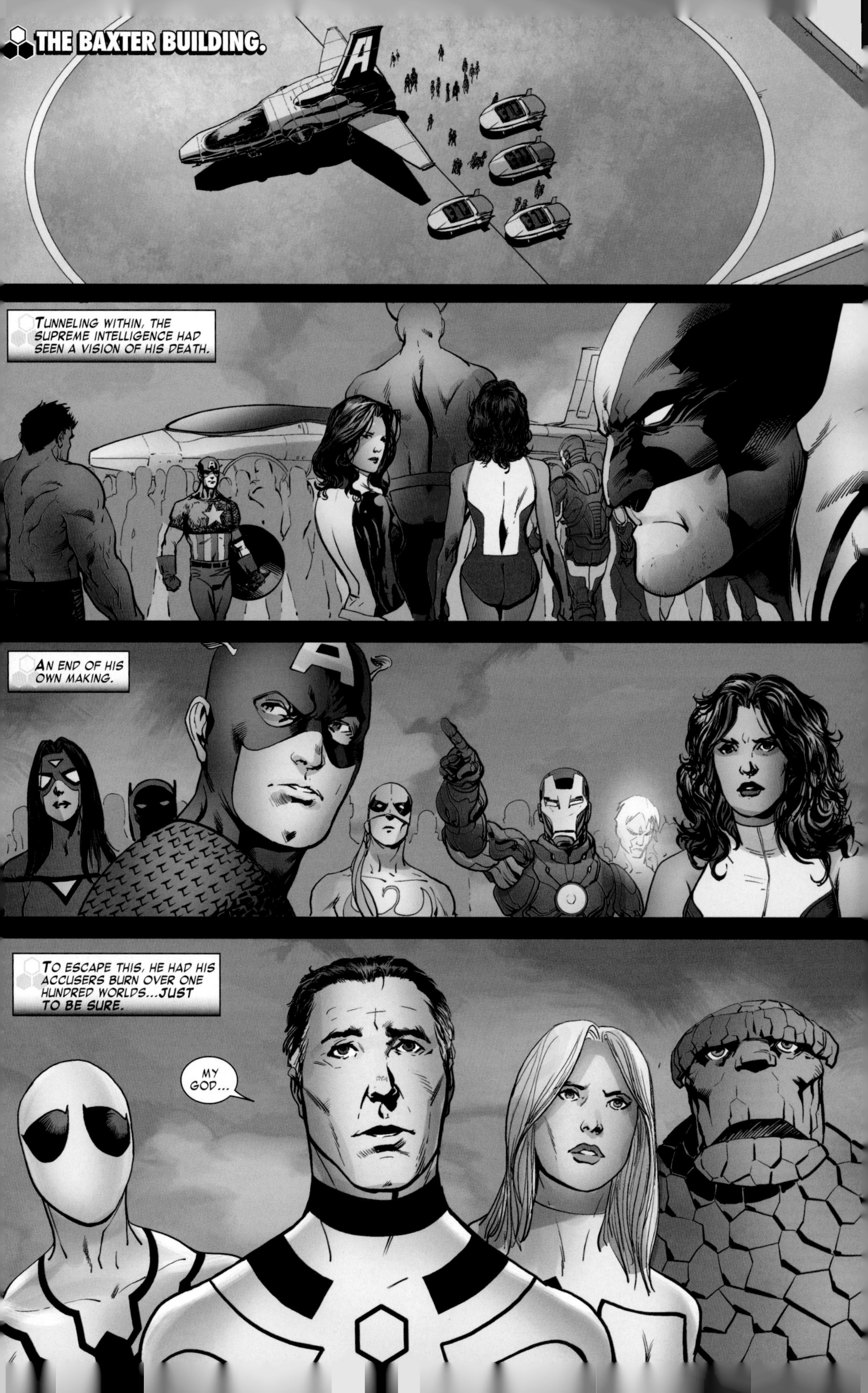
THE BAXTER BUILDING.
TUNNELING WITHIN, THE SUPREME INTELLIGENCE HAD SEEN A VISION OF HIS DEATH.
AN END OF HIS OWN MAKING.
TO ESCAPE THIS, HE HAD HIS ACCUSERS BURN OVER ONE HUNDRED WORLDS...JUST TO BE SURE.
MY GOD...

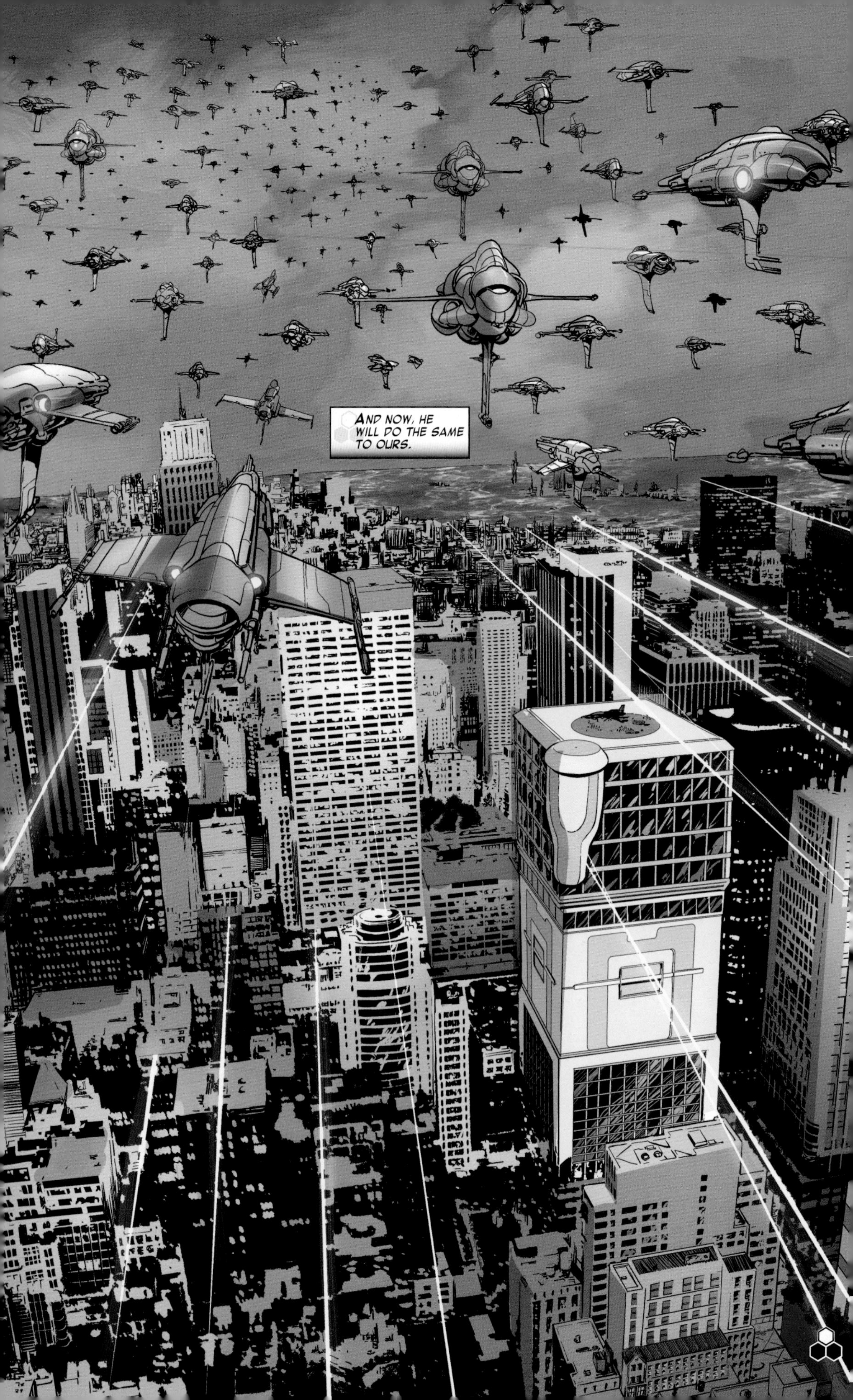
AND NOW, HE WILL DO THE SAME TO OURS.

COVER GALLERY

#6 COVER: **MARK BAGLEY, ANDY LANNING & PAUL MOUNTS**

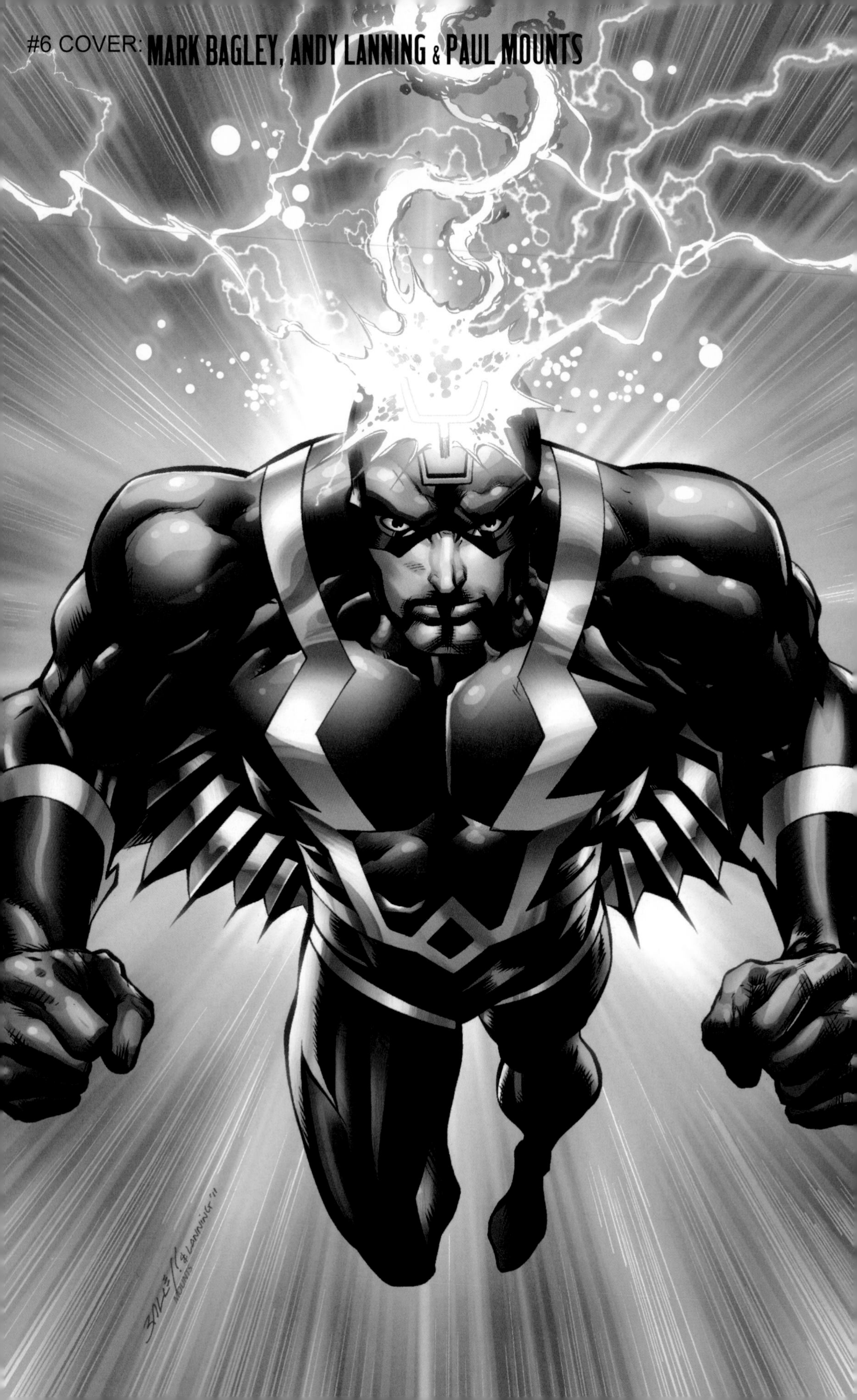

#7 COVER: MARK BAGLEY, ANDY LANNING & PAUL MOUNTS

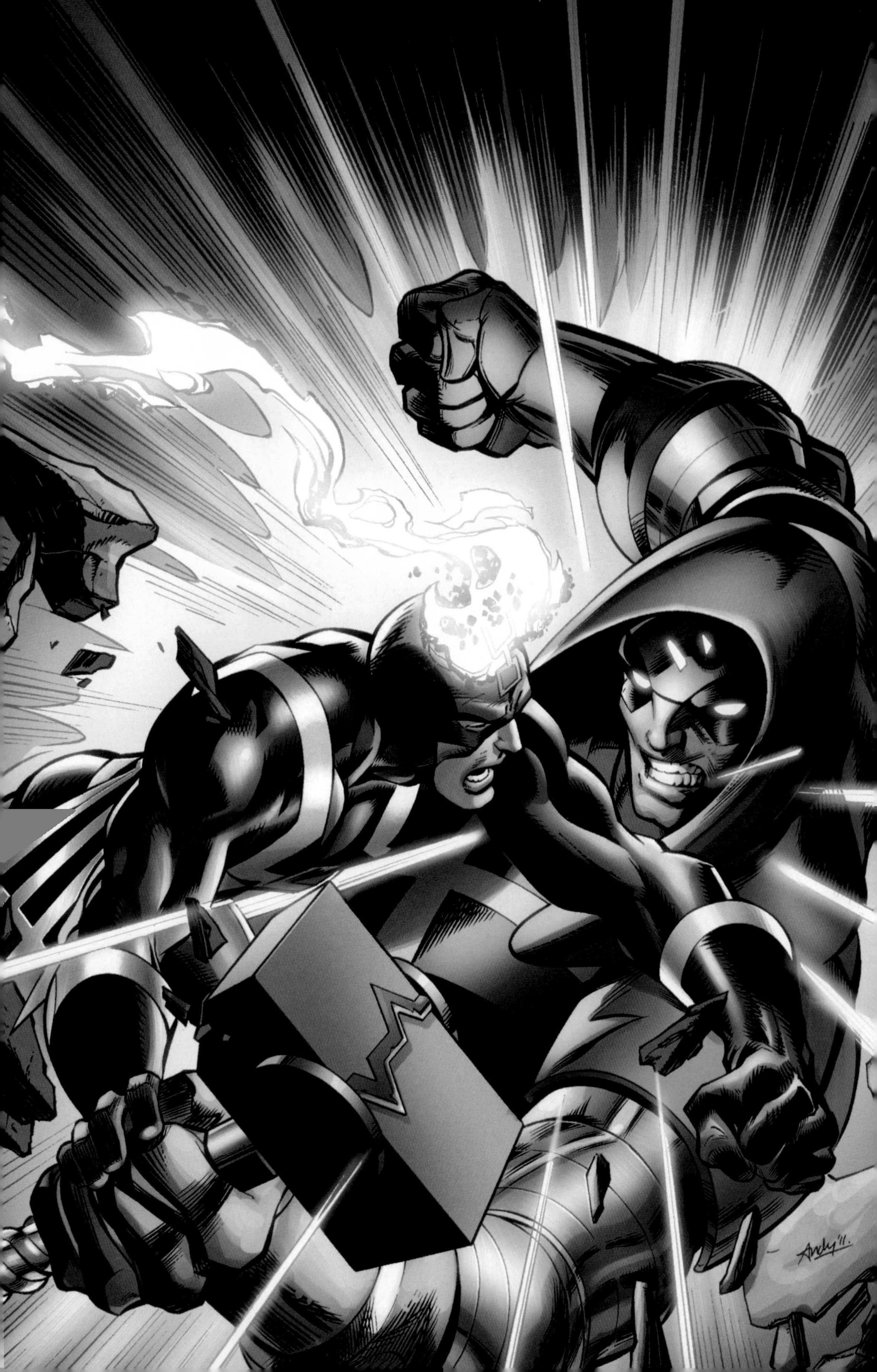

#8 COVER: DANIEL ACUÑA

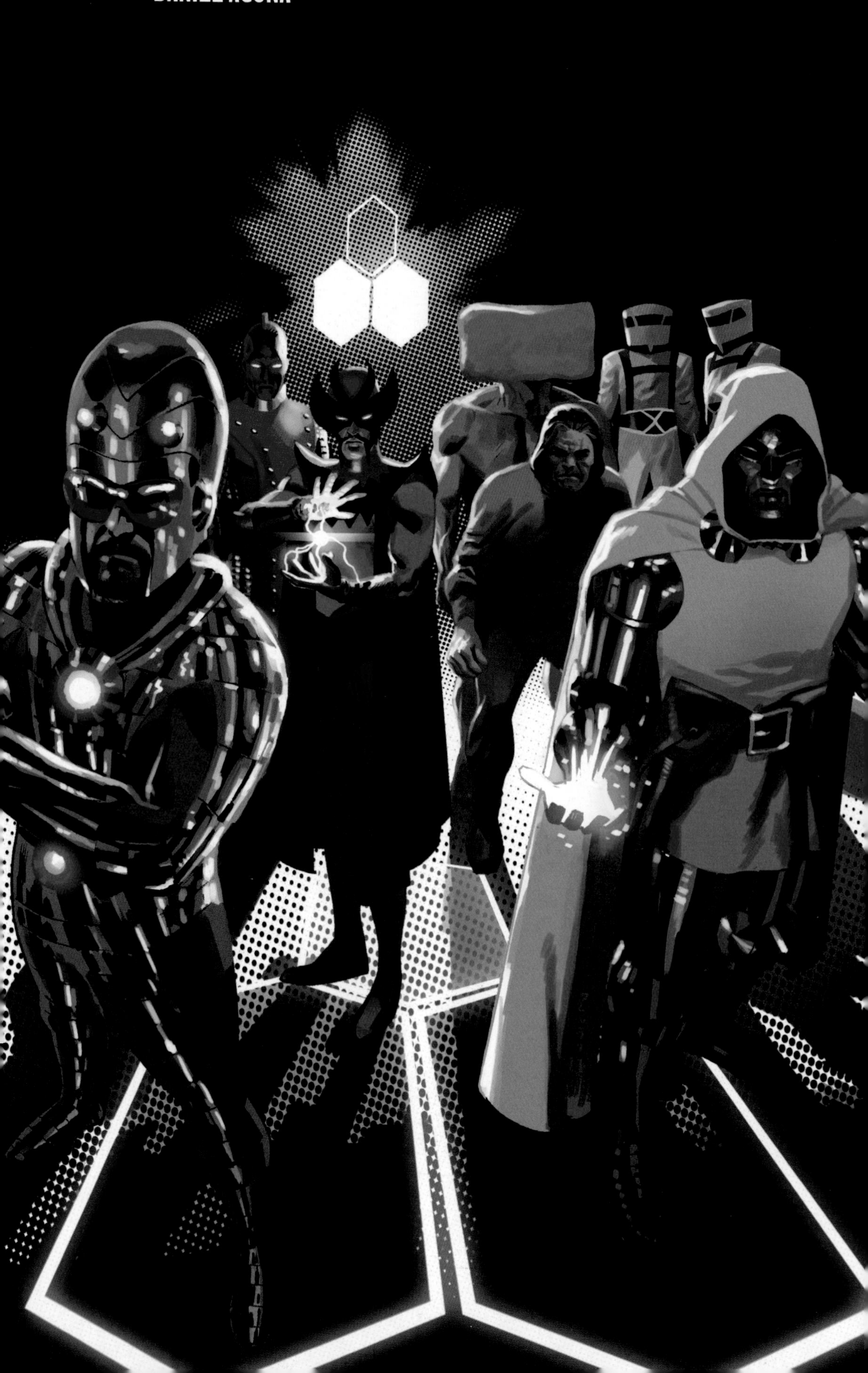

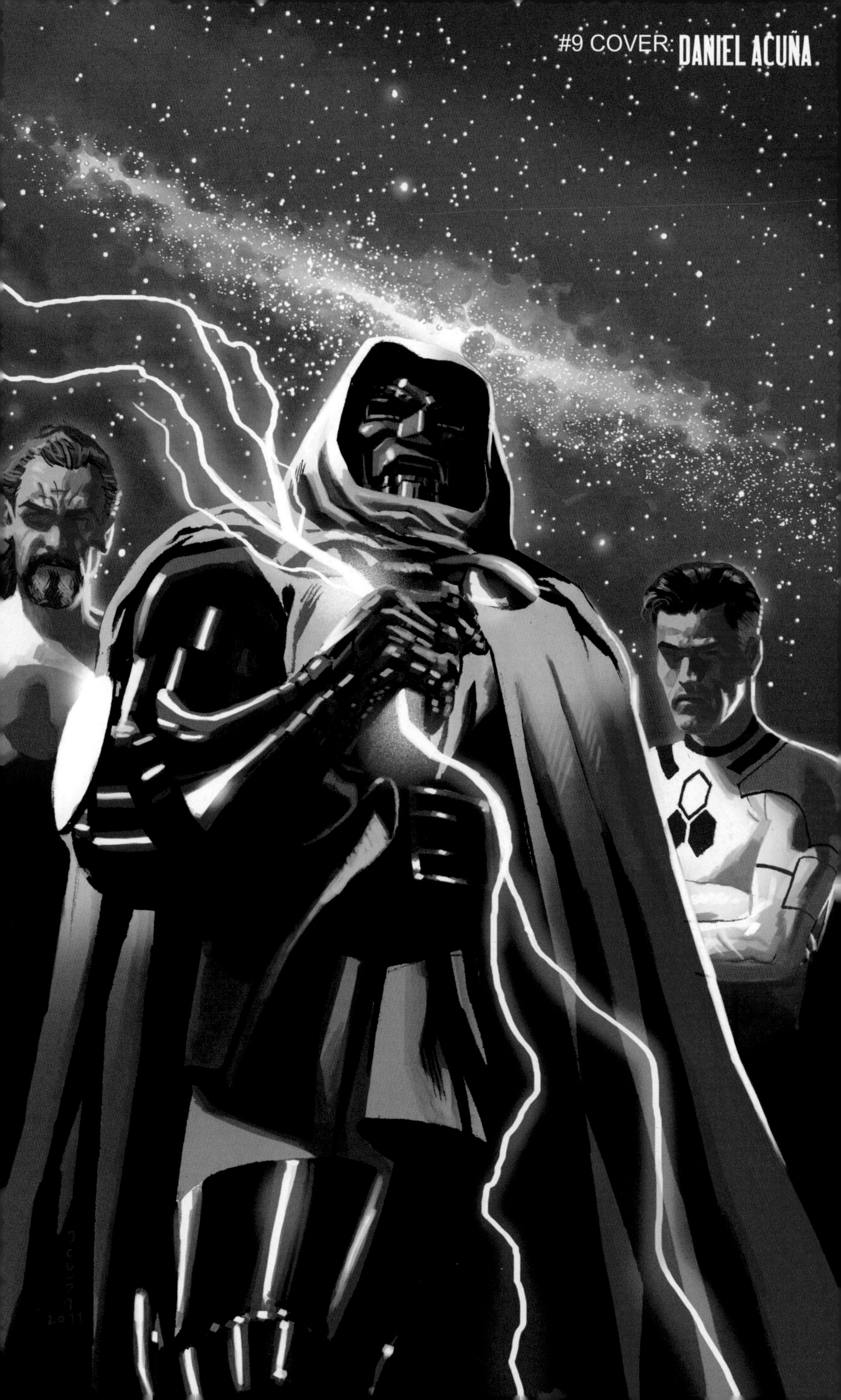

#9 COVER: DANIEL ACUÑA

#10 COVER: STEVE EPTING

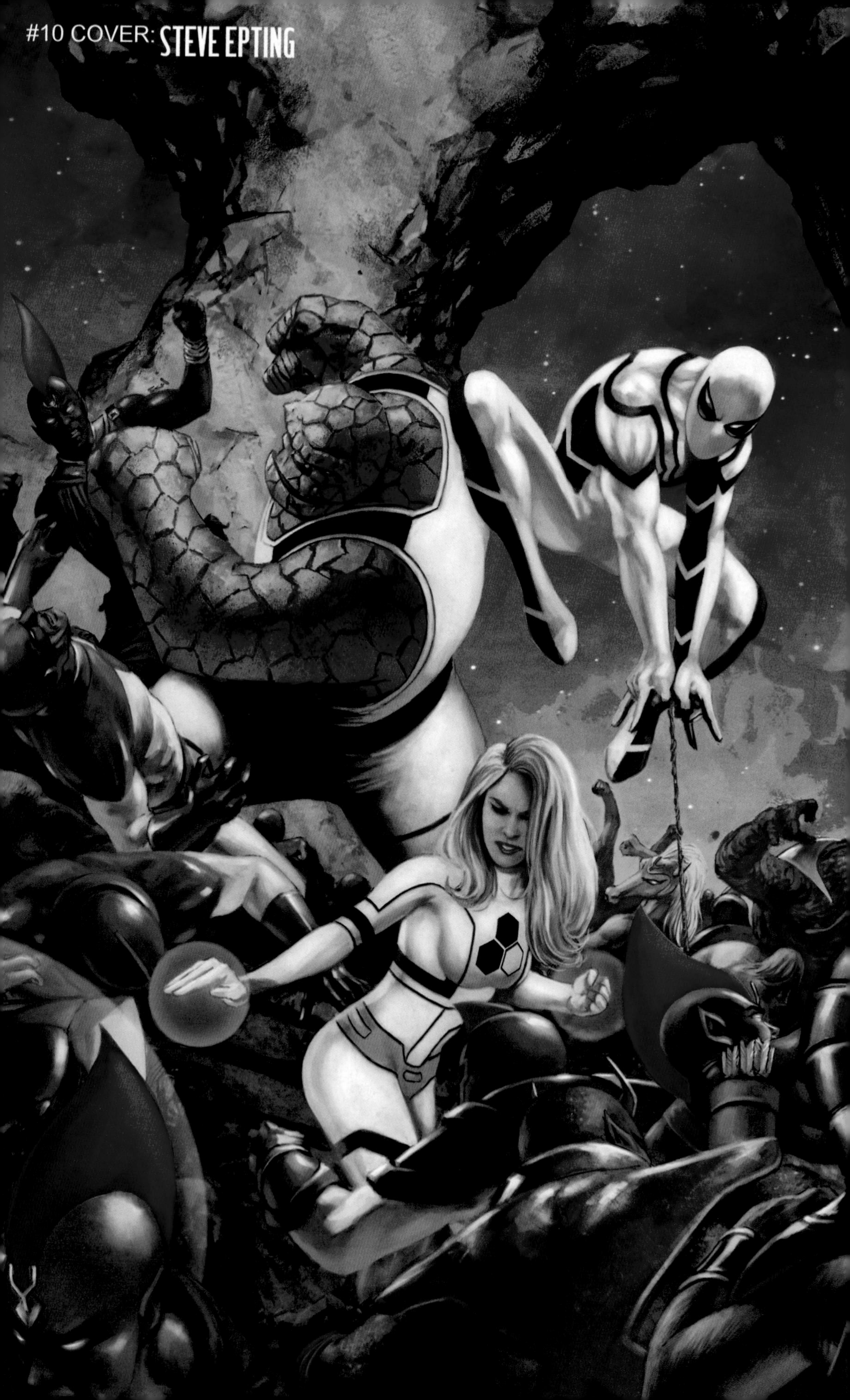

#11 COVER: STEVE EPTING

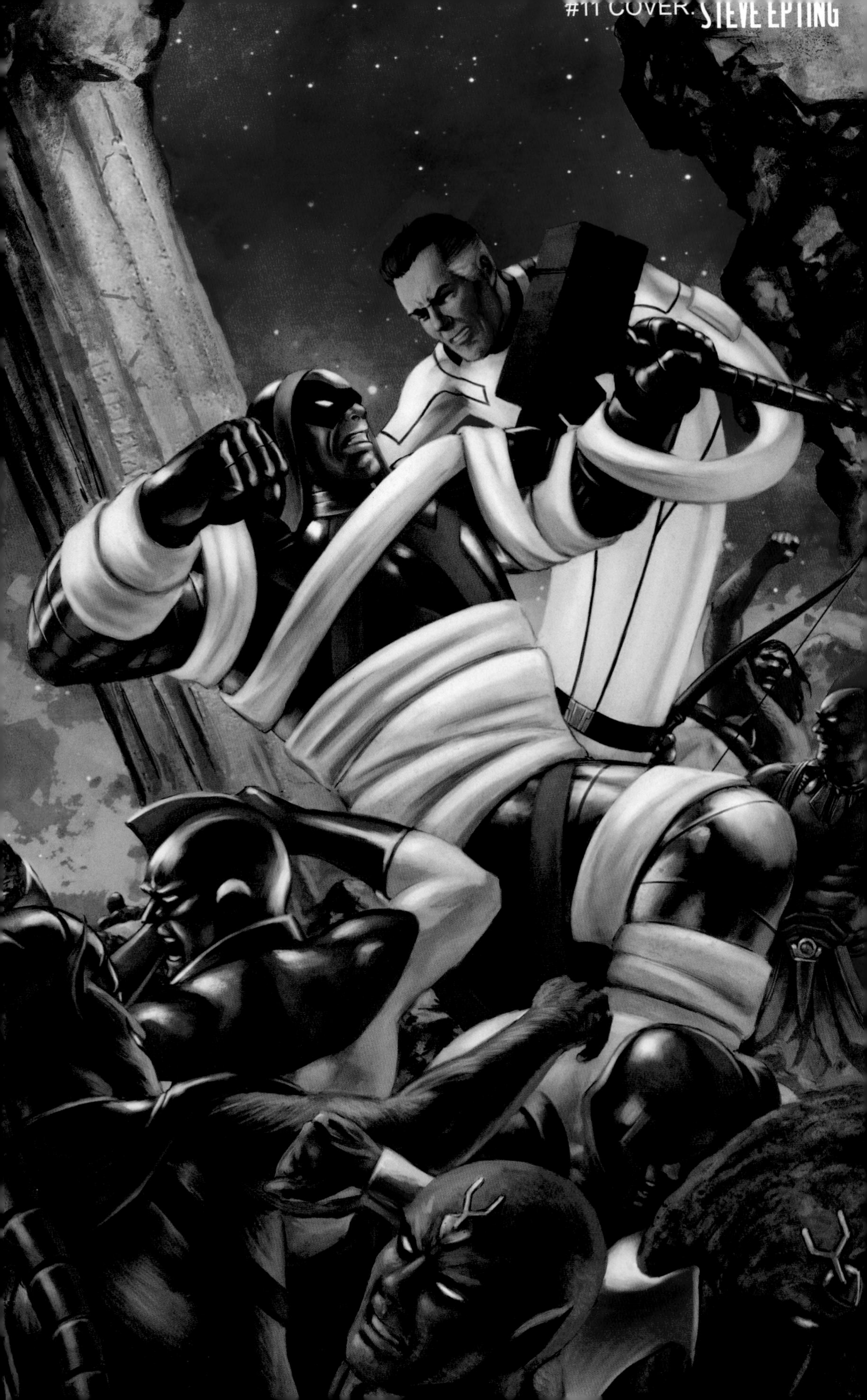

ANNIVERSARY VARIANT: STEPHANE PERGER

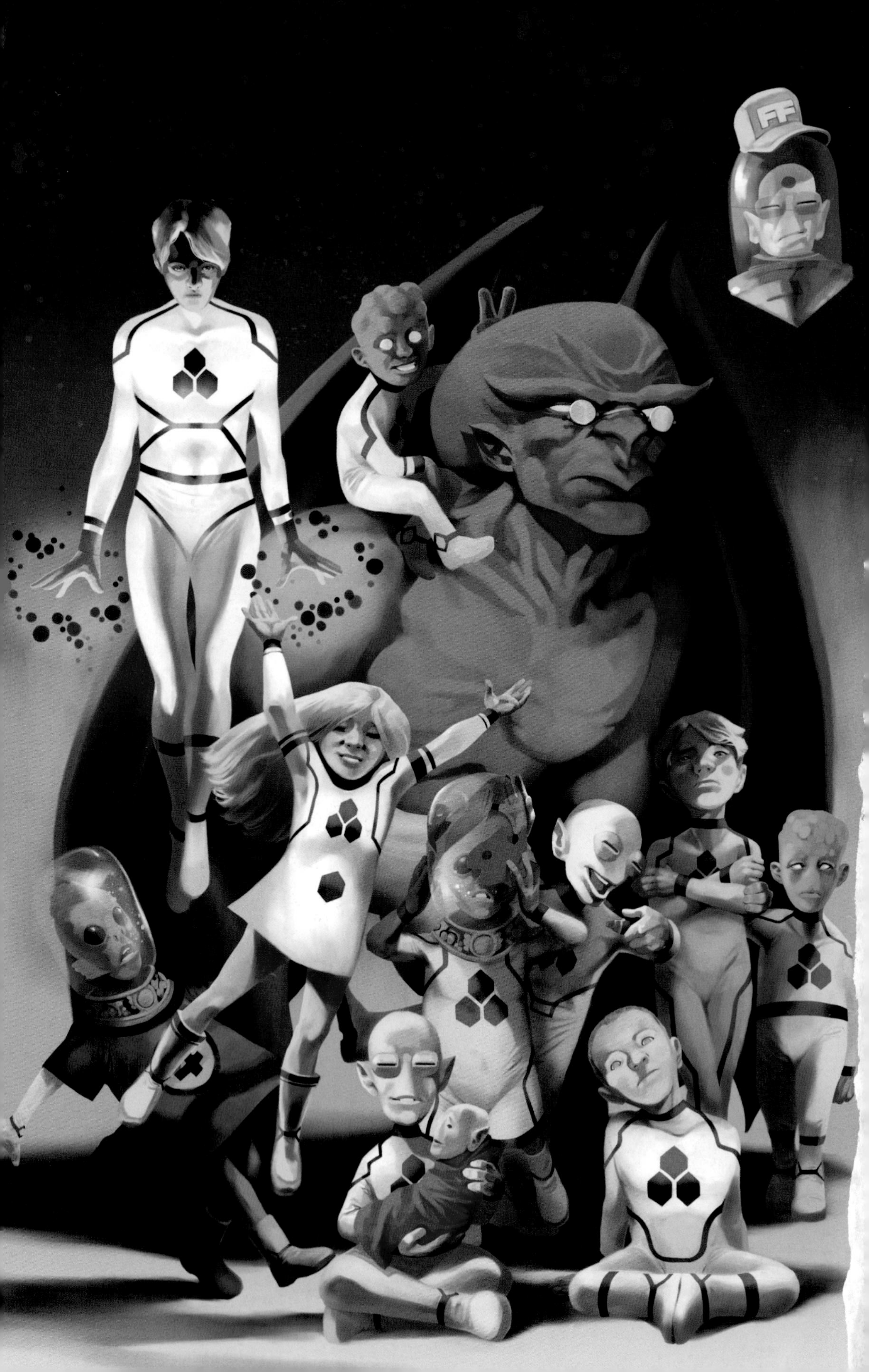
FF